THE ASSIMILATION

ROCK MACHINE BECOME BANDIDOS - BIKERS UNITED AGAINST THE HELLS ANGELS

EDWARD WINTERHALDER & WIL DE CLERCQ

ECW PRESS

Published by ECW Press
2120 Queen Street East, Suite 200
Toronto, Ontario, Canada M4E 1E2
416.694.3348 / info@ecwpress.com

LIBRARY AND ARCHIVES CANADA CATALOGUING IN PUBLICATION

Winterhalder, Edward, 1955–
The assimilation: Rock Machine become Bandidos : bikers united against the
Hells Angels / Edward Winterhalder, Wil De Clercq.

ISBN-13: 978-1-55022-824-3

1. Winterhalder, Edward, 1955– . 2. Rock Machine (Gang). 3. Bandidos (Gang).
4. Hell's Angels. 5. Motorcycle gangs—Québec (Province)—History. 6. Gang members—
Québec (Province)—Biography. I. De Clercq, Wil I. Title.

HV6491.C32Q8 2008   364.1092   C2007-907094-9

Cover Design: David Gee
Text Design: Tania Craan
Typesetting: Mary Bowness
Printing: Thomson-Shore

This book is set in Minion and Interstate and printed on paper
that has 30% post-consumer waste content.

PRINTED AND BOUND IN THE UNITED STATES

ECW PRESS
ecwpress.com

This book is dedicated to the memory of Barry Mason.
Vaya con Dios mi amigo . . .

It's a rough place, son. In fact, you have to puke twice
and show your razor just to get in. Better grow some
whiskers if you wanna go to Canada.

— Ronnie Hawkins

We are targeting biker gangs because they are not the
free-spirited, easy-rider romantics that they would have
you believe. They are criminals.

— Jim Flaherty

There's a certain breed who feel the need to put people
in their place. Not a bad bunch of guys, don't hand 'em
no lies, just stay off their case. People with angles never
should tangle with the boys who kill with words. You
don't stand a chance, you'll lose your pants.

— Phantom, Rocker & Slick

TABLE OF CONTENTS

ACKNOWLEDGEMENTS

A big thank you to my wife, Caroline, and daughter, Taylor, for standing behind me and loving me like you do. As I have said before, I would not be who I am without you both by my side.

Thanks also to the crew at ECW Press, especially Jack David, Simon Ware, and Emily Schultz, for their support and belief in *The Assimilation*.

Last but not least, I would like to thank Wil De Clercq for dedicating six months of his life turning an important page of biker history into literary reality. It has been an honor and a privilege to collaborate with you on this book. You are truly an inspiration to me.

E.W.

As a fullpatch member and national officer, first with the Rogues Motorcycle Club and then with the Bandidos Motorcycle Club, I regularly traveled all over North America and Europe to take care of business. I was a key player in the assimilation of the Quebec, Canada–based Rock Machine into the Bandidos Nation in 2001.

I got to meet dozens of fascinating people both inside and outside the biker world, which — although heavily scrutinized by the authorities, the media, and the public — is both an exclusive and secretive world. Becoming a 1%er is not like joining a bridge club — it is a long and tedious process meant to weed out those not worthy of receiving the club patch.

Some of the people I met, whether they were outlaw bikers or independent bikers, were criminals. Most, however, were law-abiding folk, albeit not your average garden-variety type. There were also the posers and wannabes, the type of people you find anywhere, in every walk of life.

I often get asked what kind of people join outlaw motorcycle clubs, or "gangs" as they are commonly called by the police and ordinary citizens. For the most part, anyone who joins a 1%er motorcycle club is a little psychologically skewed, usually as a result of an abnormal childhood. They're still looking for a sense of family; something they never found during their childhood for one reason or another.

Motorcycle clubs are first and foremost about brotherhood:

one for all, all for one. For some, it's a machismo thing, bombing along on a powerful, flashy motorcycle wearing their club colors like a rooster strutting through the barnyard. For others, it's mostly about riding their bikes with like-minded individuals, hanging out together, and having a little fun. Belonging to a motorcycle club gives many a sense of empowerment: this can be a good thing — it can also be a bad thing.

I lived the biker lifestyle for almost thirty years, and throughout most of it I was gainfully employed. Simultaneously, I lived as if every day were a holiday, for living that way is mandatory in the traditional biker lifestyle. And during that time, I was either a member of, or closely associated with, many outlaw motorcycle clubs.

Along the way, I spent time in prison; bought, sold, and built hundreds of Harleys; owned a multimillion-dollar construction management company; got married three times; and was a single parent to a young daughter. At times it was an ordeal that stretched me to limits I never knew I'd be stretched to. Being a biker has taught me a lot about human nature — the good, the bad, and the indifferent — but most of all it taught me a lot about myself. Thirty years of being a biker not only made me the man I am, but I also believe that I became a better man in the process.

Edward Winterhalder
Tulsa, Oklahoma
April 2008

I was eleven years old when Donald Eugene Chambers founded the Bandidos Motorcycle Club in San Leon, Texas. The year was 1966. Chambers, who was born in Houston, Texas, in 1930, was hooked on the motorcycle way of life from an early age. Although he didn't race, he was an avid fan of two-wheeled competition and belonged to an American Motorcyclist Association–affiliated club called the Eagles. The club's members religiously hit the road to attend and support AMA races in southeastern Texas. Eventually, Chambers migrated from the Eagles to another club called the Reapers, which, as their name suggests, was an outlaw club. In the Reapers, he attained the position of national secretary, which provided him with a solid grounding in the dynamics of how to successfully run a motorcycle club. It was only a matter of time before Chambers, who liked to do things his own way, got an itch to found his own club — a club he would call the Bandidos.

The founder of the Bandidos has often been characterized by journalists and authors alike as a disillusioned Vietnam War Marine Corps veteran who became a biker — like so many other vets — because he had an axe to grind with American society, a society that denigrated survivors of that terrible war as losers and baby-killers; that spat on them in airports; and that in many cases denied them employment. The truth, however, is in direct opposition to the myth: Don Chambers, although at one time a member of the Marine Corps, was anything but a disillusioned Vietnam vet. The closest he got to Vietnam was watching the evening news. Whether he was disillusioned or not is a moot point: it sounds good in print and gels with the clichéd portrayals of bikers. In society's collective consciousness, anybody who starts or joins an outlaw motorcycle club must be disillusioned, disturbed, antisocial, or rebelling against something — perhaps all of the above.

No doubt Bandido Don was disillusioned with American society of the 1960s, as were millions of hippies, college students, and assorted left-wingers during that turbulent decade. Another misconception that has been disseminated by many journalists is that Chambers chose the red and gold colors of the Marines for the Bandidos' patch as a tribute to the Corps. Actually, the original patch colors he chose were red and yellow, inspired by the coral snake and a southern expression "red and yellow, kill a fellow." Red and gold weren't adopted until a number of years after the Bandidos were founded. And contrary to popular belief, Chambers did not base the central image of his club's patch on the cartoon character in the Frito-Lay Bandito TV commercial. Although it makes for an interesting story, it lacks credibility, as the commercial didn't air until 1967 and then only during children's programming.

Another myth surrounding the founding of the Bandidos is that it was Chambers' intention to create an intimidating gang that would control the Texas drug trade. When the Bandidos Motorcycle Club first came into being, Chambers was a gainfully employed longshoreman on the docks of Galveston, not some kind of kingpin drug dealer as has been suggested. While it can't be denied that Bandido Don became involved with drugs — it is a matter of record that he was mixed up in a drugs-related double homicide for which he served time in prison — like the dozens of other outlaw motorcycle clubs established in the late 1950s and early 1960s, riding Harley-

Davidsons, drinking, partying, and rabble-rousing were the Bandidos' mandate.

The slogan Chambers adopted for the club — *we are the people our parents warned us about* — is the key to the mindset he harbored: Fuck the world! We're not toeing the line; we're not the conditioned little puppets churned out by the system to serve society and the ruling elite who push the buttons; we do things our own way! As an outlaw biker, Chambers' philosophy and feelings toward mainstream society were well defined: "One percenters are the one percent of us who have given up on society and the politician's one-way law. We're saying we don't want to be like you. So stay out of our face. It's one for all and all for one. If you don't think this way, then walk away, because you are a citizen and don't belong with us."

Exactly what inspired Chambers to call his club the Bandidos, and where exactly the "Fat Mexican" patch idea came from, is much less sensational than the myth surrounding it. People who were close to Chambers admit he possessed a vivid imagination, and he found inspiration in Mexican folklore, which was closely tied to the Tex-Mex community. Chambers was known to be fascinated by Mexican desperados, and he spent countless hours in his local library reading up on them. From there, it was a short path to the forming of the Texas motorcycle club that would bear the Bandidos name.

Although the original Mexican bandidos were scruffy and mean hombres who engaged in disreputable deeds ranging from raping and pillaging to causing havoc wherever they went, they would never foul up their own towns. If anything, bandidos were their town's protectors and quasi-law enforcement officers. During the French Intervention in Mexico, they even fought the invaders alongside government troops, militia, and mercenaries. The popularity of the image of the Mexican bandido as a well-fed and juiced-up pistol- and machete-wielding character wearing a sombrero and bandoleer led Chambers to adopt it for his club's patch.

The caricature of the Fat Mexican is at once humorous and menacing, and clearly sends a message: *don't mess with me, compadre!* While the idea for the Fat Mexican logo undoubtedly belonged to Chambers, the actual design was executed by a local Houston artist who had also been responsible for the logo of the Reapers. Once Chambers had a name for his club, a patch, and governing laws and by-laws put in place, he started recruiting potential members, many of whom were indeed Vietnam veterans. It was only a matter of time before the club started to spread throughout the South, Southwest, Midwest, and Northwest, and the Fat Mexican patch became ingrained in the minds of citizens everywhere.

At the time of the Bandidos' founding, there were numerous motorcycle clubs in the United States. These included AMA-chartered clubs that were dedicated strictly to the promotion of motorcycling events, including touring and racing. These were often family-oriented clubs and carried with them an aura of respectability. The first motorcycle club in America, if not the world, was founded in 1903 in Yonkers, NY, and aptly called Yonkers MC. The club actually got its start in the late 1800s as a bicycle club. Owning a bicycle back then was considered daring and different. But with the advent of motorized cycles, the Yonkers Bicycle Club became a bona fide motorcycle club in 1903. It is still active today and can unequivocally claim to be the forerunner of every motorcycle club that followed.

The Yonkers MC's main activities included recreational riding, staging racing events, and most importantly, partying! One year after Yonkers MC was founded on the east coast, the west coast got its first motorcycle club, the San Francisco Motorcycle Club (SFMC). Like Yonkers MC, it is still active today and was created with the same mandate in mind. Both clubs became among the first chartered members of the AMA, an organization that actually wasn't launched until 1924. Although latter-day Yonkers and SFMC members have been active in the outlaw community at certain times, neither club has ever worn the outlaw 1%er badge, and they are both still considered to be family-oriented clubs.

By 1966, there were plenty of outlaw clubs as well. In the public's perception, these clubs were made up of dangerous individuals who were to be avoided at all cost. This is not surprising, considering the steady diet of badass Hollywood biker movies of the 1960s, and highly publicized and exaggerated, though mostly isolated, violent incidents fed to mainstream America. The cornerstone of the modern-day outlaw motorcycle club lies in California, long known to be a magnet and incubator for off-the-wall social movements and radical concepts. Its genesis can be found with the hard-riding, hard-drinking, and hard-fisted members of two clubs: the Boozefighters of Los Angeles and the Pissed Off Bastards of Fontana. Both clubs were kick-started in the wake of the Second World War when motorcycles were cheap and sold by the thousands as war surplus.

Many of those who bought bikes gravitated into groups to ride and party together. In a story that has been told and retold countless times, the rowdy presence of the Boozefighters and Pissed Off Bastards at the 1947 Gypsy Tour Rally in the small town of Hollister, California, gave birth to the image of bikers as troublemakers and antisocial deviants. Their hard partying, heavy drinking, and crazy motorcycle stunts, although not exactly Boy Scout behavior, were totally blown out of proportion and sensationalized in news reports. The most outrageous episode that actually did occur was when two members of the Boozefighters rode their bikes into a local bar. A staged picture — taken by an opportunistic photographer and published in *Life* magazine — showed a drunk on a motorcycle clutching a bottle of beer. Ironically, he wasn't even a member of a motorcycle club.

The picture, and headlines such as BIKERS TAKE OVER TOWN, captured the imagination of the American public. Both its fear and fascination with outlaw bikers took hold, and little has changed to this day — bikers, whether independent or club members, are perceived to be a breed unto their own. Meanwhile, the AMA, horrified by the negative publicity, held a damage-control press conference stating that all the trouble was caused by the "one percent deviant that tarnishes the public image of both motorcycles and motorcyclists." This statement eventually led the outlaw biker community to adopt the term "one-percenter" to distinguish itself from the rest of the motorcycling community and citizens in general. The bikers' negative image was fixed forever in 1954, when the movie *The Wild One* — inspired by the events that occurred in Hollister — hit the big screen. Anyone on a motorcycle was now perceived to be a social outcast.

The first to capitalize on the notoriety and infamy attributed to bikers were the Hells Angels, founded in California in 1948 by dissatisfied members of the Pissed Off Bastards. They were the first 1%er outlaw club and for decades commanded the most media attention. The Hells Angels would set the standards all other outlaw clubs aspired to. Only three, however, would rise to join them at the top of the biker world's hierarchy: the Outlaws, Pagans, and Bandidos. While the Outlaws trace their lineage back to the McCook Outlaws — founded in McCook, Illinois, in 1935 — they didn't become a 1%er motorcycle club until 1963. The Pagans, which were founded in Maryland in 1959, didn't gain momentum until 1968 and today are still confined to the United States. But starting as a small regional Texas motorcycle club, the Bandidos rapidly became a force to be reckoned with, taking their rightful place alongside the Hells Angels, Outlaws, and

Pagans; collectively they are known as the "Big Four." Today, the Bandidos enjoy the distinction of commanding a world-wide dynasty with an estimated 2,400 members in more than 200 chapters located in sixteen countries.

I didn't meet my first Bandido until the summer of 1979 in Mobile, Alabama. At the time, I was a member of the Tulsa chapter of the Rogues Motorcycle Club, which got its start in Chicago in the early 1960s but later relocated to Oklahoma, the southwestern state that has been my home since 1975. The Bandido I met, Buddy Boykin, wasn't just a rank-and-file member but a Vice Presidente under El Presidente Ronnie Hodge. I was introduced to Buddy, who had been in the club for about ten years, by a member of the Outlaws Jacksonville chapter. I had built up a friendship with the Florida Outlaws and was a frequent visitor to their Jacksonville clubhouse.

Buddy, a likable and popular character, lived close to my traveling route south, so his place was a perfect overnight stopover, just about halfway between Tulsa and Jacksonville. Before long, visiting with the Mobile Bandidos became a ritual every time I ventured to Florida. I had only been a Rogue for a few years, and my experience in the outlaw biker world was restricted mostly to that club and the Outlaws. Bandidos Vice Presidente Buddy introduced me to a totally different type of motorcycle club; one that truly believed in the concept of "brotherhood." Although brotherhood was something all motorcycle clubs were supposed to represent, in my experience they often fell short of the "one for all, all for one" values instilled by Don Chambers.

It wasn't long before I started mulling over the idea of changing the entire Rogues Motorcycle Club into a Bandidos

Oklahoma chapter. Because I had a close relationship with the Mobile Bandidos, I thought the possibility of a patchover would be nothing more than a formality. Little did I know how long a process it would actually be. Despite intense lobbying, not just by me but by one of my friends in the Rogues' Oklahoma City chapter who was close to a Texas Bandido, there would be no Oklahoma Bandidos until 1997. It was, at times, a frustrating journey of ups and downs, but compared to my involvement some years later with Bandidos Canada and their precursor, the Rock Machine, it would seem like a walk in the park.

CHAPTER ONE

WELCOME TO THE GREAT WHITE NORTH

It was Saturday, January 6, 2001, a day that would go down in Canadian and world biker history as the day the Rock Machine officially ceased to exist: they were now part of the Bandidos Nation. To mark the occasion, a huge patchover party was held in Kingston, Ontario. Kingston, which traces its roots to a French settlement established on Mississauga First Nation land in 1673, lies at the eastern end of Lake Ontario, where the lake turns into the St. Lawrence River, and the picturesque Thousand Islands begin. The town, renowned for its myriad century-old limestone buildings, was chosen for the party because it was strategically located, more or less, in the geographical center of the Rock Machine's territory, which stretched from Quebec City, Quebec, to Toronto, Ontario, with members living as far west as London, Ontario. Ironically, Kingston is also home to one of the most notorious penitentiaries in North America, a prison known as the "toughest ten acres" in Ontario.

It was crucial for me to attend the patchover party and meet my new Canadian brothers. I had been assigned the task of overseeing the new national chapter of Bandidos Canada by George Wegers, who at the time was the international president of the Bandidos, as well as the president of the American Bandidos. In Bandidos terminology, he was simply known as El Presidente George.

In essence, I was to teach the Canadians how to organize and function as a Bandidos Motorcycle Club. In addition to establishing lines of communication, I was to compile and verify the entire membership roster for Bandidos Canada, including telephone number and e-mail address lists, and advise them on any necessary issues. While at first glance this may seem like a relatively easy assignment, as I actually believed it was going to be, it would prove to be anything but. I would soon discover that the Canadian Bandidos had inherited from their precursor, the Rock Machine, a disorganized mess. They had few internal records, no clearly defined mandate, and weren't even sure who was in the club.

The reason I had been given the assignment of overseeing the new addition to the Bandidos Nation had nothing to do with my pretty face. I was born with a knack for diplomacy, along with finely tuned organizational and administrative skills. I also possessed a basic knowledge of law and legalese, which I had acquired in a prison's law library while incarcerated during the early 1980s. None of my talents had escaped the notice of Bandidos El Presidente George, who had enlisted me to perform all kinds of managerial duties for the national chapter. Tasks I regularly performed for the club included coordinating the development of a Web site, assisting with putting together the monthly American Bandidos newsletter, arranging airplane flights for national officers, conducting public relations campaigns, and administering the U.S. membership phone list, e-mail list, and Bandidos support club chapter and membership lists. It wasn't like I needed any more club responsibilities heaped upon me, but I had been a vocal proponent of expanding the Bandidos into Canada, and I felt the least I could do was help make the process a success.

I had been in Canada for only two days, and all it seemed to do was snow — and it was cold as hell! But then, who in their right mind goes to Canada in January unless it's for winter-related activities, something I avoid like the plague. I do not like cold weather. I hate snow! I don't ski; I don't skate; I don't snowmobile; I don't ice-fish. And now it looked like I had made the long journey from Tulsa, Oklahoma, for nothing. After much deliberation, I had decided not to go to the patchover party even though that was my sole reason for being in the Great White North.

I had been told there were some seventy-five police officers around the former Rock Machine's clubhouse, and they would certainly be looking for me. The men in blue were engaged in their favorite outlaw biker–related pastimes: harassing people, snapping pictures, shooting video footage, checking IDs, and arresting or detaining whoever they could.

Eight fellow American Bandidos had already been detained; what would save them from incarceration and deportation proceedings was the fact that they had legally been allowed into the country. The point-of-entry stamps on their passports were proof enough. But my passport did not have a stamp. Technically, I was in the country illegally and somehow the authorities got wind of it.

A few days earlier, on a dreary and blustery afternoon, I had successfully entered Canada disguised as a construction worker in a car driven by my sister Kitty. I had contemplated a number of different border-crossing scenarios and going overland seemed like my best bet. I had been allowed into Canada in recent years but due to my criminal record and membership in the Bandidos had also been denied access at times. It all depended on who was in the customs booth at the border and how diligent they were in performing their duty.

Most of the American Bandidos who were going to the patchover party had opted to fly into Toronto's Pearson International Airport. I thought that under those circumstances, with Bandidos streaming into the city from all over the world, it would be much harder to gain entry through the airport. I had heard too many stories of Immigration Canada turning members of any motorcycle club around at the airport, even if they weren't convicted felons.

Despite the fact that it had been almost twenty years since I had last been convicted, I had little doubt I would be caught and turned around if I tried to enter at Pearson. I decided to enter Canada through the Detroit–Windsor checkpoint. Kitty lived in Michigan not far from the border and made the crossing on a regular basis.

Windsor, the southernmost city in Canada, is an automotive town like Detroit, but on a much smaller scale. The two cities are separated by the Detroit River and linked together by the Ambassador Bridge and the Detroit–Windsor Tunnel. Windsor is the western terminus of Highway 401 — Canada's busiest highway — and sees a lot of traffic flow. I assumed that if I entered the country during peak hours, border officials would be a bit more lax checking documents. My line of thinking proved to be correct: the Canadian customs officer, looking bored and cold in his booth, didn't ask for our IDs. I had my passport in hand, which he took a glance at, but all he did was ask Kitty a few questions about where we were going and how long we intended to stay.

"We're just going to the casino for a few hours," Kitty told him.

Without further ado, we were told to proceed, and I found myself in Canada, three hundred and fifty miles from Kingston, my ultimate destination. I noticed that most vehicles were entering Canada as quickly as we were. I was wondering if maybe it *was* too easy. Kitty mentioned that crossing into either country was usually a hassle-free procedure.

In the days before 9/11, no passports were required. If ID was asked for at all, a driver's license sufficed. After Kitty dropped me off, I made my way from Windsor to Kingston via London and Toronto, where I briefly stopped at the Outlaws' and Bandidos' clubhouses respectively. I finally arrived in Kingston late Friday afternoon and settled into a local Travelodge, where the other out-of-town Bandidos were staying as guests of the Kingston chapter.

After eating breakfast at the Travelodge on Saturday morning, I grabbed my laptop and went online to peruse various newspaper articles from around the world. One article caught my attention and really set my mind racing. It detailed how the police at Pearson International had caught a few Bandidos trying to get into the country for the patchover party. It went on to state that some outlaw bikers had actually gotten into the country, *including an American Bandido from Oklahoma.*

Although my name hadn't been mentioned, this hit me like a bombshell. I was the only Bandido from Oklahoma in Canada. Somehow I had "been made" and the authorities were on the lookout for me. Arresting an American Bandido for illegal entry into the country presented them with the perfect opportunity to score some points and have a media field day.

Obviously, I was quite concerned, since it meant there was a leak somewhere. I had used no credit cards since entering Canada; I hadn't made or received any cell phone calls; and I hadn't registered at the motel. I pieced together a mental list of everyone who knew I had made it into the country. I at once ruled out my sister, because I knew she would never betray me; this left a number of Outlaws members I'd had contact with after entering the country and, of course, my Bandidos brothers. As hard as it was to believe, somebody from that list had reported me to the authorities. The fact it had made the newspapers really amazed me. I wondered if this was the authorities' way of toying with my mind, letting me know they knew I was on their turf.

As much as I hated not going to the patchover party, I opted for a quiet dinner with Robert "Tout" Leger. Tout was a former Montreal Rock Machine member who was now a member of the new Canadian Bandidos. I had met him earlier in the day and discovered we had a lot in common. I had also heard of his exploits a number of years earlier, when he had gone to Texas in a bid to establish contact with the American Bandidos on behalf of the Rock Machine.

Bandido Tout had a dynamic personality you couldn't help but be drawn to. Like me, the French Canadian enjoyed working on Harleys and had owned his own motorcycle shop for many years. This in itself at once produced a common bond between us. Due to an ongoing court case, Tout was under a legal injunction that prevented him from fraternizing with any members of the Rock Machine. Although most of the Rock Machine were now Bandidos, and Tout would technically not have been breaching the injunction, he felt there was no need to delve into semantics and had decided not to go to the clubhouse either. Over dinner at the motel restaurant, he invited me to his house near Montreal to hang out for a day and then return to the United States via train through northern Vermont.

"It will probably be the easiest way to get home," he said in fluent English. "They'll never expect you to cross at the Quebec border."

Although I never underestimate the police, his suggestion made sense, and I agreed to accompany him. Hanging around Kingston and retracing my steps out of the country didn't seem like an attractive proposition. We planned to leave Kingston by 8:00 p.m. for the three-hour drive to Montreal. At about 7:00 p.m., Bandido Tout and I returned to our rooms to pack. Not wanting to use a phone, we sent a runner to the clubhouse to let everyone know we were leaving town. I threw the few belongings I had with me into my overnight bag and then went online to check e-mail. As usual, there were at least a dozen or so business-related messages, a few from my then-fiancée Caroline, and about half a dozen from fellow Bandidos club members. I answered the most important ones while I waited for Tout.

Tout joined me about five minutes later, and we hung around the room to give the Bandidos at the clubhouse time to respond. As the clubhouse was only about a five-minute motorcycle ride from the motel, we didn't expect a long wait. In anticipation, I cracked the motel room door open an inch or two using the night latch as a prop. Moments later, the door flew open, and Tout and I were confronted by members of the Kingston Police Department and the Ontario Provincial Police Biker Enforcement Unit.

"Nobody moves, nobody gets hurt!" one of the officers screamed. "Put your fucking hands on your heads. Now!"

We did what we were told and when all was deemed safe, two officers from Immigration Canada, who had waited outside the door, sauntered into the room like a couple of cats who ate the canary.

"Are you guys members of the Bandidos?" one of the Kingston cops asked.

This was a rather pointless question, as Tout and I were both sporting Bandidos logos on our belts and our shirts. We were also in a section of the motel totally occupied by out-of-town Bandidos. When we acknowledged that we were indeed members of the Bandidos, we were asked to state our names and places of residence. When I told them my full name, and that I lived in Oklahoma, the immigration officers stepped to the front of the pack — it was obviously their moment to shine.

"Is your street name Connecticut Ed?" one of them asked. I told him it was.

"If you're from Oklahoma, then how come they call you Connecticut Ed?" the other immigration officer chimed in, as if this was actually relevant.

I explained that I was originally from Connecticut and got the nickname to distinguish me from other Bandidos named Ed.

As soon as they looked at my passport to verify my identity, I was arrested for violating Canadian immigration laws, handcuffed, and shuffled out into the hallway. The Kingston police spoke with Bandido Tout inside the room and quickly established he was who he said he was, that he was not violating his bond conditions by associating with me, and that there were no illegal substances or weapons in the room. Tout was free to go, and I was now a guest of the Canadian authorities.

No one at the patchover party was surprised to hear I had been arrested. They were, however, shocked to hear I had been arrested by Immigration Canada. Local law enforcement authorities had just released a number of other American Bandidos due to the failure of the immigration authorities to arrive and take custody of them. When I learned about this, I wondered why Immigration Canada had such an interest in me. I could only guess it was due to the fact my fellow American Bandidos were rank-and-file members, whereas I had ties to the national chapter and was therefore a person of extreme interest to them. How the immigration officials knew who I was, however, was something that totally escaped me.

From Kingston, I was transported about forty-five miles east to an Immigration Canada holding cell in Lansdowne for my initial booking. So here I was, back behind bars. It wasn't an alien environment to me, but it wasn't one I particularly cared to be in either, especially in a foreign country where I didn't know the ramifications of the law — where I didn't know what to expect at all!

Ironically, Lansdowne is located less than a quarter-mile across the St. Lawrence River from the United States. I could have thrown a rock and hit the U.S. Customs Office on Wellesley Island, which is part of the Thousand Islands chain that dots the St. Lawrence like so many stars in the sky.

"Don't get too comfortable. You won't be here long. You're going to Ottawa," one of the immigration officers said as I settled into my cell, waiting for the other shoe to drop. He explained that the higher-ups had requested my transfer to Canada's capital city, where my case would receive "proper" attention. Apparently Immigration Canada was all abuzz, convinced I was a big fish and a prize catch, something the media would adore. I was soon to learn that Canadian newspapers, like their counterparts everywhere else, loved to run front-page stories about outlaw bikers — the more sensational the better.

I have to admit that the immigration officers assigned to book me were unusually respectful. I was not quite used to being treated in such a dignified manner by the authorities. Maybe it was because they really believed I was some kind of major player in the world of 1%ers. While awaiting my transfer to Ottawa, another immigration officer asked me if there was anything he could get for me. To his surprise, I requested the Canadian Immigration Statutes.

"We've got a lot better reading material than that," he said. I told him the statutes would do — I didn't bother to explain I had a knowledge of the law approximating that of a paralegal — and he was kind enough to supply me with the complete manual. I was contemplating waiving my deportation hearing, but by the time I read through the manual, I decided that I wanted to stay and fight. Why I chose to go this route, which obviously was not the path of least resistance, I'm not quite sure. Perhaps it was because it's in my nature never to back away from a confrontation. Maybe it was because I wanted to be able to return to Canada so I would be better able to do my job with the Canadian Bandidos. Maybe it was because I needed my head examined.

On Monday, January 8, I was transferred to the Ottawa Carleton Detention Centre, a maximum-security prison on the outskirts of Ottawa. I was at once placed in solitary confinement for security reasons. Apparently, the prison held a number of Hells Angels and officials feared for my safety. I was advised that my deportation hearing, scheduled for Wednesday, was being postponed for one week until January 17. On January 9, an arraignment hearing was held via telephone.

I argued the hearing myself and, over the objections of the Crown attorneys, convinced an immigration adjudicator to grant me a bail bond in the amount of $20,000. I calculated the amount of cash I would need to be released at $2,000 (10 percent of $20,000) and thought that it would be very easy to obtain. Imagine my surprise when I found out that in Canada there isn't a 10 percent bail bond system like there is in the United States. If I was to obtain my release, I was going to have to come up with $20,000 cash.

I was being held on an administrative charge, not a criminal charge. I had not been arrested for committing a crime and was not going to be formally charged with any criminal violations. Even if I was found guilty of the administrative charge, incarceration was not an option. The only punishment that could possibly be imposed on me was deportation back to the United States. But that is exactly where I wanted to be. I had a hard time grasping the logic behind my detainment because I was sure that by now they knew exactly who I was, that I had had a clean record since 1982, and that there were no outstanding arrest warrants for me in the United States — or in Canada for that matter.

For all intents and purposes, I was unable to return home because the Canadian government wanted me to stay just so Immigration Canada could "officially" deport me. It was a ludicrous situation to be in, but to the immigration people, apparently this was serious business. They were very resolute in their dealings with me and acted like I had committed a murder or something. And to make matters worse, according to Canadian immigration laws, I could be held in jail without bail for up to two years, pending my deportation hearing.

I knew that I was extremely lucky to have been granted bail, and, apparently, I was the first biker ever to receive it on a deportation matter. At this stage of the game, I figured it would all be over soon and I would be on my way back to Oklahoma, where my eight-year-old daughter, Taylor, was anxiously awaiting the return of her daddy.

As soon as I was informed that bail would be granted, I contacted one of my new Canadian brothers, Jean "Charley" Duquaire, the first national president of Bandidos Canada. He was aware of my situation, of course, and in no time I convinced him to lend me the bail money, assuring him he would be paid back within a few days. It was imperative that the money was clean, with a readily identifiable paper trail to its source. Presidente Charley obtained the necessary funds on his credit card through a cash advance at the Bank of Montreal. He converted the advance into a bank cashier's check and hand-delivered it to the Immigration Canada office in Ottawa.

Early Wednesday afternoon, January 10, I was released from custody and driven back to Kingston, where I spent a few days at the home of another new Canadian Bandido, Marc "Garfield" Yakimishan, and his family. As a condition of my bail, I had been ordered not to leave Canada, to reside in the care and custody of Bandido Garfield, and to appear at my next hearing. Garfield was, at that time, scheduled to become the new El Secretario for Canada, so staying with him for a few days was ideal. If I was going to be on an extended vacation courtesy of Immigration Canada, I thought that I might as well make the best of it. Because I was to teach Garfield what was expected of him as a Bandidos El Secretario, I wasted no time sitting down with him to give him a crash course. Although, technically, I could have split from Canada at any time, I had every intention of sticking around. Not only did I want my bond money and my confiscated Bandidos colors and passport back, I wanted to fight the deportation that was in store for me, since I was convinced I could win.

As soon as I was released from jail, I hired one of the best criminal defense attorneys in Canada, Josh Zambrowsky. Kingston-based Zambrowsky was well known for his work representing people accused of major crimes; he also had an excellent reputation with the Montreal and Kingston Bandidos. He had represented some of them a few years earlier, and they thought he was "neater than sliced bread."

As part of our plan to prepare a character defense for the hearing, two attorney friends of mine from Oklahoma, Jonathan M. Sutton and William J. Patterson, wrote tremendous character reference letters on my behalf. But our only problem was that my case was not a criminal matter — it was an administrative matter. And we were not dealing with the criminal justice system; we were dealing with Immigration Canada, which was quite accustomed to doing things however they wanted, with no interference from the justice system.

One of many newspaper articles dealing with my immigration problems appeared on the morning of my release from the Ottawa Carleton Detention Centre. It reinforced the notion that I was one of the most powerful men in the American Bandidos. Although I was on a temporary assignment for the United States national chapter, and had held the position of El Secretario (national secretary) on a number of occasions, in the scheme of things I was hardly a "big-wheel" or "high-ranking" Bandido. At the time, the only office I held in the club was secretary of the Bandidos Oklahoma chapter.

Big-wheel biker wins $20G bail

By John Steinbachs

January 10, 2001

A high-ranking Bandidos motorcycle gang member is expected to be released on bail today after cooling his wheels in an Ottawa jail.

Edward Winterhalder, 45, appeared before an Ottawa Immigration and Refugee Board adjudicator yesterday for a detention review hearing.

The adjudicator ordered that he be detained but allowed him to be released on a $20,000 bond.

The border-bouncing Bandidos biker was busted after a Kingston patchover Saturday where several local Rock Machine members were inducted into the international club.

The closed event — attended by an estimated 53 people — came just one week after the rival Hells Angels patched over dozens of members from smaller Ontario gangs.

The Tulsa biker — reputed to be one of the most powerful men in the club — was detained by Citizenship and Immigration Canada on charges that he entered the country illegally.

Winterhalder has been ordered to appear on Jan. 17 for a board inquiry, where an adjudicator will rule if the allegations against him are founded and decide whether or not to issue a removal order.

Didn't tell guards

According to a Citizenship and Immigration report, Winterhalder — who admitted to being a member of the brazen Bandidos — told investigators he entered Canada on Jan. 5 through Fort Erie but didn't tell border guards of his gang affiliations.

In 1995, he tried to cross at the same border point but was turned back by immigration officers.

The immigration report also said he has told officials that he has a criminal record, including criminal convictions for concealing stolen property, uttering a forged treasury cheque, possession of a stolen vehicle, carrying a prohibited weapon and carrying a concealed weapon. His last admitted conviction noted in the report was in 1983.

With bikers taking a higher profile in Canada recently, immigration officials have been keeping their eyes peeled for possible spottings at ports, including Pearson International Airport in Toronto.

Officers said the alerts led to the interception of four members of the Bandidos bike gang arriving here for the opening of the Kingston chapter.

Police said two members of the group's Denver chapter and one each from Washington and Amsterdam were turned around at the airport. A senior member of the Washington chapter did slip into the country but left on Sunday.

Letter from Tulsa, OK, lawyer Jonathan Sutton, offering testimony to my character.

To Whom It May Concern,
1/15/2001

I am writing for and on behalf of Mr. Edward Winterhalder, an American citizen and good friend of mine. As I am intending to provide a reference for Mr. Winterhalder, it may be important for you to know something of myself. I am an attorney practicing primarily in Oklahoma, and admitted to practice before all Courts in Oklahoma, as well as the Northern, Eastern and Western Federal District Courts of Oklahoma, the Tenth Circuit Court of Appeals, and the United States Supreme Court. I have previously worked as a corporate attorney for the United Parcel Service, and the Tulsa County District Attorneys Office, prior to establishing a private practice and firm.

I came to know Mr. Winterhalder roughly five years ago, and have enjoyed my interaction with him since. I have found him to be much like myself in many respects, specifically, a highly motivated, intelligent, tenacious individual, possessed of a strength of character and moral code so rarely found in today's society. Having worked for Mr. Winterhalder on a variety of legal issues, I can further attest to the lack of criminal allegations brought against him during the time I have known him. Clearly, I am not able to prove a nullity, thus I can only state that for the entire time I have known him, I have never known of conduct that would likely give rise to such charges. He is a loving father, a respected member of the business community, and a valued friend. I know of less than five people I would say this about, but I personally trust Mr. Winterhalder.

Truly, I wish more people in today's society were like Mr. Winterhalder: we would all be far better off. Every time he has stated he would do something, he has; every time he made a commitment, he carried it out; every time he was placed in a situation where he could do the easy thing or the right thing, he did the right thing. I have great respect for Mr. Winterhalder, and trust that whatever the situation is there in Canada, that you do the right thing and release him.

Sincerely,
Jonathan Sutton

While awaiting my January 17 immigration hearing, I went to Toronto one evening with Alain Brunette, Vice Presidente of Bandidos Canada. He had been appointed to the position by Jean "Charley" Duquaire, who as leader of the former Rock Machine had automatically become Canadian Bandidos president. I was pleased to hear Alain had received the appointment, as I had briefly met him on a previous occasion in the United States almost two years earlier.

Despite the snow that had fallen during the day, the roads had been cleared and sanded, and Vice Presidente Alain and I made our way safely into the sprawling GTA (Greater Toronto

Area) by early evening. As we approached Canada's largest city, I could see in the background the world-famous CN Tower, which pierced the darkening sky like a gigantic needle, dominating the entire skyline despite the looming skyscrapers that surrounded it.

"That's one hell of a tower," I said. "I'll bet the view from up there is amazing."

"It's the world's tallest freestanding tower," Alain said. "Going up it is a must-do tourist thing."

I asked Alain if he knew how tall it was, and he told me it was close to two thousand feet. To satisfy my curiosity, I later did a Google search and discovered the tower was actually 1,815 feet high. I definitely wanted to catch the view from the tower's observation deck, but the purpose of our trip to Toronto was not to go sightseeing. Someday, I thought.

We were in Ontario's capital city to meet with Peter "Peppi" Barilla, president of the Toronto Loners Motorcycle Club, and visit with the new Toronto North Bandidos chapter. We wanted to talk to Peppi about the possibility of patching over the Loners into the Bandidos in the near future. I had been told that Peppi wielded a lot of influence in the Toronto biker community and that he would make a valuable ally. Although he wasn't a tall individual, he exuded a powerful presence — stocky and muscular, covered in tattoos, shoulder-length sandy-blond hair, beard, and quick to flash a smile. He made you feel at ease, and yet at the same time you knew he wasn't someone to mess with. The meeting with Peppi took longer than we expected, and by the time we got to the Bandidos' clubhouse, located in an industrial area of the city, their weekly "church" (a biker term for a meeting) had just finished.

To our dismay, we discovered that the entire Toronto chapter had just voted a Bandidos prospect by the name of Eric "Eric the Red" McMillan out of the club. Bandidos Prospect

Eric was a tough young kid from Oshawa, a city about twenty-five miles east of Toronto. He apparently harbored a deep resentment for some local bikers who had joined the Hells Angels in the Toronto area. The reason for this was never revealed to me, but it was never surprising that a member of one club hated a member or members of a rival club. In many cases there was a justifiable reason; sometimes it was just the thing to do. Vice Presidente Alain and I saw Eric as one of the brightest stars of the entire Toronto chapter, but the Toronto Bandidos saw him as *too* "anti–Hells Angels."

Alain and I left Toronto harboring mixed feelings: we felt good about our meeting with Loners President Peppi, but generally bad about the Toronto Bandidos. Peppi had shown interest in our proposal to patch over the Loners — that was the good part. We didn't think the Toronto Bandidos chapter would survive — that was the bad. We also wondered if some of the members would become Hells Angels. The way they seemed to feel about the Angels — something they didn't conceal when we met them — convinced us they would.

Alain and I decided to drive directly to Oshawa, which conveniently happened to be on our way back to Kingston. As we drove out of town, I asked my new Bandidos brother to tell me a bit about himself. Usually I'm not so forthright, but I thought it was important to get to know as well as possible the new Bandidos officers I would be dealing with. I knew I wouldn't have the luxury of spending all that much time with Alain or any of the other guys. Although communicating with each other took a lot of patience, reiterating or rephrasing sentences, I discovered he was born in Montreal, grew up on the South Shore of the city across the St. Lawrence River, and had one sibling. He had been riding motorcycles since he was fifteen years old, almost the same age I was when I first threw a leg over a motorcycle.

"My first bike was a three-fifty two-cylinder two-stroke. I kinda learned how to ride on that one. Then I got a six-fifty Kawasaki, and after that a Yamaha eleven hundred. I was a pretty good rider by the time I got that beast, and then I got my Harley," Alain said. He went on to tell me he had been working since he was a teenager, mostly in the landscaping, construction, and snow-removal business. We had quite a bit in common, I thought, because I too had been working since I was a teenager, and a lot of that work had been in the construction industry.

When we got to Oshawa — a General Motors factory town — we drove to Bandido Prospect Eric's place and roused him from sleep. To make up for the early morning intrusion, we took him for a 2:00 a.m. breakfast at a local restaurant. After talking to Eric, and hearing his side of the story, we decided to reinstate him into the club. To avoid direct conflict with the Toronto chapter, we transferred Eric to the Kingston chapter, which was under the direct supervision of Alain. When we called the Toronto Bandidos to tell them what we had done, they were, needless to say, livid!

The highlight of my unintentionally extended Canadian vacation was a trip to Quebec to meet with some of the new Montreal Bandidos, including Bandido Tout, whom I hadn't seen since my arrest at the Kingston Travelodge. While I was in the area, I decided to spend some time with Tout, taking him up on his earlier invitation to visit his home. Although, technically, I was supposed to stay with Bandido Garfield in Kingston, I wasn't too concerned about breaching my bail condition. It's not like it would result in extra jail time if I got caught. Ultimately, if I lost my deportation hearing, I was just going to be booted out of the country.

Bandido Alain and I traveled from Kingston, where he actually lived, by car to Laval, a town just outside of Montreal. The journey took us east down Highway 401, which ends at the Ontario–Quebec border. The Montreal Bandidos had rented a room for our meeting in an upscale hotel in Laval, which I knew had once been the home base of the infamous Hells Angels North chapter. I don't know if the meeting was held there for my benefit or if there was some other reason, but I was quite impressed with their choice of location, away from the hustle and bustle of Montreal. The room, which was on one of the upper floors, afforded a spectacular view of the surrounding rural area and the dazzling skyline of cosmopolitan Montreal.

It had been decided prior to my meeting with the Montreal Bandidos that Bandido Garfield would not make a good El Secretario; he was not a very organized individual, and as a result, he found it difficult to comprehend what was expected of him. We definitely needed to find someone better qualified to do the job. Bandido Presidente Charley, Bandido Vice Presidente Alain, and I decided that Bandido Robert "Tout" Leger would be the perfect candidate for the job. Alain knew Tout quite well and he had assured me Tout would do an excellent job.

Despite his protestations that he didn't even own a computer, and that he didn't want the job, we somehow conned Tout into it. After the meeting, we all had dinner at a trendy Italian restaurant in Montreal, where we were joined by other local Bandidos. We had a delicious meal and everybody seemed upbeat about the future of the Bandidos in Quebec. I parted ways with the Montreal Bandidos and Vice Presidente Alain after the dinner and accompanied our new El Secretario Tout to his home just south of Montreal.

With my immigration hearing coming up in a few days, however, and the fact that I wasn't even supposed to be out of the Kingston area, I decided to make it a short visit. Still, I managed to spend two days and nights with Tout and his family and had a great time; the Leger family showed me what French-Canadian hospitality was all about. The day before my hearing, Tout gave me a ride back to the Ontario border, where we were met by Alain, who was to drive me the rest of the way to Kingston. When I said good-bye to Tout, promising him we would get together again as soon as possible, I had no idea it would be the last time I would ever see him.

To make it look like I was abiding by my bail conditions, I had Bandido Garfield drive me to Ottawa for my January 17 deportation hearing. It was another bitter cold day, and the closer we got to Ottawa — ninety miles due north of Kingston – the more snow we encountered. I noticed all kinds of dump trucks cruising around piled full of the white stuff. When I asked Garfield what that was all about, he explained the trucks were hauling snow cleared from roads and public parking lots and dumping it in the river. I couldn't believe my eyes — I had never seen anything like it.

The hearing turned out to be another big waste of time, if not a downright farce. I was beginning to wonder if the Canadian authorities and bureaucrats were actually in touch with reality. To make matters worse, Immigration Canada attorneys successfully argued that I needed to stay in Canada for four more months. I was absolutely amazed at their arrogance and lack of common sense, but Josh Zambrowsky explained it was just their way of trying to get me to capitulate — apparently they didn't like to be challenged.

Immigration Canada was under the impression that if I was forced to stay in Canada for four months, I would give up and waive my deportation. Despite the fact it was not reported in the newspapers, which ignored salient details in favor of fabricated ones, Josh argued I did not need to stay in the country, since I would be happy to return to Canada for my next hearing. The adjudicator agreed and, in his final written ruling, ordered me to return for the next hearing, which was scheduled for the middle of May. At the same time, he stated I could live "wherever I wanted" while awaiting the hearing. The adjudicator also ordered that if I decided to return to the United States, I should notify Immigration Canada at the time of my departure. I could now go back to my daughter, my fiancée, the Oklahoma Bandidos chapter, and my construction management business.

On Friday, January 19, I said my good-byes to everyone who had helped me and crossed the border, fittingly enough, at Lansdowne, where a few weeks earlier I had spent two nights in an Immigration Canada holding cell. Once I was in the great state of New York, I headed to Syracuse, where I caught a night train to Cleveland, Ohio. In Cleveland, I boarded a Southwest Airlines flight to Tulsa. Soon I would be back in the American heartland.

My Immigration Canada deportation hearing on January 17 put me back in the headlines. An article published in the Ottawa Sun *gave a fairly accurate report of what transpired at the hearing. It is interesting to note, however, that the writer of the story had me cross the border at Fort Erie instead of Windsor. The two cities are separated by a distance of 248 miles.*

Bandidos departure stalled — Biker told to stay in country until May

By John Steinbachs

January 18, 2001

Bandido biker Edward Winterhalder is accused of being in the country illegally, and Citizenship and Immigration Canada wants him out.

That's why it seemed bizarre yesterday when a lawyer for the government asked for a four-month adjournment during Winterhalder's Immigration and Refugee Board hearing, effectively stranding him on Canadian soil until May.

If he leaves the country and tries to come back, he'll be denied entry by Immigration and forfeit his bail money.

The border-bouncing Bandido — reputedly one of the highest-ranking men in the organization — was busted at a Kingston Travelodge after a biker patchover Jan. 7 where several local Rock Machine members were inducted into the international club.

After five days in jail, he was ordered released on $20,000 bail.

Winterhalder, who says he owns a construction company, wants to go home to take care of his young daughter.

But the adjudicator at the hearing, who admitted his hands were tied in the matter, ruled for an adjournment and denied Winterhalder's request that he be allowed to return to Oklahoma and return for the May hearing.

He ordered Winterhalder to remain on bail and be back in Ottawa for the May hearing.

Immigration officials say they need more time to put together their case against him, which includes entering the country illegally with a criminal record and being a member of the Bandidos, an alleged criminal organization. Winterhalder bristled at the suggestion.

"It's certainly not a criminal organization," he said of the Bandidos after the hearing.

He said he didn't enter the country fraudulently and was waved through the border stop in Fort Erie before he could identify himself and describe his criminal record.

CHAPTER TWO

REFLECTIONS

On the flight back to Oklahoma, all I could think about was the Canadian Bandidos. I also thought of how I got involved with their precursor, the Quebec-based Rock Machine. My mind wandered back to an occasion a few years earlier in Washington State.

It was springtime in the northwestern most state of the continental USA. I thought it always rained there, but it was one of those rare and beautiful days of unexpected sunshine. I was flying into Seattle with my young daughter, Taylor; we were both struck by the towering magnificence of Mt. Ranier, which loomed over the entire region like some giant snow-capped rock god. Once on the ground, it didn't seem to matter where we were: Mt. Ranier dominated the background. Taylor and I were met at Seattle–Tacoma International Airport by Bandido Tim "TJ" Jones. For the duration of our short visit to Seattle, I had decided to stay with TJ and his wife, Sheryl; they had kids around the same age as five-and-a-half-year-old Taylor, so I knew she wouldn't feel lonely when I wasn't around.

The reason for the trip to Washington state in April of 1999 was neither business nor a holiday: I was there to attend the funeral of Bandido Mississippi Charlie. He had died while having sex with his girlfriend. In many cases, when a hardcore biker meets an untimely end, it's a violent end. This was definitely different. If it wasn't for the fact that it was a somber occasion, the whole scenario could have been taken as humorous. Actually, it was kind of humorous: no one can deny that dying while making love isn't such a bad way to go.

There were hundreds of bikers gathered at a small-town cemetery just outside of Seattle where the funeral was taking place. Most of them were Bandidos, but there was a solid representation of other clubs, most of which were from Washington state. I recognized quite a few of the guys and the patches they were wearing, but there was one individual who stood out in the crowd. There was something about him that caught my eye, and it wasn't his rotund size. The first thing I noticed was his patch. It was very unusual. The top and bottom rockers and the center patch were silver on black, with red stitching on all the edges. The center patch depicted a stylized eagle's head that did not look familiar to me. I maneuvered through the throng to get a closer look at the rockers so I could identify the club. When I got within range of the large, mysterious man, whom I estimated to be in his mid-thirties, I realized I was looking at a fullpatch member of the Rock Machine. I knew little about the club, other than that they were exclusive to Canada and basically confined to the province of Quebec. I was also aware that there was a lot of bad blood between the Rock Machine and the Canadian Hells Angels. This was the first Rock Machine member I had ever seen, and I was surprised to find him so far from home attending the funeral of an American Bandido. Unless the brother being laid to rest is a high-ranking club member, it is rare to see foreign bikers — whether from the same club or other clubs — at the funeral. There was also the chance, of course, that the lone Rock Machine had been a friend of Bandido Mississippi Charlie, but somehow I doubted that.

My ever-calculating mind tried to think of another reason why this foreign biker had ventured all the way across the continent. Perhaps it was business-related; perhaps he was on a goodwill mission to bring the American Bandidos and Rock Machine closer together. As recently as the fall of 1997, there had been unsuccessful overtures made by the Rock Machine to the American Bandidos, expressing their desire to become part of the Bandidos Nation. Earlier that year, Australian Bandidos Presidente Michael "Mick" Kulakowski had traveled to Canada to discuss a possible patchover of the Rock Machine, discussions I would learn much later had been very favorable.

Unlike the American Bandidos, the Australian, as well as the European Bandidos, were in favor of expanding the club into Canada. After discussions between Presidente Mick and the Rock Machine hierarchy concluded, the merger was apparently all but a done deal. This turn of events, however, was scuttled when Presidente Mick, along with two other fullpatch Bandidos, was assassinated in the basement of an Australian nightclub on November 9, 1997. If Mick had not died, it is almost certain that the Rock Machine would have become Bandidos by Christmas 1997. The situation with the Hells Angels would no doubt have turned out very differently if the patchover had occurred at that time. The Rock Machine was a much stronger organization then than they were by the time they were finally accepted into the Bandidos Nation in December 2000. Becoming Bandidos would have given them more clout and put them in a much better position to negotiate peace. Conceivably, the turf war with the Hells Angels could have come to an end right then and there.

After ascertaining what club he belonged to, I took the liberty of introducing myself to the Rock Machine member; in heavily accented English, he told me his name was Alain Brunette and that he was from Montreal. We exchanged a few words and then concerned ourselves with the task at hand: shoveling earth onto the coffin of our deceased Bandido brother. I felt like I was the only American Bandido to show any kind of interest in, or spend any time with, the French Canadian. Perhaps the reason no one else would even try to communicate with him was the fact that Alain spoke only broken English, or maybe it was because he was a Rock Machine. I'm not sure why I approached him, other than to sate my curiosity. It could also have been my natural inclination to gravitate toward people who both exude and command respect. In any case, I found myself drawn to him like the proverbial moth to a flame. I had no idea why, but I found myself intrigued by Rock Machine Alain Brunette. There was no way I could have known at the time what an important part of my life the French Canadian would become, or the role I would play in the world of the Rock Machine after their eventual patchover to the Bandidos. In retrospect, I can only ascribe it to fate.

I knew I wouldn't have time to attend the funeral after-party (wake), so I tried to find Rock Machine Alain again before we all dispersed from the cemetery. But it seemed as though he had vanished into thin air, and with a plane to catch, I headed back to Bandido TJ's house to pick up Taylor. Something inside me told me, however, that I would cross paths with the Canadian biker again.

The next Rock Machine member I saw was at the Red River Biker Rally in New Mexico in late May 1999. The memory is distinctive because it was the year after the Oklahoma Bandidos officially became fullpatch members of the Bandidos Nation. I was taken aback to see that the Rock Machine's patch had changed: it was red and gold now, no longer silver and black. Prior to attending the rally, I had heard a rumor that Bandidos Europe had recently designated the Rock Machine as a "hangaround" club; subsequently, the Rock Machine had changed their colors to the Bandidos' red and gold standard. As the shock wore off, I found myself pleasantly surprised to discover that the rumor was indeed true. I was aware that most of the older, hardline U.S. Bandidos were against expansion — an antiquated sentiment I didn't share — and was glad to see the Rock Machine had made some headway in their quest to wear the Bandidos' "Fat Mexican" patch.

Ever since I became aware of the problems in Quebec, I had admired the Rock Machine for standing up to the powerful and wealthy Montreal Hells Angels and their elite Nomads chapter. The Angels were trying to decimate the Rock Machine in a vicious gang war that had left scores dead, wounded, and missing. I especially admired the Rock Machine's tenacity in their efforts to establish a Bandidos chapter in Canada. This was something I could readily identify with, as establishing a new Bandidos chapter was something that had consumed my life for many years.

The fact that the Rock Machine had managed to become a Bandidos hangaround club — an existing club that wants to join a larger motorcycle club — spoke volumes to me. Being accepted as a hangaround club puts everyone in the biker world on notice that a smaller club wants to merge with a larger club and that the larger club is considering the change. In the Bandidos world, after at least one year of carrying on an association with the hangaround club, members vote as to whether the smaller club is worthy to wear the Bandidos patch. If the vote is affirmative, the smaller club is upgraded to probationary Bandidos status. Taking the recalcitrant attitude of the U.S. Bandidos into consideration, I wasn't sure if the Rock Machine would ever achieve their goal. But as a proponent of Bandidos expansionism, I was certainly hopeful for them. Little did I know then that eighteen months later I would find myself in the thick of things when the Rock Machine officially were upgraded from a hangaround club to a Bandidos probationary club.

In mid-November 2000, Bandidos business took me to Denmark, the country that gave us Carlsberg and Tuborg beer. A world meeting was being held outside of Copenhagen, and Bandidos El Presidente George Wegers had personally requested my presence. Because only national officers are allowed to attend a world meeting, I had been appointed an El Secretario just for the occasion. The purpose of the meeting was to discuss issues that concerned Bandidos clubs across the globe. These meetings were usually intense and stressful, condensed into one or two days of practically round-the-clock talks. I wasn't aware of it when I was summoned to Denmark, but the Rock Machine's situation in Canada, with the problem of the Hells Angels and a possible patchover, was going to be included in the agenda.

Instead of flying directly to Denmark, I flew to Frankfurt, Germany, where airport officials paid much less attention to motorcycle club members than their counterparts in Copenhagen. Maybe the Danes were more vigilant; maybe it was the lingering aftereffects of the shooting at Kastrup Airport in March 1996 that had left one Bandido dead and three wounded. A friend and motorcycle business colleague of mine, Dieter Tenter, picked me up at Frankfurt International Airport, and I spent one night with him and his family. The next day, I met up with El Presidente George and El Vice Presidente Jeffrey "Jeff" Pike. George had made the long trip from his home in Bellingham, Washington; Jeff had flown in from Houston, Texas.

We were making the overland trip to Denmark with three German Bandidos, including European Vice Presidente Leslave "Les" Hause and European Sargento de Armas (sergeant-at-arms) Hans Jurgen "Diesel" Herzog. We all piled into a late-model minivan and headed north on the autobahn for the five-hundred-mile journey to Copenhagen. On the way there — before we even got out of Germany — a nondescript car pulled alongside us on the high-speed autobahn. The passenger started making all kinds of histrionic hand gestures in order to attract our attention, and he was definitely succeeding!

"What the hell is going on? Are these guys for real?" El Presidente George said, obviously concerned that we might be in for some kind of unpleasantness.

I must admit, I was wondering myself what this charade was all about. In my mind it could be only one of three possibilities: rival club members looking for a confrontation; the police on a mission of biker harassment; or not-too-bright "citizens" out to taunt "bikers." That begged the question: how did they know we were bikers? There was no visible evidence of that on the exterior of the van, and nobody was wearing their colors inside the vehicle, as per Bandidos tradition.

"They're for real, all right. They're Polizei [German police]. Looks like we're going to get pulled over," Bandido Les, who was driving, said matter-of-factly.

The unmarked cruiser lurched ahead and then veered into our lane, installing itself right in front of us, so we were now following the Polizei. Suddenly, a lighted screen popped up at the bottom of the car's rear window with a message in German that instructed us to follow. When we approached an exit, the lead dog signaled intent to leave the highway, and we followed suit. No one had any idea why we were being pulled over; we could only surmise it was because we were all Bandidos. No doubt, if their intelligence was up to snuff, the authorities knew the van was full of high-ranking Bandidos — a prize engagement for any cop.

"Just be cool. It could be anything," Bandido Les said, appearing unperturbed.

Cool was the word and cool it was. It could indeed have been anything, and for the American contingent aboard the van, the worst-case scenario was deportation. As soon as it was safe to stop, the police car pulled over to the side of the road, and Les came to a stop behind them. To my surprise, he got out of the minivan and walked over to the cops who remained in their vehicle. I found this very odd, because in the United States the cop always comes to you — you don't ever go to the cop. As a matter of fact, they get real antsy if you step out of your car unless you've been instructed to do so. If that is the case, chances are good they already have their weapon drawn.

Bandido Les and the driver of the police car exchanged some banter, and Les handed over his driver's license and vehicle documents. In less than five minutes, glancing up to the sky as if looking for a plane or helicopter, the European Bandidos Vice Presidente returned to the minivan and the police car drove off.

"A speeding ticket. Can you believe that?" Les said, shaking his head. He got back behind the wheel of the minivan, fired up the engine, and headed back toward the highway. Les explained he had been issued a fine for driving too fast through the construction zone we had passed some twenty miles earlier. Even on the fast-paced German autobahn, speeding through a construction zone was a definite no-no. Les said he didn't remember speeding and was convinced he had obeyed the reduce-speed posting. The last thing he wanted was to get stopped by the Polizei; like bikers everywhere, avoiding needless encounters with the police was high on Les's priority list.

"Makes you wonder if they have us under surveillance and just wanted to make sure they had the right van," Les said, shrugging his shoulders.

It was indeed a strange scene; but strange scenes are part and parcel of the 1%er world. Why it took so long for the cops to react, we'll never know, but at least we weren't subjected to a major hassle and delay. We eventually arrived at our destination in a rural area of eastern Denmark around 7:00 p.m. It was shortly after nightfall, and our surroundings were pitch-black except for the odd streetlight, porch light, or a muted glow filtering through the windows of the few houses we passed.

Although I was still suffering from jet lag and didn't feel well, I was glad to see Bandidos from all over the world had congregated in this out-of-the-way location for the meeting. Included in the group was European Sargento de Armas Helga from Norway; European Sargento de Armas Johnny and European Nomad Clark from Sweden; European Presidente Jan "Jim" Tinndahn from Denmark; European Vice Presidente Mike from Denmark (who controlled Scandinavia); European El Secretario Gessner from Denmark; European El Secretario Munk from Denmark; European Vice Presidente Les (who controlled Germany) and European Sargento de Armas Diesel from Germany; Australian Presidente Jason Addison and El Secretario Larry; El Presidente George, El Vice Presidente Jeff, and myself from the USA.

The meeting was held out in the middle of nowhere in a house that was surrounded by farmers' fields, woods, and a contingent of armed Bandidos. Once we had arrived, we were not allowed to leave or even go outside for a breath of fresh air by ourselves. We were told this was a precautionary measure put in place for our own safety. Although the Scandinavian bike clubs had lived in relative peace since 1997, our hosts didn't want to take any chances. Still fresh in everyone's minds were the murders of two Bandidos and an associate in Lahti, Finland, in early February 2000. The three had been assassinated while eating lunch at a restaurant. Bandido Bjorn Isaksson, president of the Helsinki chapter, Bandido Sakke Pirra, and Juha Jalonen, a member of the Black Rhino Motorcycle Club, were all killed in a hail of gunfire. Within days, local police arrested about a dozen members of the former Lahti chapter of the Cannonball Motorcycle Club, of which three were suspected of direct involvement in the shootings.

According to the authorities, the attack was payback for the attempted assassination of a Cannonball member in October 1999; he survived the attack with a bullet in the leg. The Bandidos members allegedly responsible for that shooting were appearing in a Lahti court around the time of the slayings. It was definitely not a good start to the New Year.

Shortly after we settled in, we were informed that there were three Rock Machine members in the area who would soon be joining us. They were identified as Martin "Blue" Blouin, Alain Brunette, and one other guy I only got to know as "Will" Williamson. I was quite surprised to hear that Alain was in the area and found myself anticipating his arrival.

With meetings scheduled for the entire next day, I knew I needed to get a good night's sleep. As usual, after flying to Europe I was totally jet-lagged, even a few days later. I looked around for a place to bunk down and found a tiny sauna room where I thought I could try to get some sleep. That notion was supplanted when European Sargento de Armas Johnny decided to engage me in an all-night game of Ace of Spades, which involved him trying to sneak up on you while you were sleeping and put an ace of spades on you without waking you up. I had told Bandido Johnny that I was a very light sleeper and that he would be unable to tag me.

"You have to be more than a light sleeper to beat me Ed, because I'm a very light walker, like a cat," he told me, convinced he would succeed. By the end of the night, and numerous attempts, Bandido Johnny found out that Connecticut Ed was indeed a light sleeper. He was fortunate that I am not a gambling man, or he would have been relieved of the money he wanted to bet me.

The next day, we had meetings off and on all morning and afternoon. We would meet for a while, take a break, watch some television — the European Bandidos were especially enamored with American westerns — resume our meeting, and then eat a meal. The cooking was done by the European Bandidos members and supervised by European Vice Presidente Mike, who had actually gone to culinary school. Over the next few days we discussed a myriad of issues that were of club importance worldwide, none of which concerned illegal activities. For anyone eavesdropping, the business covered would have sounded rather mundane, especially if they were expecting incriminating dialogue.

World Meeting – Europe – November 15, 2000

Old Business

1. USA to provide Europe & Australia with disc of correct patch design.

2. Call Tutti regarding German MC club about patch — advise German Bandidos.

New Business

1. Canada — someday soon is ok — currently there is peace — RM removed SYLB patch & HA changed colors on support club — as part of the peace — peace is very important to keep.

2. Relationship with Outlaws in Canada, USA, Australia & England — stabbing of Bandido by Outlaw Probate in Guernsey. George will talk to Frank and set up meetings worldwide between us and the Outlaws.

3. Consider updating Fat Mexican — drawings to be submitted.

4. Check and see if probationary members in USA are wearing 5 yr charter patch — if so, remove immediately.

5. Actual color of gold on patches to be determined by patch reps (USA, Europe & Australia) and standardized.

6. The shield is the official 5 yr patch worldwide.

7. Patch reps (USA, Europe, and Australia) to make decisions on officers' patches. President, Vice Pres, Sgt at Arms, Sec-Treas, Secretary, Treasurer, Road Captain with no periods.

8. Europe — return history books to George via CT Ed.

9. Patch reps (USA, Europe, and Australia) to make decision on Life Member patch.

10. No more mandatory visits to other countries for Europe and Australia members.

11. Whispering Jim & Uncle Mad — giving away ENM patches in Europe.

12. Switzerland HA incident — Munich chapter — Sep 00 — rest area.

13. Relationship with HA in USA, Europe, Germany, Scandanavia, & Australia.

14. Outlaws friendship with Black Ghostriders in Germany; Pagans friendship with Bats in Germany.

15. Thailand — support club — Diablo MC.

16. USA runs are: Birthday Run (1st week of March) & Memorial Day Run (last weekend in May) & Sturgis (1st full

week of August) & Labor Day Run (1st weekend in September) & Thanksgiving (last Thursday in November).

17. Australia's triangle international patch is ok to be given to USA & Europe Brothers that have visited Australia — all gift patches given to Australia & Europe Brothers are not to be worn on vest without approval from their National officer.

18. If your death is the result of a suicide, you are not deserving of a Bandido funeral.

19. If you a borrow a bike, ol' lady, or any other Bandido-owned property while visiting another area, chapter, or country, leave the property in the same or better condition than what you received it in when you leave.

Most of what was discussed at the world meeting is reflected in the minutes I took: it is hardly the stuff a police official or "citizen" would anticipate.

During the afternoon meetings, the subject of the Rock Machine possibly becoming Bandidos was discussed many different times. By now, the Rock Machine had been a hangaround club for about eighteen months and something needed to be done. The European and Australian Bandidos were adamant that the Canadians should become Bandidos immediately. It was a notion that I shared. Conversely, my compatriots El Presidente George and El Vice Presidente Jeff were of the opinion that they should never become Bandidos.

According to rumors, the El Presidente had made a deal with both the American and Canadian Hells Angels; the gist of the agreement was that the Rock Machine would never become Bandidos. Allegedly, George had concurred with the Angels' stance that the Bandidos should never patch (take in) an enemy of the Hells Angels. Whether or not the rumor was true, I didn't know, but the subject made for long and sometimes heated discussion. I didn't realize that George, who had many good intentions and who wanted to please everyone, was prone to making promises he would never be able to keep. Although at the time I never would have believed that George was capable of such duplicity, in the next few years his true nature would manifest itself over and over again. After a lot of bickering on day two of the meeting, a compromise was reached late in the afternoon. The American, European, and Australian Bandidos settled their differences and finally agreed that when peace was firmly established between the Rock Machine and the Hells Angels in Canada, the Rock Machine could become Bandidos.

Early that evening, Alain, Blue, and Will from the Rock Machine arrived. They had shown up just in time to join us for dinner, which consisted of a tasty stew concocted by our resident chef, Bandido Mike. After we ate, we all caught up on personal matters and then sat down around a big table to discuss the Rock Machine becoming Bandidos. Alain, Blue, and Will were told the Rock Machine would continue to be a hangaround club for the time being. If they could broker a lasting peace with the Hells Angels, then, and only then, would the Rock Machine be allowed to become Bandidos. Everyone at the table supported the proposal, but in my opinion, El Presidente George agreed only because he was certain peace would never last and that it was only a matter of time before the Rock Machine capitulated. George probably wasn't the only one to think along those lines, if indeed he did. When you took into consideration the long-running turf war between the Rock Machine and the Hells Angels, and how the Angels appeared to have the upper hand, only the most optimistic of people could have believed a positive outcome was in the cards.

But unbeknownst to the American Bandidos at the meeting

was the fact that the Rock Machine and Hells Angels Canada had sat down for talks just a couple of months earlier on September 26, 2000. For the first time ever, Rock Machine President Frederick "Fred" Faucher and infamous Hells Angels' Nomad President Maurice "Mom" Boucher met in a room at the Quebec City courthouse to discuss a preliminary plan for peace between the two clubs. The unusual choice of location, selected by lawyers who represented Faucher and Boucher, apparently did not sit well with Quebec justice officials when it became known their hallowed ground had been used for a biker powwow.

Two weeks after the courthouse meeting in Quebec City, Faucher and Boucher announced that the war between the Rock Machine and the Hells Angels was officially over. This time a much more public place was used for their meeting, the venerable Bleu Marin restaurant in Montreal. A photojournalist from the weekly Quebec crime tabloid *Allô Police* was on hand to take pictures of the two leaders shaking hands. Fred and Mom and their respective entourages had a great dinner, and the get-together proved to be a timely photo op, but that's about it. Not long after the dinner meeting, rumors circulated that the Rock Machine was going to join the Hells Angels. Even though Mom Boucher — sometimes referred to as the "John Gotti of the bikers" — may have dreamed of such a merger to further his own agenda, the Rock Machine had every intention of becoming Bandidos, not Angels. It was no secret that Faucher had met with then–Vice Presidente George three years earlier in October 1997, hoping an invitation to patch over the Rock Machine would materialize. No such invitation was extended, but despite George's resistance, it was the beginning of a dance that would result in exactly what Faucher had hoped for.

Shortly after the sit-down meeting came to an end, Alain and I had time to talk for a while. I hadn't seen him since the funeral in Seattle nearly eighteen months earlier. I wanted us to pick up where we had left off and get to know each other a little better. With the real possibility of becoming a Bandido, Alain was pretty upbeat, and he appeared in fairly good health despite all the stress that came with being a member of the Rock Machine. Alain was a marked man, and it wasn't unusual for him to wear a bulletproof vest when he ventured out onto the streets. The brutal war that raged in Canada between the Hells Angels and Rock Machine had been taking its toll on everyone concerned, including the public.

I was surprised to learn that in the days following the world meeting in Denmark, the European and Australian Bandidos had somehow convinced El Presidente George that the time had come to change the Rock Machine into Bandidos. After the meeting, on their way to a fullpatch party for German Bandidos in Aachen, Germany, Australian Presidente Jason and European Presidente Jim hammered away at El Presidente George and El Vice Presidente Jeff, urging them to see it their way and patch over the Rock Machine. Jim and Jason were still angry with George over a Bandidos world meeting in Thailand earlier in 2000. Apparently, the El Presidente had given his approval for the merger at the Thai meeting but then changed his mind by the time he got back to the United States. No doubt the reason for this arbitrary decision was that he didn't want to admit to the American Bandidos, who were adamantly against the merger, that he had approved it.

Meanwhile, Alain, Blue, and Will had arrived in Aachen from the world meeting in Denmark one day ahead of El Presidente

George and his entourage. Like the rest of us, they were going to attend the fullpatch party for the German Bandidos. When they got to Aachen, Alain, Blue, and Will met with current Rock Machine leader Jean "Charley" Duquaire and advised him of everything that had transpired at the world meeting. Charley decided to force El Presidente George to do the right thing and patch over the Rock Machine or, as the French Canadian put it, "pull his pants up and act like a man." Without conferring with the rank-and-file members of the Rock Machine in Canada, Charley made the decision to tell George that his club was ready to change over and become Bandidos. Not wanting to lose the momentum generated at the world meeting, Charley knew he had to capitalize on the situation as it then stood or risk more delays. The turf war in Quebec with the Hells Angels had already caused much damage to both clubs, but especially to the Rock Machine. No more time could be wasted.

The biker war that had erupted in Montreal in 1994 and fanned out across the province of Quebec had left more than 160 dead and scores injured. Quebec bikers had a reputation for being the meanest and deadliest on the planet, and this grim toll certainly underscored that. Sadly, one of the victims included an eleven-year-old boy, Daniel Desrochers, an innocent bystander killed by shrapnel from a bomb that had been planted under a vehicle owned by Marc Dubé, a small-time drug dealer who reportedly had run afoul of the Hells Angels. Dubé was killed instantly that fateful day in the Hochelaga-Maisonneuve district of Montreal in August 1995; the boy died four days later from a head wound. In military terms, his death would have been referred to as collateral damage and barely raised an eyebrow; in Quebec, the incident sparked such public outrage that it led the Canadian government to implement Bill C-95. This legislation was enacted specifically to target organized crime and increase jail terms for convicted offenders who were proven to belong to established criminal organizations. Eventually, using the bill as their calling card, authorities in Quebec started coming down heavily on the biker community, including the Outlaws, Hells Angels, and the Bandidos.

Charley, like most of the Rock Machine's membership, was counting on the fact that a merger with the Bandidos would bring an end to the senseless bloodletting in Montreal. During the fullpatch party that night, Charley met with Presidente Jason, Presidente Jim, El Presidente George, El Vice Presidente Jeff, and a few other high-ranking Bandidos members and told them that the Rock Machine was ready to be part of the Bandidos Nation and that now was the time to begin the assimilation. George had no choice at this point but to capitulate, and he did so to the accolades of everyone in the room except for El Vice Presidente Jeff, one of a vanguard of American Bandidos who wanted nothing to do with the Canadians.

After the Denmark world meeting finally wrapped up late on the second day, I caught a ride into Copenhagen, where I planned to look up a friend of mine, a Bandido named Kemo. I had met Bandido Kemo on an earlier trip to Europe and we had stayed in touch. Although it seemed like the meeting had been held in the middle of nowhere, a good half hour later I found myself on the outskirts of Denmark's capital city, one of the oldest in Europe. Within no time I was ringing Bandido Kemo's doorbell, hoping I would catch him at home. To my delight, he answered the door and ushered me inside, insisting I spend the night. After finally getting a good night's sleep, I felt refreshed enough to do a bit of sightseeing, and I tooled around the city with Kemo the following day. I had been fascinated by Copenhagen when I first saw the city a few years earlier and was again enjoying the sights. While driving around town, Bandido Kemo pointed out a brand-new store that was run by the Denmark Hells Angels. It looked very upscale, and because I had never seen anything like it, I convinced Kemo to stop so we could go inside and have a look around.

"Sure, if that's what you want to do," he said. "You can go in and check it out. I'm sure it will be okay."

We found a parking spot, got out of the car, and after putting on our colors so we would be readily identified as Bandidos, we headed across the street to the Hells Angels' store. We entered the building that housed the store, but Kemo did not seem intent on going into the store with me.

"You go ahead. I'm going to say hello to a buddy of mine who owns the tattoo shop downstairs. Don't worry, it's cool. He's a friend. I'll come looking for you in about five minutes," Kemo said and then headed down a spiral staircase that led to the tattoo shop in the basement.

I wondered if Kemo actually thought my dropping into the store was reason for concern. There had been some serious issues between the Denmark Bandidos and Hells Angels earlier in the decade, but that was water under the bridge now. From early 1994 till mid-1997, a war had raged across all of Scandinavia (Denmark, Norway, Finland, and Sweden) between the Bandidos and the Hells Angels and their respective hangaround and support clubs. The weapons of choice had included home-made bombs, hand grenades, anti-tank rockets, knives, and guns.

In the wake of the Scandinavian biker war, eleven people were dead and ninety-six injured. Five of those killed were Bandidos, including Bandidos Sweden President Mikael "Joe" Ljunggren; Bandidos Finland Vice President Jarkko Kokko; Uffe Larsen (Denmark Bandidos); Bjorn Gudmandsen (Denmark Bandidos); and Bandido Prospect Jan Krogh Jensen (Norway). Another victim of the carnage was a young

Norwegian woman. Like the eleven-year-old boy in Montreal, she died from injuries sustained when a car bomb exploded. The bomb, which leveled the entire Bandidos clubhouse in Drammen, Norway, amazingly claimed no other casualties.

Scandinavian authorities attributed the violence to control over the "criminal underworld." More informed, or perhaps more forthright, officials later called it what it really was: macho bullying that was meant to prove which club was the best, the toughest, and the most prestigious of them all. After things had settled down, one police official echoed those sentiments and stated the conflict had been "childish maybe, but very deadly."

The war had started with the shooting of a Hells Angel in February 1994 and ended with the shooting of a Bandidos prospect in June 1997; an official truce wasn't declared until a few months later. Since that time, things had been relatively peaceful, and I saw no reason not to sate my curiosity by entering the store. Besides, I had been in Denmark in the spring of 1998 when things were still simmering down. To ensure my safety, I had been surrounded by local Bandidos bodyguards the entire time, but there had been no incidents at all and I didn't expect any now.

When I walked into the store I was amazed by how spotless, elegant, and well lit it was. Although Hells Angels support stores were nothing new, this one was a cut above the norm. I had never seen such a classy biker store. Having a background in the construction business, I could see that no expense had been spared fitting out the place. Although the exterior was modest enough, the interior, resplendent in chrome, teak, mahogany, and hardwood cherry, reminded me of the type of upscale establishment you'd find on Fifth Avenue in New York City or Rodeo Drive in Beverly Hills.

All the merchandise carried by the store, from T-shirts to jogging suits, was related to the Hells Angels and effectively displayed on expensive shelving or hanging on stainless-steel tube racks. I noticed about a half-dozen club members inside the store, and from their expressions, it was obvious they were completely thrown for a loop. They gazed at me as if I had dropped in from another planet, utter disbelief etched on their faces.

"How you doing? My name is Connecticut Ed," I said, offering my hand to the closest Angel. "Nice place you got here."

"Uhm . . . yeah . . . thank you," he said, eyeing me with suspicion.

It was obvious they didn't get too many Bandidos in their store. The fact that I was an American must have confused the issue even more. I'm sure they didn't know what to make of me, or if they thought there was some purpose to my visit other than just admiring their store.

"Mind if I have a look around?" I asked.

"Only if you buy something," the Angel said, studying me for a reaction, which he didn't get. He then snickered and said, "I'm joking. Go ahead."

As I started looking around, I noticed the Angel I had spoken with make a head gesture to one of the other guys, who then called up to a second-storey balcony office that overlooked the store. A moment later, a large man with a shaved head sauntered purposefully down the stairs. I assumed, rightly so, that he was in charge. He said something in Danish to the Angel who had called him, who in turn just pointed at me. He walked over to me under the watchful eyes of his brothers.

"Hello, I'm Blondie. And you are an American Bandido," he said with a hint of a smile appearing on his face. He thrust his hand out to me and I shook it. The rest of the guys started to ease up after we shook hands and introductions were made. I found myself face to face with Bent "Blondie" Nielsen. I had never met him before, but I knew him by reputation. Bent

Nielsen was a well-known leader of the Denmark Hells Angels and highly respected figure in the European outlaw biker community. I knew that Nielsen had been instrumental in ending the Scandinavian biker war and, like most of us, he just wanted to coexist peacefully with other clubs. It had been a major media event when Hells Angel Blondie and Bandidos European Presidente Jim appeared on Danish television September 25, 1997, to announce the two clubs would cease hostilities. Although an undercurrent of tension is always present where rival outlaw clubs are concerned, everything had been more or less copacetic between the Scandinavian Bandidos and Hells Angels since the symbolic handshake.

"We don't have many American Bandidos visit us," Blondie said. "I think you're the first. We're honored. So, you like our store, huh?"

As Blondie and I chatted, the atmosphere in the store became more relaxed and unthreatening. The motorcycle club patches and ideology were no longer of prime importance. This was about a brotherhood in which motorcycles were the common denominator, a brotherhood I had known for many years, not just with fellow Harley riders, but with motorcyclists in general. The feeling is pervasive in the motorcycle world, whether it's oriented toward recreational riding, transportation, racing, or making a statement . . . or, in some cases, all of the above.

Blondie and I talked briefly about motorcycle club politics, why we should all get along, and the concept of the store, which was obviously his pride and joy. Our conversation was cut short when Kemo entered the store. He exchanged greetings with Blondie and the rest of the Angels; they all knew one another and seemed to be on friendly enough terms.

"So we owe it to you, the visit of an American Bandido," Blondie said to Kemo as they shook hands. "Can I offer you a coffee or something?"

The question was directed at both of us, but Kemo said we had to go. He explained that I was on a tight schedule and that he wanted to show me some more places in the city before I left Denmark. I promised Hells Angel Blondie that I'd drop by the store again next time I came to Copenhagen, and Kemo and I left to resume our tour of the beautiful city.

On November 22, 2000, one week after the world meeting in Denmark, Bandidos El Presidente George had a secret rendezvous at Peace Arch Park on the west coast of the North American continent with Richard "Dick" Mayrand, a high-ranking member of the Quebec Hells Angels. The sixty-seven-foot arch, located between Vancouver, British Columbia, to the north and Bellingham, Washington, to the south, has one foot anchored in American soil, the other in Canadian. It was an ideal place for an American and a Canadian to get together for talks without the risk of being detained at the border.

At this meeting Bandido George confirmed what up to that point had just been rumors as far as the Hells Angels were concerned: the Rock Machine would soon be members of the Bandidos. This news was not well received by Mayrand, especially after the El Presidente had made it known earlier that the Bandidos would not take in the Hells Angels' enemies.

Shortly after the Peace Arch Park meeting, the Rock Machine Motorcycle Club ceased to exist. On December 1, 2000 the Bandidos Motorcycle Club Canada was born. A patchover party was planned for January 6, 2001 at the former Rock Machine clubhouse in Kingston, Ontario, where it would be announced to the world that the Rock Machine were now officially Bandidos.

CHAPTER THREE

A MATTER
OF FATE

It had been a bizarre two weeks in Canada, and I was happy to finally be back home. Oklahoma was a sight to behold; it had never looked so good. But the joy of being home was overshadowed by the news that on the evening of January 18, 2001, the night before I had left Canada, the biker killings had resumed. Real "Tin Tin" Dupont, a fullpatch member of the Bandidos Montreal chapter, was shot to death while sitting in his car.

Bandido Tin Tin had been keeping a low profile by staying away from other club members, one of the conditions of his parole. Up until now, the victims of the Quebec biker war had been members of the Hells Angels and Rock Machine or their support club members and associates. Tin Tin was the first Canadian Bandido to die. For Bandidos worldwide, this was a very serious situation. We had anticipated that our arrival in Canada would keep the peace, not provoke more violence. The turf war with the Hells Angels was obviously anything but over.

Before we got over the death of Tin Tin, another setback

befell the Canadian Bandidos, although this one had been anticipated. As Bandidos Vice Presidente Alain and I had feared a few weeks earlier, the Toronto North Bandidos chapter fell apart. Most of them were *too* pro Hells Angels to be like us. We had tried to convince them that they needed to have regular employment. If they wanted to be big-time drug dealers or get involved in other illegal activities, they needed to leave the club.

We also tried to teach them that to get respect you had to give respect. You could never receive and maintain respect through fear and intimidation. We were of the opinion that to survive long-term as a member of a 1%er club, you had to have visual means of support: gainful employment, income from a disability pension, or a wife or girlfriend who worked and didn't mind a biker for a househusband.

Selling drugs or engaging in other criminal enterprises to make a living usually proves, sooner or later, to be counterproductive. Most of the Canadian Bandidos understood this. It appeared that the majority of the Toronto North chapter did not. After the collapse of their chapter, all but a handful became Hells Angels. Those who chose not to join the Angels retired from the 1%er world and became independent bikers.

The Toronto Sun'*s article about the demise of the Bandidos Toronto North chapter proved to be fairly accurate. Although the newspaper reported that there was a Bandidos chapter in London, this was incorrect. Some of the Toronto Bandidos did try to establish a chapter in London, but it never got off the ground.*

Toronto bikers close up chapter

By Rob Lamberti and Jack Boland

February 6, 2001

The Bandidos biker gang has shut down its Toronto chapter.

It's the second Ontario chapter to close since the Hells Angels arrived in the province last year.

The rapid implosion follows the defection of more than a dozen Ontario Bandidos since the Hells swallowed four Ontario gangs Dec. 29.

The Hells moved into Ontario in response to the Rock Machine — with chapters in Montreal, Quebec City, eastern chapters in Kingston, Toronto and western in London — becoming probationary Bandidos on Dec. 1.

Police said the Hells' plan was to squeeze competition from the world's second-largest biker gang out of the province.

'Ontario Phenomenon'

When the Rock Machine became probationary Bandidos, five members instead joined the Hells Angels, including Paul "Sasquatch" Porter, president of the Eastern chapter.

About 10 members of the Bandidos' Toronto chapter quit with president Bill Miller and last week joined the Hells' Lanark County chapter — west of Ottawa — headed by Porter.

The four remaining members of Toronto's Bandidos chapter refused to join the Hells and have retired.

"It's an Ontario phenomenon," said Surete du Quebec Sgt. Guy Ouellette.

"These guys are there just to enjoy the advantages of being bikers, money-wise."

Joe Halak, who briefly became the Bandidos' Toronto president, refused to comment.

The Rock Machine and Hells Angels were locked in a bloody six-year turf war in Quebec until hammering out a truce last Thanksgiving.

A little more than a week later, bullets were flying again. Bandido Vice Presidente Alain came within an inch of his life on February 13, 2001, while driving his white Pontiac Grand Am along Highway 15 in the rolling hills and eroded mountains of the Laurentians near Mirabel. It was a stroke of sheer luck that Alain and a passenger in the car, Bandido Prospect William "Bill" Ferguson, survived. Despite having a bullet pass through his belly — one of the most painful of gunshot wounds — and coming very close to death, Alain was in good spirits when I spoke with him on the phone as he lay recovering in his hospital bed.

"It all happened so quickly," Alain said. "Those guys were next to us in no time, and all hell broke loose!"

Alain explained that he had been driving down the highway when he and Bill noticed a car tailing them from some distance behind. At first they thought it was the police, not an implausible assumption considering how often 1%ers are followed by law enforcement. By the time they realized it wasn't the authorities, the assassins' car was beside them, and the shooting had started. In just seconds, Alain's Grand Am was riddled with bullet holes and had most of its windows blown out. To save their lives, Alain swerved the Pontiac into the opposing lanes and drove the wrong way against oncoming traffic.

"It would have been really crazy if we ended up smashing into another car and getting killed that way," Alain mused. "I think it was fate that we made it out of there."

Not long after the shooting, police in Piedmont — about

twenty miles from the scene of the attack — found a handgun and bullets, as well as a burned-out car. No one had to tell us that the Hells Angels had sent the shooters. The torched vehicle, a common trademark of a biker shooting, matched the description of the assassins' car. It appeared the Angels had left their calling card. Whereas Tin Tin's murder could arguably have been unrelated to biker rivalry, this incident left no doubt the truce between the Bandidos and the Angels had been broken.

On the same day as the attempt on Alain's life, more discouraging news came our way. The president of the Bandidos Quebec City chapter, Fred Faucher, who had been held in jail on multiple drug charges since his arrest in early December 2000, was charged with the attempted murder of a number of Hells Angels. Bandido Fred had been at the forefront of assimilating the Rock Machine into the Bandidos, and had actually become a member of the Bandidos while incarcerated. He had also been instrumental in getting the Hells Angels to agree to a truce when he met with Mom Boucher six months earlier in Quebec City. Bandido Fred was now accused of a total of twenty-six criminal acts, seven of which involved the manufacturing of bombs.

Some three months later, Faucher would plead guilty to the crimes he had been charged with and received a twelve-year prison sentence. At the same time, another prominent Quebec City Bandido, Marcel "LeMaire" Demers, pled guilty and was sentenced to nine years in prison. Bandido LeMaire had been arrested with Bandido Fred in December 2000 on numerous drug charges.

We were still dealing with Alain's narrow escape and the negative publicity surrounding Bandido Fred when, one day after the botched assassination, another hit was carried out — this time successfully. Michel Gauthier, a friend of some of the Montreal Bandidos, was killed as he drove off in his car around 8:00 a. m.

A few days after what newspapers had labeled a "flare-up" of the biker war, our luck seemed to change. At a Holiday Inn near Montreal, police arrested eight Hells Angels who were planning to murder members of the Montreal Bandidos. Seven of the arrested were either prospects or fullpatch members of the Quebec Nomads Hells Angels chapter. The Nomads, founded by Mom Boucher in June 1995, were comprised of an elite group of Hells Angels whose main focus was criminal activity, establishing new Hells Angels chapters, and eliminating rivals. As their name implies, and unlike regular Hells Angels chapters, the Nomads were not confined to any particular region or clubhouse; this ultimately made it more difficult for their enemies or the police to monitor their actions and plan countermeasures.

When arrested, the Nomads were in possession of an incriminating "hit list" that even included recent pictures of their intended victims. One of the names and pictures on the list was that of Bandido Vice Presidente Alain. Because Mom Boucher, president of the Quebec Nomad Hells Angels chapter, was already in jail, we hoped that this signaled an end to the renewed hostilities. It was also an indication that the police were all over the Hells Angels and determined to eradicate them from Canada. Of course, that begged the question of what was on the cards in the future. It no doubt meant "today the Angels . . . tomorrow the rest of the clubs."

The other shoe dropped on March 28, 2001, when more than 125 Hells Angels and their associates were arrested. Also included in the sweep were all the members of the Rockers and Evil Ones, Quebec Hells Angels' puppet clubs. Many of them were charged under a new federal anti-gang law, C-95. At least sixty-five fullpatch members of the Hells Angels in Quebec were now behind bars or were going to be arrested as soon as they were located. We were convinced the killing would now stop.

In mid-March, at the annual Birthday Run for all U.S. Bandidos, Bandido El Presidente George asked me to continue supervising Bandidos Canada until the end of their probationary period in December 2001. The El Presidente wanted me to handle all the legitimate club business with Canada, which included communications and the hiring or firing of national officers.

In early April, I replaced Bandido Presidente Charley, who had gone to Europe to avoid dealing with the Canadian legal system, with Bandido Alain. I was convinced Alain was the best man for the job, not because he had become a good friend, but because no other candidate had as much heart, courage, and insight into the biker world.

By the time May rolled around, things were running about as smoothly as could be hoped for, and I started making plans to return to Canada for my absurd deportation hearing. To my surprise and dismay, however, Immigration Canada requested a postponement of the hearing. They claimed to need at least six more months to investigate my case. The adjudicator, who appeared to be the only sane person involved with the case, ruled against Immigration and set the new hearing date for October 5, 2001.

Meanwhile, progress was being made with our Bandidos Canada expansion efforts, something that was crucial to the long-term viability of the club. On May 22, 2001, twelve members of the Toronto Loners Motorcycle Club formed a new

Bandidos chapter with headquarters in a suburb just outside of the city. Ever since Bandido Alain and I had met with Peter "Peppi" Barilla in Toronto in mid-January, we had stayed in close touch with him and other club members.

After the collapse of the Bandidos Toronto North chapter in February, it had been our intention to open another Toronto chapter; we just needed the right group of guys to do it. Not only did the Toronto Loners seem to be the right bunch, the Loners had chapters in Italy that were aligned with the European Bandidos. The Canadian Loners also had a fairly long history. The club had been founded in Ontario in 1979, although it ceased to exist in 1986 when many of the original members joined the Outlaws Motorcycle Club.

In 1990, a number of ex-Satan's Choice Motorcycle Club members rekindled the Loners, and by 1999 there were chapters in Woodbridge, Richmond Hill, St. Thomas, and Amherstburg, all in Ontario. In 2001, after the majority of the Canadian Loners patched over to the Bandidos, only the Loners Woodbridge chapter remained.

To oversee our growth in the Toronto area, Bandidos Presidente Alain appointed Peppi Barilla as Vice Presidente of the Canadian Bandidos, a position Peppi would shoulder in addition to his duties as Toronto Bandidos chapter president. Since Alain and I had met Peppi on that frigid January day, I had developed a great deal of respect for him and thought he was an excellent choice. Bandido Peppi had been a member of the Loners since the early 1990s, and he knew everyone in Toronto's motorcycle club world. He was even on speaking terms with some of the Hells Angels in that area, guys he had known in other clubs prior to their becoming members of the Angels.

By early July, everything was going well. It looked like the deadly conflict between the Hells Angels and Bandidos was now over for good. And with summer in full bloom, many of the new club members were cruising around on their bikes: for the first time they were able to proudly wear their Bandidos colors. What was really encouraging was the fact that about half of the members of Bandidos Canada in Quebec were gainfully employed — ditto nearly all of the Ontario Bandidos. Many others were stay-at-home husbands whose wives or girlfriends were working and supporting them. Of course, there were also some who were doing their "own thing," something that is inevitable in the biker world.

Meanwhile, I was still making headlines in Canadian newspapers. We all took notice when the *Ottawa Citizen* ran a major article about my convoluted battle with Immigration Canada. I couldn't believe my eyes when I noticed the article actually stated that I was a legitimate businessman and contributing member of society. To the best of my knowledge, this was the first article in a Canadian newspaper to portray an outlaw biker in such a fashion.

The Ottawa Citizen*'s Gary Dimmock wrote an interesting article about my immigration situation. It was anything but favorable to Immigration Canada.*

Canada fights to ban biker kingpin — Senior US gang member insists on right to take up with Canadian brothers

By Gary Dimmock

July 21, 2001

Edward Winterhalder, reputed to be one of the most powerful members of the U.S.-based Bandidos, a ruthless, worldwide biker gang, is trying to position himself closer to new Canadian chapters, mostly ex-Rock Machine bikers, amid police fears of an intensified street war against the gang's rival, Hells Angels.

Though Mr. Winterhalder, 46, insists the gang's presence "brought an end to the supposed [biker] war," the federal government is trying to stop him from entering the country because of his criminal record and alleged links to organized crime. They say he is a danger to the public.

The highly placed biker told the *Citizen* he's determined to fight the Immigration and Refugee Board to win the right to travel freely across the border.

"I'm absolutely fighting it. It's a case of personal liberty, and I want to travel," Mr. Winterhalder said.

It's also a matter of business.

"I'm not an undesirable. I'm a legitimate businessman," said Mr. Winterhalder, a single father of a young girl who describes himself as a respected member of society.

Corporate records filed in Oklahoma list Mr. Winterhalder as owner of a construction firm that won contracts worth $20 million U.S. in the past two years — including the construction of a county courthouse.

And his business keeps him moving, according to statements recorded during an immigration hearing.

"In the process of conducting my construction company, I have traveled frequently all over the world," he said.

The Texas-based Bandidos, formed in 1966 by disillusioned Vietnam veterans, is organized much like a corporation, with approximately 5,000 members and more than 100 chapters in 10 countries, including Sweden, which recently saw the gang engage in a murderous war with Hells Angels. They turned the countryside upside down, using shoulder-fired anti-tank missiles to attack rival compounds.

The gang's expansion into Canada in January brought about

60 former members of Rock Machine into probationary membership. The probationary chapters include Eastern Ontario, Montreal and Quebec City.

Intelligence agents say the probationary members are trying to prove themselves by making money for the outlaw empire any way they can — including money laundering, drug distribution, loan sharking and prostitution.

The Bandidos prospects have waged war for Quebec's drug market since 1994. So far, the battle has claimed the lives of more than 150 people — including an 11-year-old boy killed in 1995 when he was hit by shrapnel from an exploding bomb.

Besides the death toll, the biker war has seen 124 attempted murders, nine missing persons, 84 bombings and 130 reports of arson.

Intelligence agents fear that if Mr. Winterhalder wins the right to enter Canada, it will grant him a license to take care of business.

Police say the criminal corporation will flourish with much bloodletting in what they call an intense attempt to wrest control of the drug market from the Hells Angels, who currently have a tight grip on 75 per cent of the trade.

Mr. Winterhalder told immigration authorities there is little to worry about.

"I am certainly not a danger to society. My criminal convictions in the early 1980s were for a non-violent activity. I am a member of the Bandidos motorcycle club, but our presence (in Canada) has brought an end to the supposed war. Since November, there is no more war, and now that we are here, there will be no more war," Mr. Winterhalder said.

Intelligence agents dismiss his declaration of peace, saying the war is bound to escalate now that ex-Rock Machine members are linked with the Bandidos, the second-most powerful motorcycle gang in the world.

And any suggestion that the drug war has been over since November is dead wrong, police say.

So far this year, there have been several biker gang fistfights, a bombing and a handful of shootings.

In February, four armed members of the Nomads, an elite Hells Angels crew, gathered around a table in a suite at Montreal's Holiday Inn Crown Plaza while a security detail kept watch in the hotel lobby.

It was a study of the enemy, with each elite member taking turns thumbing through photographs of probationary Bandidos, police say.

They included snapshots of Denis Boucher, a rival biker who was almost killed last September, and Alain Brunette, reputed president of the Bandidos chapter in Kingston.

Earlier in the week, Mr. Brunette had been targeted in a drive-by shooting while making his way down Highway 15 outside Mirabel.

That same week, Michel Gauthier, a Bandidos associate, was found dead in his car on a lonely road in the Laurentians. Some 20 kilometres away, police discovered a burned-out car — the trademark of a biker contract killing.

The shootings made clear that the biker war is far from over, with the Hells Angels unable to accept a shared drug market.

But police could be wrong about an escalation, judging from how Bandidos do business south of the border.

In Oklahoma, where Mr. Winterhalder was the reputed leader of a chapter in Tulsa, county, state, and federal law agencies report no problems with the Bandidos.

Most of the gang members, according to a U.S. intelligence agent who monitors bikers in Oklahoma, make honest livings. Of the 10 motorcycle gangs operating in Oklahoma, the Bandidos have been the most quiet. And there is no biker war.

"It seems to be bloodier up there in Canada. Down here they

all seem to get along pretty good," said Lieut. Alan Lansdown, an intelligence officer with the Osage County Sheriff's Office.

The last known time Mr. Winterhalder crossed the border was Jan. 5 at Fort Erie, Ont.

Seated in the passenger seat of a van, Mr. Winterhalder had his passport ready in his hand. He had been turned away in 1995 because of his criminal record, and he did not know if he would be allowed to cross the border.

The border guard spoke briefly with the driver and waved them through.

They then drove to Kingston to oversee the induction of about 60 probationary members, mostly ex-Rock Machine bikers.

But the visit didn't last long for Mr. Winterhalder. It wasn't long after checking into a Travelodge that Immigration officer P. Cooper, accompanied by a special police team, arrived at his door.

In an interview with the Immigration officer, Mr. Winterhalder appeared co-operative. He had only $217 U.S. in his pockets.

Police later arrested him, saying he had entered the country illegally. They said he posed a danger to the public because of his alleged links to organized crime.

They also said he lied to Immigration officers, saying he should have identified himself as a gang member to border guards.

But it was the driver that did all of the talking at the border, and if the border guard had inquired about his membership, Mr. Winterhalder would have likely told the truth. He says it is against club law to lie.

And they said he had a duty to tell them about his criminal history, a record that led Mr. Cooper to believe the U.S. visitor would do something against the law.

Mr. Winterhalder says he paid his debt to society years ago.

His last conviction was in 1983. His crimes include carrying a prohibited firearm (a .45-calibre handgun), possession of a stolen vehicle and forging a $5,000 U.S. cheque.

Under the Immigration Act, an exception can be made for visitors with criminal records, so long as they are reformed and that at least five years has elapsed since the end of the person's last sentence.

Mr. Winterhalder finished serving his sentence some 14 years ago.

In any event, police threw him in jail for three nights until he appeared at a detention review hearing. Immigration officer Lynn Leblanc portrayed Mr. Winterhalder as a dangerous criminal who should remain locked up.

Mr. Winterhalder then made his case, saying he is not a flight risk, nor a danger to society, and that he is reformed.

The board adjudicator, Rolland Ladouceur, released Mr. Winterhalder on $20,000 bail on the condition that he would appear at an upcoming hearing — which he did.

Immigration officers then requested that Mr. Winterhalder be detained in Canada for up to six months so they could have time to look into certain criminal allegations against the biker.

The adjudicator concluded that the government's motion was unreasonable because the visitor would be separated from his daughter and business in the U.S.

Mr. Winterhalder has enlisted a respected lawyer to help him fight for the unfettered right to set foot in Canada at an upcoming hearing.

CHAPTER FOUR

STURGIS HIGH . . .
MONTREAL LOW

"If you attend only one rally in your life, Sturgis is the one to attend," I told Alain. "You won't believe it. It makes most other rallies look like a backyard picnic."

Sturgis, South Dakota, is home to the largest biker event in the United States, if not the world. It takes place in the first full week of August, and hot, dry weather is practically guaranteed. Actually, the event, simply known as the Sturgis Motorcycle Rally, gets underway on the Friday before the first full week and ends on the following Sunday, running some ten days in total. It has been estimated that in the past few years more than 750,000 people, and a staggering 500,000 motorcycles, have gathered in Sturgis for this rally.

The Bandidos Motorcycle Club has a chapter and clubhouse near Sturgis at Rapid City, and every year Sturgis has been a major event for the entire Bandidos club. For me, the 2001 Sturgis Rally was going to be exceptional, for I had convinced Bandido Alain to come to Tulsa and ride with me all the way to South Dakota and back.

When Alain mentioned that he wouldn't have a bike to ride, I assured him I'd stick a set of wheels beneath him.

"Well, okay then. I guess I'm going to Sturgis with you," he said in his charming French-Canadian English.

Sturgis has always been one of my favorite destinations. Located in the Black Hills of South Dakota, the region's scenery and solitude are second to none. Its roads are ideal for cruising on a motorcycle. Within a few hours of Sturgis are such western American landmarks as the sweeping Badlands and the imposing Devil's Tower, featured in the movie *Close Encounters of the Third Kind*, among others. Also nearby is Sylvan Lake, known as the "crown jewel" of Custer State Park. These majestic places are a feast for the eyes — nature at its best.

Like many events that have attained legendary status, the Sturgis Motorcycle Rally began simply enough as a low-key affair. The first rally, which wasn't even a true rally, saw the light of day in 1938 when Clarence "Pappy" Hoel and some of his friends from the Jackpine Gypsies Motorcycle Club — a club Hoel had founded in 1936 — decided to hold a motorcycle race and stunt competition.

Hoel, a motorcycle shop owner in Sturgis, persuaded local business owners to put up a $500 purse, a small fortune at that time. Only a handful of racers entered the inaugural event to bang handlebars on the town's half-mile oval and participate in hair-raising stunts, which included board-wall crashes and ramp jumps. Although few spectators showed up to watch the action, the event quickly took on a life of its own, especially after the Second World War when motorcycling gained in popularity.

In addition to half-mile flat-track racing, the program evolved to include motocross, short-track racing, drag racing, and hill climbs. Touring was incorporated within a few years of the rally's launch; today it makes up the lion's share of the Sturgis Motorcycle Rally.

Motorcyclists from all walks of life — ranging from factory workers to teachers, doctors, nurses, engineers, and numerous other professions — are represented at the Sturgis Rally. And there is always a sizable presence of 1%ers, representing many clubs from across the United States.

Bandido Alain arrived in Tulsa a few days before our planned departure for Sturgis. Looking like a regular citizen, and with his tattoos concealed, he had taken a Greyhound bus from Toronto, hoping to blend in with the rest of the passengers so as not to draw attention to himself at the border. The plan worked well, but he paid the price by having to endure an uncomfortable 1,180-mile bus journey of more than twenty hours to Tulsa.

For someone of Bandido Alain's size, a ride that long in the cramped seat of a bus approximates sheer hell. When he finally got to my home outside of Tulsa, he spent two days recuperating from the trip. It was great to have a Canadian brother around, and Caroline, Taylor, and I truly enjoyed his company. Alain had a way of making us all laugh, and after a while we became quite adept at understanding his French-Canadian English.

To make the trip to Sturgis, I borrowed a 1999 Harley FXDX Superglide for Alain from my attorney friend Jonathan Sutton. I was going to ride my own 1999 Harley FXDL Superglide, which was very similar to Jonathan's machine. On Saturday, August 4, Alain, Caroline, and I set out for Sturgis. Ahead of us was a 950-mile odyssey that would take us through Missouri, Nebraska, and South Dakota. It was trip I had made on numerous occasions and one I never tired of. Although I was an east-coast boy by birth, I had long ago become a Midwesterner at heart and considered the plains my stomping grounds.

Accompanied by the distinctive rumble of two hot-rod Harley engines, Alain and I rode side by side like the consummate bikers we were, every once in a while exchanging a thumbs-up out of sheer joy. I'm sure that for much of the time we had contented grins on our faces, mirroring the passion we felt for our bikes, the open road . . . and being Bandidos. There is no better feeling than blasting down the highway with another guy on a motorcycle, especially a club brother. Well, actually, there might be: blasting down the highway with dozens, if not hundreds, of other club brothers — a deafening convoy of modern-day cowboys slicing through the country-side on their iron horses.

Caroline, an avid motorcyclist in her own right who owned a Sportster when I met her, had her arms wrapped around me. She was enjoying being a carefree passenger and letting her eyes wander over the passing scenery. We left Oklahoma behind and traveled northeast up Interstate 44 into Missouri, the only state other than Tennessee that is bordered by eight other states.

As we cruised along past Joplin and headed toward Springfield, I couldn't help but think again about the first time I had met Alain and my subsequent involvement with the patched-over Rock Machine. I was proud that I had done my part to get Bandidos Canada to where they were, and I knew I would have a long association with them. I was prouder still to be riding next to Alain, a brave soul who had gone from being a rank-and-file Rock Machine to the enviable position of Bandidos Canada Presidente.

"This is the first time in a long time I have been able to ride a motorcycle without worrying that somebody might shoot me off it," Alain mentioned while we were fueling up at a gas station along the way. "I'm sure glad you talked me into coming."

In early August, southwest Missouri is especially beautiful country to be traveling through, with many tree-covered areas that provide quite a bit of shade and pockets of cooler air. In the stifling heat, we were extremely grateful for the trees. One of the stops on our itinerary was Springfield, where we were scheduled to rendezvous with two Arkansas members of the Ozark Riders Motorcycle Club — a Bandidos support club — who were going to ride with us to Sturgis.

I also made arrangements to see a childhood friend of mine, Kurt Newman, who had lived in Springfield for some ten years. After lunch, and reminiscing with Kurt, we met up with Andy and Nick, the two Ozark Riders. By mid-afternoon, Bandido Alain, Ozark Rider Andy, Ozark Rider Nick and his girlfriend, and Caroline and I had ridden out of Springfield and traveled another sixty miles northeast, close to Ozark Lake, where we were scheduled to visit a group of guys who had expressed interest in joining the Ozark Riders.

This was a good opportunity to combine a little business with pleasure. Considering that club business usually is pleasure, the meeting was a bonus. We arrived at our destination near Ozark Lake early in the evening, with a blazing sunset coloring the darkening sky. After dinner and a short meeting, we retired for the night. We had been well received at the meeting, and the group of guys we spoke with would eventually become Ozark Riders.

Early the next day, we set out for Kansas City, Missouri, where we had planned to stop and pay our respects to the local chapter of the Boozefighters Motorcycle Club, popularly known in American folklore as "the original Wild Ones" because they were part of the inspiration behind the first biker movie, *The Wild One*. It was our intention to get to Kansas City before the heat became unbearable, but unfortunately we didn't manage it. By the time we got to the north side of Kansas City, it was very hot and probably close to 100°F. Most of us southerners could tolerate the heat fairly well, but Bandido Alain — a denizen of the land of ice and snow — was having some difficulty coping with the broilerlike conditions. He was beginning to look like an overripe tomato, so stopping for the afternoon was a welcome relief.

We spent a few hours in Kansas City, situated at the junction of the Missouri and Kansas Rivers, and considered to be one of the most beautiful cities in the United States. It is renowned for having more boulevards than any other city in the world except Paris and more fountains than any other city except Rome. Although nothing beats the grandeur of nature in my eyes, Kansas City is a visual delight, a perfect example of diligent city planning.

After relaxing a bit and enjoying a good meal, we left Kansas City around 6:00 p.m., hoping to make Omaha just after dark. This time we were on schedule. We found a decent motel and spent a restful night recharging our batteries for the next leg of the journey. It had been a good day with no major breakdowns and plenty of water breaks, food, and gas stops. The following day would be another story. We were now far away from all the shady trees and rolling hills of Missouri and would soon be heading into the hot, dry plains of South Dakota.

The next morning, Monday, August 6, we got up early and headed for Sioux Falls, South Dakota. We knew that we needed to be there by late morning if we wanted to avoid the stifling heat predicted for that day. By high noon, temperatures of 100°F were predicted, under a blazing plains sun that was just too hot for comfort: it wasn't good for the bikes, and it surely wasn't good for us. And I was very worried about Bandido Alain: the heat was really kicking his ass!

Despite the sunblock he and the rest of us had been generously slapping on any exposed skin, Alain's face and neck were an alarmingly bright red. Fortunately, the ride went well, and men, women, and machines held up. Just after noon, we arrived in Sioux Falls, known as the "Gateway to the Plains." I was scheduled to meet another 1%er friend of mine, Mike, who rode with the Sons of Silence Motorcycle Club in Minnesota. Mike was going to join our group, which now included five riders and two passengers, for the rest of the ride to Sturgis.

Sons of Silence Mike and I had previously agreed to meet at a Sioux Falls tattoo shop where we had a mutual friend. Mike and I knew the shop's "piercing girl," who was the widow of a Bandido from Louisiana. We spent most of the early afternoon just hanging out, relaxing, catching up on things, and watching TV in the air-conditioned shop. Later that day, after the temperature had dropped and much of the heat dissipated, we all headed west on Interstate 90 for Chamberlain, South Dakota, our final stop of the day. By now, I-90 was crammed full of Harleys — hundreds and hundreds of them — heading west toward Sturgis. It was a sight to behold, and the thundering of the many motorcycle engines was music to my ears.

We were hoping to reach Chamberlain, some 210 miles east of Sturgis, just before nightfall and meet up with about fifty other members of the Sons of Silence. While at the tattoo shop in Sioux Falls, we had made reservations at a motel in Chamberlain. Fortunately, we had been able to find one with some vacant rooms. I had been this way many times before and knew it was very easy to get stranded in these environs without gasoline, water, food, or lodging.

We made good time and cruised into Chamberlain around dusk. We had no trouble finding our motel in the small town whose population at that time was around 2,338 residents. This number probably included the cats and dogs, because there was hardly a soul to be seen anywhere. I was surprised by how much the heat had affected everyone. Even with the layover in Sioux Falls, during the worst part of the day, everyone was drained and looking forward to a good meal and kicking back for the night. Although I was only in my early forties, it seemed the older I got, the harder the ride got.

Although he was more wrecked than the rest of us, Alain still behaved like a kid in a candy store. Despite his discomfort, the journey from Tulsa to Sturgis was a ride of discovery for him. He was thrilled to see new places on the vast expanse of the American Midwest and enjoyed meeting all kinds of new people. By now Alain was quite sunburned, especially his face; thinking of a new name for him, I asked him what "head" and "tomato" were in French.

"Head is 'tête' and tomato is 'tomate,' which is pronounced in English as 'tight toe mat,'" he explained.

From that time on, we all affectionately called him "Tomato Head" or, in French, "Tête Tomate."

After settling into my room with Caroline, I took a quick shower and then headed to the local bar to visit some of the Sons of Silence; and there were plenty of them there — some forty in total. But I didn't last long at the bar and was barely able to keep my eyes open. After only a few ginger ales — I had given up drinking alcoholic beverages in 1986 — I was toast. It seemed way past my bedtime, and after bidding everyone good night, I went back to the motel around 10:00 p.m. I wanted to get a good night's sleep because, once again, we were going to try to get an early start in order to stay ahead of the blast-furnace heat the weathermen had predicted.

We figured if all went well, we could make it into Rapid City around noon, and had it not been for the Probationary bottom rocker Bandido Alain was wearing, we probably would have. In the world of 1%ers, when the Bandidos accept a patch holder who has been in another club, it is a rule that he becomes a probationary member for at least one year. This is based on the fact that a probationary member already has some motorcycle club experience, and that this previous experience will give him a good foundation to build upon while learning what it is like to be a member of the Bandidos.

Probationary members are easily identified by their bottom rocker, which says exactly that, "Probationary." After making it through the probationary period, a new member receives the 1% patch and a chapter bottom rocker, which replaces the "Probationary" bottom rocker. Usually, the chapter bottom rocker designates the geographical area the member resides in. In Bandido Alain's case, his bottom rocker would eventually read "Canada." In the early days of outlaw motorcycle clubs, the bottom rocker indicated the name of the city the chapter was located in. This practice has largely been replaced by listing the state, province, or country on the bottom rocker. The reason for this is twofold: to confuse law enforcement, other clubs, and the public so that no one can pinpoint the location where the member resides; and to create the illusion that there are a lot more members than there actually are.

We managed to get everybody out of bed by seven o'clock the following morning. Chamberlain wasn't much more active at this time of day than it had been when we rode into town. We enjoyed a breakfast of bacon, eggs, sausage, pancakes, and toast, washed down with orange juice, milk, and coffee. Keeping to our plan, we were back on the road before 8:30 a.m. This was a good thing, because the weather forecast had been right on the money. Another scorcher was unfolding. On a motorcycle, the heat emitted from the engine easily increases the temperature by fifteen to twenty degrees; at times like this, the prospect of an air-conditioned car is very attractive. But we were bikers, and dealing with sauna-like riding conditions comes with the territory during the hot summer months. We continued our journey down I-90 toward Sturgis, happily zooming along at the speed limit and minding our own business.

About mid-morning, without any warning, a South Dakota Highway Patrol car nosed right into the middle of our entourage, effectively cutting us into two groups. We were very fortunate that he didn't cause an accident. It was obvious he pulled this reckless maneuver with full intent, not caring about the consequences. The officer behind the wheel looked like he was pointing at Bandido Alain and signaling him to pull over to the side of the road. Although it seemed pretty obvious that Alain was being singled out, Ozark Rider Andy, who was riding next to Alain at the rear of the pack, pulled over with him just in case. When someone in a biker convoy gets signaled by law enforcement to pull over, everyone behind him will follow suit; all those ahead of him keep going to the next exit.

It became pretty clear Alain was the main man of interest because the first thing the cop did was order Andy to get lost. When it looked like Andy wasn't going to desert Alain, Alain nodded that he better follow the cop's advice. Taking the cue from Alain, Andy did the smart thing and hightailed it. At the time, we had no idea why Alain got the short end of the stick, but we learned later that the state trooper wanted to know who the new probationary Bandido riding a bike from Oklahoma was. It has always been the task of law enforcement officers in South Dakota to determine *who we are*, but this one wanted to know so badly he didn't seem to mind if some of us got killed in the process.

The frontrunners of the group, which included me and Caroline, continued riding farther down the road for about four miles until we came to the next exit. We parked under the highway overpass to shield ourselves from the blazing sun. It didn't take long for Ozark Rider Andy to catch up with us. By now, we knew that the cop's sole interest was in Bandido Alain, and we wondered what was going to happen to him. We were quite concerned that he would be arrested for some kind of immigration violation. I can only imagine the look of surprise on the cop's face when he discovered Alain spoke English with a heavy French accent; that he was a Canadian Bandido riding a motorcycle he had borrowed in Oklahoma; and that he had a driver's license from Quebec.

It took the lawman quite a while to check out our French-Canadian brother. Fortunately, he came up empty; he didn't even discover that Alain Brunette was the president of Bandidos Canada. To ensure his effort wasn't a complete waste of time, the trooper wrote Alain a $100 traffic citation for having an exhaust system that was too loud. This was interesting because the bike was brand new and still had the stock factory exhaust installed on it. Actually, the cop didn't even bother to test the exhaust system; no doubt he knew if he had done so, the monitor would have indicated that the exhaust system met the required noise level standards.

This scenario reminded me somewhat of an incident on the Autobahn in Germany, when we were ticketed for supposedly speeding in a construction zone. When you're a biker on the road and you get pulled over by the authorities, you can bet your bottom dollar it's going to cost you money, especially if you fail to satisfy their suspicions that there must be some kind of warrant floating around for your arrest.

Biker protocol says that when someone in a group gets pulled over, the rest of the convoy waits at the next exit for at least an hour. If he's not coming down the road by then, you know he was taken into custody. That's why we were all overjoyed when we finally saw Bandido Alain barreling down the highway in our direction. He joined us underneath the bridge and gave us a thumbs-up as he coasted to a stop.

"Well, that was really interesting for sure. I thought I was gonna be in deep shit, but all I got was a ticket for a noisy muffler. Go figure," Alain said.

"Yeah, go figure," I said. "But at least you're still going to Sturgis, and that has to be considered a good thing."

We all let out a war whoop, fired up our bikes, and got back on the highway. In the back of my mind, I was hoping we weren't going to be pulled over again a few miles down the road. This had happened to me many times before; you get stopped once, chances are you'll get stopped twice. Alain had been lucky because he could just as easily have ended up in the same predicament I had in his country, dealing with immigration officials who got their jollies messing with people's lives — all in the name of doing their duty, of course. The last thing I wanted was for Alain to be a guest of Uncle Sam. In total, the encounter with the State trooper cost us more than an hour and it was getting very, very, hot!

The final stretch of our journey was pleasantly uneventful, but we did have to stop more often for water. We seemed to be dehydrating as quickly as we were hydrating. We got into Rapid City about 1:00 p.m. and headed straight to the Bandidos clubhouse property on the east side of town. Everyone at the clubhouse was very happy to see us, and quite surprised to see Bandido Alain. Alain was just happy to be there, period — still in one piece but very sunburned. For him this had been the longest ride on a bike in his entire life — it was, as he called it, his "grand adventure."

We spent almost four days in the Sturgis–Rapid City area. We had actually arrived on the morning of August 7, and would eventually leave around 4:00 p.m. on August 11. When we got to the chaotic downtown core of Sturgis, Bandido Alain — still behaving like a kid in a candy store — couldn't believe his eyes. The town's historic Main Street and central five blocks — open to motorcycle traffic only for the duration of Rally Week — were an ocean of multicolored bikes and equally colorful people of all shapes and sizes. Add into the mix close to one thousand 1%ers, four hundred of whom were Bandidos at the 2001 Rally, and you had soap operas, reality shows, and circuses to appease even the most jaded visitor. During Rally Week, Sturgis is a place both to see and be seen. The streets are also lined with vendors selling a wide selection of goods ranging from leathers to the ever-present souvenir T-shirts, jewelry, and, of course, motorcycle parts of every description. And there's plenty of food to be had, ranging from old standbys like hamburgers and fries to the exotic, like alligator, ostrich, and jambalaya.

In addition to hanging out and taking in the madness, I made sure that Bandido Alain got to see some of the more popular tourist attractions in the surrounding area. The highlight of our out-of-town tour was Mount Rushmore, the famous site of the humongous head sculptures of the former U.S. presidents George Washington, Thomas Jefferson, Theodore Roosevelt, and Abraham Lincoln. Like good tourists, we took the requisite photos to show the folks back home.

When we weren't sightseeing or carousing in Sturgis, we spent our nights at a house we rented in Rapid City. The entire Oklahoma Bandidos chapter stayed there, plus Andy and Nick from the Ozark Riders, as well as all of the Canadian Bandidos who made it across the border. It was a decent, completely furnished four-bedroom house in a nice neighborhood; it had a very handy kitchen, which kind of became grand central during our stay. The ladies cooked huge meals every day; we made sure there was always plenty of food in the fridge. In the basement was a huge open room where different groups congregated at all hours of the day. We had bought a stack of inflatable mattresses at Wal-Mart, which we used for everyone to sleep on and then shipped home by mail the day we left. By the end of the week, the house had been a hotel for more than twenty people, and we left it just like we found it — immaculate! For anyone buying into the stereotypical biker image and expecting the place to be trashed, seeing the vacated house in such condition would have come as a big shock.

Late in the week, a carload of Bandidos from Canada showed up at the house. In the group was Bandido Vice Presidente Peppi from Toronto — the ex–Loners Motorcycle Club member who had become a Bandido a few months earlier — and another Bandido named Luis Manny "Porkchop" Raposo. Bandido Peppi and Bandido Porkchop drove all the way to Rapid City from Toronto nonstop, spent two days there, and drove all the way back nonstop. I felt bad for them because all they ever saw while they were there was the clubhouse property and the house we rented. They never had a chance to really experience what Sturgis is all about during Rally Week or see the sights, like Bandido Alain did.

I had really hoped that Bandido El Secretario Robert "Tout" Leger was going to be with Peppi and Porkchop, but unfortunately he was not. I had spoken with Bandido Tout nearly every day since I had left Canada. From the time Bandido Alain arrived in Oklahoma, we had both been on the phone with him whenever the opportunity presented itself. We both tried unsuccessfully to talk Tout into coming to Sturgis; on one occasion, we actually thought he was going to join us.

"Hey, guys, you know I would really like to come, but if I get busted in the States for any reason whatsoever, I'll really be screwed. I don't know what to do," Tout said. "My heart says go, but my mind say no. You know what I mean?"

Despite wanting him with us, we did indeed know what he meant. Bandido Tout was very hesitant about leaving Canada because, at the time, he was subject to bond stipulations that prevented him from leaving the Montreal area. In the end, he decided it was too risky to take the chance. I spoke with him two or three more times while I was in Sturgis, and I had to agree that he had made the right decision.

"Don't feel bad for me, okay? I'll be cool. I'm going to my house in the country to spend the weekend there with my family. We can use a break," he told me during our last conversation. "I'm sure we'll all get together sometime soon."

After four days of revelry, fun in the sun, and getting together with Bandidos from all over the world, Alain, Caroline, and I hit the road for the long ride back to Oklahoma. We left late on Saturday afternoon, August 11, and rode all the way to the railroad town of North Platte, Nebraska, a distance of about 325 miles. In North Platte, we grabbed a motel room for the night, where we fell asleep shortly after arriving. We had planned on making the trip in just two days. Bandido Alain was scheduled to fly back to Canada on Tuesday morning, and he wanted a day to relax before the flight.

We got up early the next morning to tackle the remaining six hundred miles to Tulsa. It was a cloudy day and rain had been predicted. On our way out of town, we rode past the Union Pacific Railroad Bailey Yard, the largest railroad classification yard in the world. This humongous yard covers a staggering 2,850 acres and reaches a total length of eight miles. As we rode eastbound on Interstate 80 across Nebraska, it started to look like we were definitely going to get rained on. When we finally encountered the rain, we turned south, then east, to get around it. Dealing with hot weather when traveling on a bike is one thing, rain is quite another, and I'll do just about anything to avoid it. Detouring around the rain took us way off the beaten path, but soon we were under clear, sunny skies. We traveled down a strip of county roads, which, except for some local vehicles, was devoid of traffic.

Although we were losing valuable time, we got to see a slice of Nebraska no tourist ever sees: quaint little country towns and miles upon miles of cornfields. Baking under the hot plains sun, a sweet smell wafts into the air from those cornfields; it's no wonder they call Nebraska the "Cornhusker State."

At one desolate point on our journey, I thought I was going to run out of gas. Because I was packing Caroline with me, I burned more fuel per mile than Alain, even though we were on nearly identical bikes. That day, I discovered the Superglide FXDL would go nearly twenty-five miles on reserve, which turned out to be just enough to find a gas station. After refueling, we crossed into Kansas, running south on State Highway 81, heading through the wheat fields for Salina and Wichita.

We finally crossed the Oklahoma border in the very late afternoon and stopped just north of Blackwell on Interstate 35, at a Conoco Service Station, for more fuel. While at the station, I took the opportunity to check my cell phone for messages and noticed there were quite a few. They weren't for me, however, but for Alain. All of the messages, coming from urgent voices, basically relayed the same thing: call home "immediately." I had checked for messages two hours earlier at the last gas stop, and there hadn't been any — obviously something was up. I handed Alain my cell and watched him nervously punch in some numbers.

"I do not think this is good," Alain said. "I hate messages that say to call home immediately. It is never good news."

I knew it was really bad when I saw a tear slide down Alain's face before he even got off the phone. I had no idea what was going on because he was talking in French; the only word I recognized was "Tout." It was worse than bad news: it was the worst news I had heard for many years. When he got off the phone, Bandido Alain sadly explained to me and Caroline that Bandido El Secretario Robert "Tout" Leger had been murdered by the Hells Angels.

"The bastards shot him right in front of his wife and kids at their country house. He had seen them coming and got in between them and his family," Alain said in a faltering voice. "You won't believe this, but Tout was a Rock Machine prospect for almost seven years. Not because he was a screw-up or anything. I don't think he really cared if he ever made it into the club. Tout was his own man. He was one hell of a biker. We all looked up to him and respected him."

Alain went on to explain that one assassin had fired a machine gun and the other a pistol, riddling Bandido Tout with bullets. I couldn't believe my ears. I had only known Tout for a short period of time, but I felt like I'd lost a lifelong friend. We sat in stony silence at the gas station for what seemed like an eternity. It was a sad day for all of us — for all Bandidos. Tout was the first national chapter officer in the history of the Bandidos to be killed by members of another motorcycle club.

"You know, Tout died as he had lived. He was a man of courage and action, always thinking of others before himself," Alain mumbled after a long silence.

I knew it was best to give Alain some quiet time, and I retreated into my own jumbled thoughts. Caroline, with her emotions in check, just stared into her own space, thinking about who-knows-what. I reflected on some of the Rock Machine history Bandido Tout had told me about during the brief eight months I had known him. Back in the mid-1990s, Tout had been the first Rock Machine to ever venture into the United States. He had a clearly defined mission ahead of him: make contact with the Bandidos and talk to them about the Rock Machine wanting to patch over. Because Tout spoke excellent English, he had been sent to Houston to search out members of the Bandidos. As there had been no advance communication, any members of the Bandidos he could track down would have to do.

"I didn't know a soul in Texas. Nobody! But we figured I would have nothing to lose, so I went," Tout had told me. "We really hated the Angels because they figured they could tell us and everybody else what to do."

Somehow a self-assured and resourceful Tout managed to locate a group of Bandidos at a bar in Houston. When he mentioned he was a member of the Rock Machine from Canada, and that he had been sent there to make contact because they wanted to become Bandidos, they told him in no uncertain terms to get lost.

"When I think about it now, that was a pretty crazy thing to do. I was fortunate not to have my ass kicked all the way back to Canada," Tout said, laughing. "We were pretty naive to think that we were going to be received with open arms by the American Bandidos.

I suddenly felt Caroline's hand on my shoulder, giving me a little nudge. Alain was already sitting on his bike.

"I think we should go now," Caroline said. "Alain looks like he's ready to hit the road."

With a heavy heart, I got back on my Harley, and we set out to complete the last hundred miles or so to Tulsa. We rode east and stopped about halfway, just south of a town called Pawhuska. This was the site of Biker Days, a huge annual biker party that was Oklahoma's version of Sturgis, albeit on a much smaller scale. I had promised Alain we would stop and take his picture at the actual location of the site. He had always wanted to attend the event, but had never been able to. At least now he could say he had been at the place where the party was held every year.

The picture Caroline took of us will always trigger for me the memory of that fateful day: a red-faced Bandido Alain and me, trying to look happy when we were clearly not. Our final hours on the road were a horrible end to a wonderful week. But such is life: a complex tapestry of ups and downs, joys and sorrows — you simply have to take the good with the bad. We resumed our journey and got to my house just after dark on Sunday night.

Everyone took a hot shower, had a bite to eat, and went straight to bed. I fell asleep thinking about Tout and the senselessness of his death. I knew that violence, death, and tragedy sometimes were the unpleasant flip side of the outlaw biker lifestyle, but the brutality of what had been going on in Canada — and prior to that in Scandinavia — numbed my mind. In the United States, which has a high concentration of 1%ers, unbridled slaughter was relatively rare. As I drifted off to sleep, my last waking thoughts were on the fragility of life . . . and my childhood. I was happy to be still among the living.

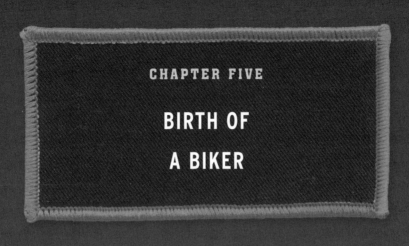

CHAPTER FIVE

BIRTH OF
A BIKER

I came into this world in Hartford, Connecticut, in the summer of 1955. In addition to being the capital city of Connecticut, Hartford is best known for its numerous insurance companies. They have earned the city the moniker of "insurance capital of the world." Hartford is also home to the renowned firearms firm Colt's Manufacturing Company, founded in 1847. Later in life, I would face criminal charges in Oklahoma, Texas, and Florida, each time for the possession of one of Colt's famous 45-caliber automatic handguns.

On the day after my birth, my mother gave me up for adoption, and I was sent to a foster home. At the time, my father had no idea what was going on. He was in the process of getting divorced from my mother, and they had no contact with each other. As soon as he became aware of my fate, he tried unsuccessfully to gain custody of me. Perhaps this inauspicious beginning contributed to the path I would take in life: a life of adventure and misadventure — a life that would eventually lead to my becoming a 1%er outlaw biker.

Six months after I was born, I was adopted by a childless couple, Warren and Helen "Dolly" Winterhalder. They resided in Hamden, Connecticut, a quiet suburb of New Haven and birthplace of Academy Award–winning actor Ernest Borgnine. Warren was a business forms salesman and Dolly a homemaker. They were wonderful people, and it was a stroke of good fortune for me that they were the ones who liberated me from the foster home. I spent my first five years happily playing in our Gorham Avenue neighborhood and went to kindergarten nearby. In the summer of 1961, we moved to a brand-new house smack-dab in the center of a middle-class neighborhood in Northford, Connecticut, a town of less than one thousand residents.

Our new home, about a half-hour drive from Hamden, was a three-bedroom, split-level house located on Carlen Drive, a cul-de-sac that had a turnaround circle with a basketball hoop located in the center of it. There was also a large pond at the end of the cul-de-sac, formed by a dammed-up creek. The creek had a footbridge across it that led to a huge field where neighborhood kids played baseball in summer and football in autumn. Behind the field was a wooded area that looked like a small forest to me. For a six-year-old kid, this place was heaven on earth. Even though I wasn't given free reign of the place until quite a while after we had settled in, I was thrilled to find myself in these new surroundings.

I started first grade at the William Douglas Elementary School in the fall of 1961. I went from being just another inconspicuous new kid to the talk of the school when I got run over by a bunch of fifth graders playing football during recess; this mishap fractured my left leg. In the fall of 1963, when I was eight years old, I changed schools and started attending the Stanley T. Williams Elementary School in Northford.

By the time fourth grade rolled around, I had become aware that I was fairly intelligent; my ease of learning and straight-A grades were testimony enough. I spent a lot of my time reading, something I do to this very day. Although it was mandatory reading in junior high, *The Outsiders* by S.E. Hinton was one of my earliest favorite books. I discovered later that the author happened to be from Tulsa. (While in New York City promoting my first book, *Out In Bad Standings*, I had the pleasure of meeting Ms. Hinton and was able to tell her how much *The Outsiders* had meant to me.)

Although I liked to read, I also loved watching television. Among my favorite shows growing up were *Bonanza, Wagon Train, Route 66*, and *Mission Impossible*. I found out years later that my biological dad actually played bit parts on *Wagon Train*. There I was, glued to the television set, unknowingly watching my real father acting in one of my favorite westerns.

I was also very keen on music and soon developed a fascination with Myron Floren, the feature accordion player on *The Lawrence Welk Show*. I convinced my parents to let me take accordion lessons at the Betty Revegno Accordion School in Wallingford, Connecticut. This no doubt qualified me as a bona fide weirdo because, even at that time, the accordion was hardly the choice of instrument of most kids. I was so absorbed with the accordion eighteen months after my first lesson that I won first place in a state competition for ten-year-old players. It didn't take me too long, however, to discover that the instrument was not very hip. The guitar was much cooler, thanks to all the guitar-driven groups that were surfacing at the time, both American and British. Soon I wanted to play guitar like my new heroes.

Despite continuously ragging on my parents to buy me a guitar and let me take lessons, Mom and Dad would not cave in. But I found a way to get what I wanted: I continued my accordion lessons just so I could learn to play guitar from another teacher at the studio. I would usually go there early, and the guitar teacher would let me sit in the room and watch as she gave her students lessons. After my accordion lesson, I was able to borrow a school guitar and practice what I had learned. It would be years before I could put all those guitar lessons to good use, but I eventually did. As I got older I wrote a lot of songs, and by the time I was thirty-five, I had self-produced and recorded three albums under the stage name of Warren Winters.

Other than being ostracized by most of the kids in my neighborhood for being too "brainy," my life was fairly normal until I was eleven years old. I was a good boy by conventional standards: I toed the line and followed the straight and narrow. Like many kids blessed with some degree of intelligence, I was not much good at sports. Even America's favorite pastime, baseball, proved to be a tall order for me. Although I joined an organized Little League Baseball team for one year — at my dad's urging — my main position was mostly that of benchwarmer. I played some outfield and second base for the team, but with disastrous results. I quickly realized that sports were clearly not my forte, and I rapidly moved onto what I considered to be bigger and better endeavors: earning money!

When I was about eleven, my entrepreneurial spirit began manifesting itself. I started shoveling snow in winter and mowing lawns in summer to earn some cold hard cash. Although cutting grass and shoveling snow back then wasn't that unusual, working at a local dairy farm was something most kids from the suburbs shied away from. Not me — if there was a buck to be made, I was up for it. The work didn't pay all that much, but I was able to buy things I wanted, like Beatles 45s at

Barkers, the local discount store. I was a huge Beatles fan and I bought all their early singles and albums.

A favorite pastime of mine was watching the construction of new houses in my neighborhood. This was the original era of urban sprawl, and houses were going up left and right. For reasons unknown to me at the time, I was fascinated with the construction process: it was as if building was ingrained in my soul. Thirty years later, I would learn that my biological dad, grandpa, and great grandpa were all builders and carpenters. As the saying goes, the apple doesn't fall far from the tree, and I would eventually follow in their footsteps.

I began junior high school in North Branford, Connecticut, where I entered the sixth grade. Northford, the area I lived in, was a small section of North Branford, and I had to travel about five miles to get from home to school. At the time, I thought it was a long way! The social scene at North Branford Junior High was totally different from what I was used to at the elementary school I had graduated from; it didn't take long before I fell in with what most parents would call the "wrong" crowd.

But I felt right at home with these kids for reasons I did not then understand. No doubt it had to do with the fact that for the first time in my life I finally felt what it was like to actually have some brothers. These kids didn't mock me or judge me on my IQ, or condemn me for my lack of talent on the sports field. They accepted me as one of their own, and soon I was one of the group's leaders and main instigators.

Not surprisingly, I was beginning to use my "smarts" to come up with the best pranks and ways of getting into trouble. During my first year at North Branford Junior High, I went through a massive amount of change. I had been a model student and son, but now I was starting to question all types of authority. It was also around this time that my parents told me I was adopted. Although initially I was shocked when I heard the news, the stark reality of the situation explained a lot of things. The thought that I might have been adopted had crossed my mind more than once. Now I knew why I was so different from Warren and Dolly in appearance, mentality, and character.

Although Mom had always been supportive and was proud of my high intellect, Dad, an average man who carried a lot of emotional baggage, for some reason resented it. One time, he got very upset when I managed to put together a Christmas present I had received when I was seven or eight. He had been unable to put it together and must have felt embarrassed. He never bought another present for me that needed to be assembled.

I developed new friendships at North Branford Junior High that would have a monumental impact on me. The first and foremost was with Peter "Pete" Hansen. Pete was the sixth of seven sons and he was my age. Pete had two older brothers that I knew of, Walter "Walt" Hansen and Harry "Skip" Hansen. Ironically, Skip would eventually play a larger part in my life than Pete. After Skip moved to Oklahoma, some years later when we were all adults, we would become close friends. He even worked for me on one of my building projects, and he would be a founding member of the Oklahoma Bandidos with me.

The Hansens were all big, tough kids who had serious reputations for not taking crap from anybody. They were my kind of people. Pete and I became the best of friends and were almost inseparable. We did a lot of stupid things together, none of which made our parents very proud of us.

By now, I was totally disgusted with the accordion. To my parents' dismay and disappointment, I quit taking lessons and totally gave up practising the instrument. Making money had become one of the most important priorities in my life; I had figured out that money made the world go round. The summer before, when I was eleven, I had mowed some twenty lawns each and every week using my dad's old Simplicity riding lawn mower.

Back then, a riding lawn mower was a novelty, and I felt like the king of the hill racing around on the machine. At the end of the season, the engine finally gave up and died from my abuse. The fact that I drove the mower like a hot rod no doubt helped it along to the scrap heap. Dad, wanting to teach me a lesson, went out and bought himself a brand-new riding mower at my expense. To my horror, he spent every dime I had made that summer. I was very upset and vowed to find another source of income. Although I still cut one or two lawns on my day off, the summer I turned twelve I went to work at a local dairy farm. After some problems with the dairy farm's foreman, however, I left to work at a vegetable farm, where things were more to my liking and a lot easier.

I made a decent income at the farm, which belonged to a friend's dad, and pretty well did what I wanted to financially. It was there I learned to drive the farm's old six-cylinder Chevy flatbed pickup truck, which was used to collect the boxes of harvested vegetables. Even though the truck came with a standard transmission and required clutching to shift gears, I soon found that driving came naturally to me. It was something that should have been a blessing, but it actually ended up being a curse.

Seventh grade was the beginning of the end for me as far as being a problem-free child was concerned. I became the bane of my parents' existence. Studies were a breeze and I was bored stiff. To me, school was becoming a waste of time, and I felt I needed to move onto other things. I had firmly established myself in the crowd of troublemakers who ran the school, not through brawn but with my brain.

In the late fall of 1967, Pete and I skipped school — something we did quite a bit — and went roaming aimlessly, looking for trouble. We ended up at a Forte's Market grocery store where we intended to purchase some cigarettes. Instead, my eyes caught the welcome sight of a car that had been left with the keys dangling in the ignition. It was like waving a red cape in front of a bull. I wasted no time climbing into the car, starting it up, and taking off down the street. Pete wisely refused to join me on my joyride. It was the adventure of a lifetime for a twelve-year-old, and I eventually found myself back in Hamden, about twenty miles from my home and school. I was barely tall enough to see over the steering wheel, so it did not take long before an observant Hamden police officer noticed me when I stopped at a school crossing.

I was duly arrested and transported to the Westbrook Barracks of the Connecticut State Police, where I was forced to wait in a jail cell until my embarrassed and very angry dad came to get me. The worst thing about it all wasn't being arrested or sitting in jail, but having to endure the long, silent ride home, wondering what kind of punishment I was going to be subjected to. After a solid lecture and stern warnings, Dad grounded me for three months.

Although this would have seemed like a life sentence to most kids, it didn't bother me all that much; I knew there was no way I was going to carry out that sentence. Soon I would sneak out of my room at night and go cavorting with my friends. From that point on, it was all downhill, and things at home got worse every day.

Somehow I made it through the seventh grade, despite all the trouble the stolen car had gotten me into. I had an itch that needed scratching. I was always in search of a challenge, something to stimulate my brain.

Regularly stealing cars soon became the answer; and it became a bad habit I could not shake off. I found the adrenaline rush intoxicating — the aura of invincibility I felt was almost as powerful as the crime. And as a bonus, I soon found the parameters of my playing field had grown twentyfold. I could easily travel just about anywhere I wanted to go.

I turned thirteen in June 1968, one year after the so-called Summer of Love. The idealistic 1960s were starting to fade out on a bad note, and an entire generation was becoming increasingly disillusioned with their government, the Vietnam War, and the world at large. Robert F. Kennedy had just been murdered in San Francisco, and Martin Luther King Jr. had met an assassin's bullet a few months earlier in Memphis.

It was also the time of badass American muscle cars, which were much more interesting to me than local, national, and world affairs. When it came to stealing high-performance cars, I was an expert. Just about every model — from the Dodge Charger Hemi, Plymouth Barracuda, Ford Mustang, and Pontiac's GTO and Firebird — was prey for me. My cars of choice, however — because I happened to be a Chevy man — were Chevrolet's Nova ss, Chevelle ss, and Camaro ss.

Although I sometimes targeted mundane family sedans and station wagons when nothing else was available, almost every weekend I would cruise around in some kind of Chevy hot rod. On rare occasions, if my cash flow was a bit on the low side, my friends and I would dismantle a car and sell the parts to a local salvage yard. Muscle cars and the precious parts they harbored, like engines, transmissions, rear ends, and bucket seats, were the most in demand and therefore the most profitable. Every once in a while, we would simply trash a car with sledgehammers and sell the whole thing for scrap. When I didn't feel like liberating somebody's car, I would sneak Dad's car out of the garage after my parents had gone to sleep, and sneak it back into the garage before they woke up in the morning. Life was good!

Eighth grade went by really fast — I even passed all my subjects with flying colors, and before I knew it, it was the summer of 1969. There was a huge music festival in Woodstock, New York, supposedly about peace and love, which I did not attend, and America went to the moon, which I watched on television. Closer to home, at the North Branford Carnival, a monumental event occurred that would alter my life forever. While hanging out at the carnival, girl-watching with a few friends, I suddenly heard a loud, unusual sound — almost a rumble — that overshadowed the blaring music and human and mechanical cacophony of the carnival. I tuned into the sound and sought out its source. A pack of Harley choppers was coming my way. The guys riding the bikes actually pulled to a stop right next to where I was standing with my friends.

The bikers riding the chromed choppers were members of a local motorcycle club from New Haven. I was mesmerized by the aura of power and intimidation they projected and noticed how everybody stepped aside for them as if they were celebrities. In addition to the actual bikers, I was totally in awe of the beautiful Harleys they were riding and vowed that someday I would own a motorcycle just like the ones I was looking at. But what really caught my eye was the two guys who stood out from the rest of the group: they were Hells Angels.

I had never seen or heard of the Hells Angels, and I was completely taken in by these two men who, to me, represented the epitome of coolness and attitude. The way they parked their bikes and shut off their engines; the way they got off their bikes; and even the way they walked projected sheer confidence with a message attached that said, *Don't fuck with me*. The winged death's-head emblem they were wearing on their sleeveless blue jean jackets — I didn't know they were called patches or colors at the time — made them look like harbingers of trouble. I knew that I had just discovered my reason for living: I was going to become a biker!

One night early that summer, I "borrowed" my dad's 1967

Pontiac Lemans for a final ride to freedom. I had had it with living at home and was leaving for greener pastures. Pete and I broke into an Elk's Lodge to finance a trip to Florida. With two girls and another friend along for the ride, Pete and I headed south down Interstate 95 for the Sunshine State. We made it all the way to South Carolina, almost one thousand miles from home, before we ran out of money and gas.

While siphoning some fuel from a car in a rural neighborhood, we were spotted by a police officer and promptly arrested. We were incarcerated in the Orangeburg County Jail at Orangeburg, South Carolina, while we waited for Pete's dad, my dad, and one of the girls' dads to come and get us. The twenty-mile ride from the Westbrook Barracks two years earlier, after getting busted for my first car theft, would pale in comparison; it was more than nine hundred miles back home to New Haven! When we got home, I was read the riot act and grounded for one year; that, however, lasted about one day because I just ignored it and snuck out as usual.

It was September 1969 when I started the ninth grade at North Branford High School. I was fourteen years old and considered brilliant for my age. Unfortunately, I channeled most of that brilliance into the wrong areas of endeavor. By now, I had fallen in love for the first time in my life. The object of my affection was Cathy Newell, a girl I had met at a church-sponsored dance. Cathy was one year younger and a real sweetheart. I spent many a night hitchhiking across town — I didn't always steal cars and wanted to make a good impression on her parents — just to be with her for an hour or two. I dated Cathy for the better part of two years and thought we would be together for the rest of our lives.

By the time I turned fifteen in the summer of 1970, I was becoming quite an accomplished car mechanic. I seemed to have a natural ability when it came to things mechanical, and I loved tinkering with cars. Some of my older friends let me work on their vehicles with them, and I learned a lot in the process. I knew that as soon as I was old enough, I would seek out some kind of mechanic's job, preferably at a Chevrolet dealership. Later in life, I found out why I possessed such a knack for working on engines. My biological grandfather on my mother's side had been a mechanical engineer — it was in my genes.

By now, my reputation as a car thief was preceding me all over Northford. And I made sure I lived up to that reputation by swiping as many cars as I could. But in late November, I got caught again — and this time things did not go very well. I had stolen a Mercury station wagon that I kept for way too long, stashing it in the woods behind the family home at night and driving around with it during the day, even to school. I almost started to believe the car was mine.

One day, as I was cruising around, some observant police officer recognized the car as belonging to the local pharmacy owner. I was busted! Inside the car, to complicate my situation, was a plethora of stolen items like tools, automotive parts, and liquor that I had bought for resale or was fencing for somebody else. As dumb as it might seem to drive around with "hot merchandise," the cars I stole served as a mobile storefront from which I would sell my wares.

My goose was cooked and I knew it. This time I wasn't just held at the local cop shop until my dad came to get me; I wound up at the Orange Street Juvenile Detention Center in New Haven, Connecticut, where I stayed until just after the New Year. After spending more than a month in a very real prison environment, I was released into my parents' custody. Before that occurred, however, I had to make a solemn promise to the judge that I would stay out of trouble and never appear in front of him again. But I would have promised anything to get out of jail, and I knew damn well I would not keep it.

As it turned out, I kept my promise to the judge for a few months. Late in my sophomore high school year, in mid-May 1971, with my grades failing and my attention elsewhere, I sealed my fate one day just before math class. One of the guys I hung out with had an M-80 firecracker, and he dared me to light it and put it in the toilet in the boys' lavatory. Not being a chicken, but obviously lacking common sense. I lit the M-80 — which was supposed to be the equivalent of a small stick of dynamite — and tossed it into the toilet, flushing right when I dropped the firecracker into it.

I figured that the water would snuff out the fuse and the flush would cart away all of the evidence. I was not as smart as I thought I was; before I got out of the lavatory door, a huge explosion rocked the entire school. Pieces of porcelain showered over me as I came through the door. I ran to my next class hoping for the best but expecting the worst: the worst wasn't long arriving. Five minutes after class started, I was summoned to the principal's office. By this time, the principal was thoroughly sick of me and looking for any excuse to expel me from his school. This was the opportunity he had dreamed of, and he wasted no time suspending me for the rest of the school year.

"I must be out of my mind, Winterhalder, because I'm not going to press charges against you if you pay off the damages you caused before the summer holidays start," he said. "And you can even come back to write your final exams. I think I owe that much to your parents, bless their souls. You I owe nothing, keep that in mind."

Once again my parents were extremely disappointed in my behavior but by now had resigned themselves to the fact that I was going to do what I wanted to do. They knew there wasn't much they could do about it. I was out of control. I tried my best to mellow out a bit while putting some distance between myself and my latest exploit. Because I was in danger of going back into the custody of the State of Connecticut for more rest and relaxation at one of their juvenile detention centers, I worked feverishly to pay for the toilet facilities and plumbing repair bill. And despite missing more than sixty days of school, I managed to pass my exams and graduate to grade eleven.

I turned sixteen in the summer of 1971, a milestone in any American kid's life; I was able to obtain a driver's license and legally operate a motor vehicle. Despite all the trouble I had been in, and much to my surprise, I was granted my driver's license by the Connecticut Department of Motor Vehicles. With four years of driving experience behind me, I passed the exam on my first try with flying colors.

I spent part of the summer working at a car wash and hated every minute of it. At the end of the summer, I landed my first dream job, pumping gas at a local ARCO service station in downtown Northford. I saved up enough money to buy my first car, which cost $300, and promptly blew the engine in it three weeks later by over-revving it, showing off in front of the guys.

That summer, my friend Pete Hansen moved up the shore with his family to a small seaside town called Old Saybrook. His mom and dad had a boat not far from there in the town of Westbrook. I started going to Old Saybrook almost every weekend; if Pete's parents were on the boat, we had the house to ourselves — if his parents were at home, then we had the boat to ourselves.

Both locations provided us with abundant opportunities to play house with our girlfriends, or just a place to hang out with the guys. In the fall, I somehow got talked into going back to school for what would have been my junior year, and somehow the school allowed me back in. I always wondered who pulled that one off.

By now, I was a legend at school and knew that the first sign of trouble would spell my doom. It only took one day: some slacker called me out during lunch hour to fight him. An hour later I was history: permanently expelled from high school. At that point, I didn't really care, for I felt as if a huge monkey was finally lifted off my back. I knew there were bigger and better things waiting for me down the road.

Sometimes strange things happen for strange reasons: call it serendipity, destiny, coincidence, or fate. In the spring of 1974, my life took a drastic turn, and it all started with someone pounding on my apartment door in Wallingford, Connecticut. At first, I thought it was the police, but to the best of my knowledge I wasn't in any kind of trouble. Not only that, when the police are pounding on your door, they usually announce themselves.

I opened the door and found myself confronted by an irate biker who accused me of stealing his stereo. I honestly didn't know what he was talking about, and I told him as much. He explained that somebody had broken into his house and stolen his stereo, which, he pointed out, was worth a ton of money. He also mentioned he had it on good authority that I was the culprit who took it. I denied responsibility for the burglary and invited him to search my apartment. After he looked around and didn't find his precious stereo, he insinuated that I must have sold it.

"Look, I didn't steal your stereo, okay? I don't go around stealing other people's stereos. I can afford to buy my own. I work down the street at Cooke's as a heavy-equipment mechanic," I said.

"Yeah, I'm impressed. Whatever! I'll find out who stole my stereo and when I do, his ass is grass. I hope for your sake it isn't going to be yours," he said and stormed out of my apartment.

I thought that would be the last time I saw the guy, but a few days later he showed up again. This time, he knocked on my door in a civil manner. I was surprised to see him, clutching a case of beer.

"I guess I owe you an apology. I found out who stole my stereo. Anyway, I brought you a case of beer," he said, pushing the case toward me.

I thought this was a very commendable gesture on his part, so I asked him to come in and join me for a drink. He introduced himself as Richie Doolittle and went on to explain that he had recovered the stolen stereo and given the thieves an attitude adjustment in the process. We started making small talk as we sipped our beers, and the subject of motorcycles naturally came up. I asked him what kind of bike he rode and immediately it was obvious I had asked what he considered a dumb question.

"A Harley! What else is there?" he said.

I readily agreed there wasn't any other kind of bike to ride. Since the fall of 1973, when I returned home after a two-year stint in the U.S. Army, I had thought of nothing else but owning a Harley. I had worked with a guy at Connecticut Truck and Trailer who rode one, and every time I saw him on the bike, I looked at it with a certain type of lust that can only be described as envy. I knew I wanted nothing more than to own a Harley myself. I had learned to ride a bike on a 50cc Benelli when I was around fourteen years old. It was an old clunker that belonged to a friend of mine, and everybody rode around on it. Compared to a Harley, the Benelli was a mere toy and certainly not something I ever dreamed of owning. Richie and I talked about Harleys for a while, and then he switched the conversation to cars, another topic close to my heart.

When Richie brought up the fact that he owned a Corvette, I mentioned in passing that I loved working on Chevrolet products and that they were actually my specialty. He got really excited about this and told me that nobody in town seemed to be able to work to his satisfaction on his Corvette. He asked me if I would come down to his place and help him do some wrenching on the car. I readily agreed, and that summer we started hanging around together on a regular basis. I helped Richie work on his Corvette, and he introduced me to the world of Harley-Davidsons. It seemed like destiny had come calling — an appointment that would eventually lead me to the world of 1%er outlaw bikers.

In the fall of 1974, I sold my Nova — a car that I really valued and had put a lot of work into — and bought a 1963 Harley Panhead chopper for $2,500 from one of Richie's friends, a charismatic guy named Cecil Pullen. Cecil was a local biker who, like Richie, was not in any motorcycle club. Guys like Richie and Cecil were known as independent bikers. Cecil was also one of the best Harley mechanics around, so it was an honor to end up owning one of his bikes.

This particular Harley was very special, for the frame had been altered by "Gene the Bean," a legendary local welder whose forte was altering motorcycle frames. Gene had added about five inches to the down-tubes and about three inches to the top rail of the frame, which paved the way for an eighteen-inch over-springer style front end. Although the bike was mechanically sound, and ran like a dream, I wanted to take it apart and paint it so it would be uniquely mine.

After stripping everything off of it, I took the frame to a fantastic auto body man and painter in Meriden, not far from New Haven. He painted the frame pearl ice blue and the gas tank and fenders a dark midnight blue. On the gas tank, he painted a mural of the tattoo I had on my arm: crossed pistons and a skull on the top and bottom. I thought I had died and gone to heaven — I was just nineteen years old and owned one hell of a mean Harley. And not just any Harley: this one was a chopper that turned everybody's head.

Even though it was way too cold to be out on a motorcycle, the first place I rode my showstopper to was my girlfriend Toni's high school. I had promised to pick her up, and I didn't want to let her down. Much to my dismay, I dropped the bike in the parking lot in front of about a hundred kids. Fortunately, the bike escaped unscathed, but my pride certainly didn't. Although I finally owned a Harley, I was just a guy on a motorcycle and obviously had a ways to go before I could call myself a biker.

As 1974 turned into 1975, Cooke's Equipment Company was losing work left and right. I was barely getting in forty hours a week, and it looked like I would soon be laid off. The prospect of that was not unattractive, as I hated the cold New England winters with a passion and had been thinking about relocating for quite some time.

In February 1975, I convinced Toni — now almost seventeen years old — to move to Tulsa, Oklahoma, with me. My uncle had lived in Tulsa for about ten years in the 1960s, and he told me there was a lot of work there for anybody who wasn't afraid to get his hands dirty. The weather was also a lot more agreeable than it was in Connecticut. When we arrived in Tulsa, it was a beautiful sunny day, and the temperature was in the mid-seventies.

We pulled into a cheap motel at the corner of 11th Street and Memorial and stayed there for the night. I immediately rolled my pride and joy out of the trailer and took it for a ride around town. Within a day, I had located an apartment complex that was willing to trade out some maintenance work toward payment of the rent. It was called the Orchard Park Apartments and was located just off 64th Street and Peoria in a nice area not far from Oral Roberts University. I was able to maneuver the Harley through the sliding door at the back and parked it inside my bedroom, where I knew it would be safe. To make ends meet, I took a temporary job as a laborer on a framing crew while canvassing the local heavy construction equipment dealerships for a mechanic's job. By early April, I landed a position at a John Deere dealership and settled into a regular routine. I would work during the day as a heavy equipment mechanic and as a maintenance man around the apartment complex during evenings and weekends when required.

What little time I had to myself I would use to ride my motorcycle a few miles down to the local Arby's Restaurant, which was right in the middle of what was known as Tulsa's "Restless Ribbon." The Ribbon was a two-mile strip of Peoria Avenue where all the kids in town hung out on summer nights. Different groups and cliques congregated at different hangouts, and because I now considered myself a biker — I was no longer dropping my Harley — I usually joined the town's bikers who congregated at Arby's.

After pulling out of the parking lot one night, I was stopped by the police because I wasn't wearing any goggles. When the officer discovered I had a Connecticut license plate on the bike, he decided to impound it. I had no idea he could do such a thing and adamantly voiced my disapproval. The situation quickly escalated into a resisting arrest charge. In no time at all, my bike was dangling from the back of a wrecker sling, and I was hauled off to jail. Needing $300 for bail bond, and not having a soul to call — Toni resisted employment as if it were a disease and didn't have a penny to her name — I had no idea which way to turn.

While I was mulling over my predicament, I was pleasantly surprised when suddenly I was notified that my bail bond had been paid, and I was released from jail. When I walked outside, I found some of the bikers I hung out with at Arby's waiting for me. They had seen me arrested, watched as my bike was impounded, and realized I was in a jam. They went down to the jail, and one of them bailed me out. Next, they escorted me to the impound lot and paid to get my Harley released. Three hours after I had been arrested, I was back at Arby's. I had never experienced such a sense of brotherhood and a feeling of belonging.

By the spring of 1976, I had moved a number of times and had also been through a few job changes. Around this time, I experienced a bit of a cash-flow problem, so, with a heavy heart, I sold my prized 1963 Harley Panhead in order to pay the bills. But I wasn't going to deprive myself of owning another bike: I used some of the money to buy an old Harley frame and most of an engine. This time I wanted to build my own motor, which was going to be an 80-inch stroker.

I went out to the Harley shop in Sand Springs and found a set of ULH 80-inch flywheels and a set of decent cases for which I was charged next to nothing. I sent all of the engine parts to Truett and Osborn in Wichita, Kansas, and had them build an ass-kicking stroker motor. Meanwhile, Toni had decided it would be a good idea to actually contribute to our living expenses, rather than just being an expense, and she was holding down a job at a local bar.

One day, I was at the bar with Richie, who had joined us in Tulsa, and another friend, Chris, when Toni told me a customer was giving her a hard time. I looked over to see a biker sitting in a corner by himself, so I went over to see what was going on. Before I even said a word, he snarled that he would fight all three of us if that's the way it was going to be. He came across more humorous than intimidating. I told him we had no intention of fighting — that all we wanted was for him to come over and join us for a beer.

"I'm Ed, and those are my friends, Richie and Chris," I said as I ushered him over to our table. He introduced himself as Lee McArdle and mentioned that he had just ridden into Tulsa from Maine. Lee told us that he had been raised in Detroit, lived in New Mexico for a while, and then spent a year in Maine. He had worked as a landscaper, an electrician, and a chef in a fancy restaurant. He sounded like my kind of people, and I liked him at once. That afternoon, we forged the kind of friendship that we knew would last a lifetime, rapidly becoming inseparable and spending all of our free time together. In June, just in time for my birthday, the engine from Truett and Osborn arrived from Wichita, and I spent the next few weeks putting the finishing touches on my new bike.

Soon, I was back hanging out at Arby's with the biker crew and discovered that one of the regulars, Johnny Cook, had started prospecting for a club called the Rogues. This was a big deal to us independents, and we all looked up to Johnny with new admiration. Although he was a family man and older than the rest of us, we considered Johnny one of us, and he was well liked.

One night, while we were all hanging out at Arby's, Johnny rode into the parking lot wearing his new prospect colors. A stranger, driving a car, followed him into the lot. As Johnny got off his motorcycle, the stranger got out of his vehicle, walked up to our group, and threatened the Rogues prospect by pointing two sawed-off shotguns at him. Knowing that Johnny was the type of guy who didn't have a beef with anyone, I assumed right away that the stranger had a problem with somebody in the Rogues, and he had no idea who Johnny was.

I did a very stupid and impulsive thing and got in between the shotgun-wielding stranger and Johnny. With about twenty people watching from ten feet away, I told the guy to go ahead and shoot me; I was not going to let him shoot Johnny. I explained that Johnny was a friend of ours and that he was a married man with a bunch of little kids. I ended my conversation by telling him he needed to settle up with the actual Rogues he had problems with, not with Johnny just because he happened to be a prospect in the club. I wasn't sure which way this was going to go, but to my relief, he got back into his car and drove off. All I could say after that was that I needed a beer, and a thankful Johnny was more than happy to oblige.

In late September, as a direct result of the incident at Arby's, the Rogues Motorcycle Club invited me to attend one of their meetings. They were very appreciative of what I had done for one of their own, and they wanted to see what I was all about. One of the other guys who regularly hung around at Arby's, Rickie "Smoker" Miles, came along with me. We were introduced to all twelve members of the Tulsa chapter, four of whom were prospects.

We found out that the Rogues had been started in Chicago in the early 1960s by ex-members of the Outlaws Motorcycle Club. In 1966, one of its founding members, Fred "Thumper" Knippenberg, moved to Oklahoma and started a chapter in Oklahoma City; a few years later the Chicago chapter folded, and Oklahoma became the home state for the club. Although it was essentially an Oklahoma organization, there were a few chapters in northern Texas and southern Kansas as well.

The Tulsa chapter had been founded the previous year by Edwin "EJ" Nunn, Roy Green, Marvin Brix, Robert "Rob" Reynolds, Charles "T-Chuck" Schlegel, Dennis "Rev" Isaacson, and Keith Vandervoort. Being a couple of young bucks, Smoker and I were very impressed with the Rogues, the first outlaw club I had been this close to. I thought back to the bikers I had seen at the North Branford carnival some seven years earlier, thinking how cool it would be to belong to a motorcycle club. I couldn't believe my ears when we were invited to prospect for the Rogues Tulsa chapter.

I wasn't exactly sure what prospecting would entail except that we would have to do all sorts of things — like being at the beck and call of the fullpatch holders 24/7 — to see if we were worthy of becoming members. They told Smoker, who owned a Kawasaki kz1000, he would have to buy a Harley if he wanted to join the club. Outlaw bikers don't ride "rice rockets," one of the guys said. Although I wanted to join the club, I didn't just jump at the opportunity; neither did Smoker.

We were told it would be a full-time commitment and that the club would come before all else in our lives. Holding down a day job was fine, but the rest of our time belonged to the club. It took us a few days to make up our minds, but we decided to give prospecting for the Rogues a try. Smoker found himself a beat-up old Harley Sportster, and a week later we both started hanging around. I officially began prospecting a few weeks after that and proudly sewed my prospect patches onto an old blue jean jacket.

Unfortunately, I had only been a Rogues prospect for a few months when I found myself unable to make ends meet in Tulsa, and I grudgingly accepted a job offer with a heavy-equipment dealer in Richmond, Virginia. It broke my heart, but I had no choice: I had to quit the Rogues. Everybody in the club was supportive and understanding of my situation and told me I would be welcome back at any time and could pick up where I left off.

Toni and I packed up our belongings and moved to Virginia just before Thanksgiving 1976. Shortly after we arrived in Richmond, however, we got into a huge argument, and she went back to Tulsa. Considering our relationship revolved around fighting like cats and dogs one minute, then fluttering around like a couple of peachfaced lovebirds the next, breaking up and getting back together was par for the course. I knew she'd be back, and I settled into an apartment on the north side of Richmond.

Within a few days of arriving in Richmond, I started working at the Rish Equipment Company, an international construction-equipment dealer whose history went all the way back to 1934. As I hadn't forgotten the mechanical skills I had learned at Cooke's Equipment in Connecticut a few years earlier, I worked my way up to a field-truck position in just a couple of weeks. This meant I wasn't stuck at the shop, but roamed around various locations, working on construction equipment on site without a supervisor bossing me around or leaning over my shoulders. And the best part of the position was that I had all of my mechanic's tools with me when I went home at night, which facilitated my ability to work on my bike. I was continually fiddling around with it, making it better and more reliable, while at the same time boosting my confidence as a motorcycle mechanic.

Now that I was making good money, I started traveling back and forth to Connecticut, buying and selling Harley parts to pay for the trips. I was becoming quite the wheeler-dealer in Harley parts, and had built up a nice inventory of front ends, Shovelhead top ends, and transmissions. I also had an extra Harley rigid frame, a set of engine cases from which I had removed the serial numbers because they were stolen, and an Oklahoma builder's title. In essence, the builder's title came with a serial number that allowed the holder to assemble a motorcycle using different parts and then stamp that serial number onto the frame and engine cases.

Although I knew there was no way I could afford one, it didn't take me long to locate a fairly new Superglide with only one hundred miles on it. The owner was a total jerk, a biker wannabe who had bought the Harley right off the showroom floor and then decided he wanted to sell it. I guess he realized he wasn't cut out to be a biker. Maybe his wife had ordered him to sell it, or maybe he needed the money. I didn't ask. He let me take it for a test ride on my own — a bad mistake — and I promptly neglected to return it.

It seemed like my old ways — when I regularly stole cars — had left some residue on me, and it didn't bother my conscience in the least. A few hours later, back at my apartment, I had taken the bike completely apart and then disposed of the frame and engine cases in a local river. A week later, I set out for Cecil Pullen's house in Durham, Connecticut, with my Harley rigid frame and the parts from the Superglide I had taken for a test ride.

I had been seeing a lot more of Cecil since I had been living in Richmond. This historic city, one of the oldest in the United States and a key center in the Revolutionary and Civil Wars, was only about eight hours away from his house. Cecil had a well-equipped motorcycle shop in the basement of his house where he let me build my new bike. Every other weekend or so, over the next few months, I traveled back and forth to Connecticut to work on the motorcycle. When all was said and done, I owned another awesome Harley. The bike was, in essence, a brand-new Superglide stuffed meticulously into an old Harley rigid frame, electric start and all. Once again, I had a stunning paint job applied to the frame and fenders and the gas tank emblazoned with crossed pistons and a skull. I was prouder than a peacock when I brought the finished bike back to Virginia. I now had two Harleys squeezed into a small one-bedroom apartment. I just knew it was going to be a great summer.

It was still winter outside in March 1977 when I took my beautiful new bike for a spin, but I was so excited I hardly felt the cold. After showing off the bike to some friends at my local bike shop, I took a little tour around Richmond and was promptly stopped by a police officer. After looking at my bike and my registration papers, he called in the local auto-theft detectives. Fifteen minutes later, I watched my precious Harley get loaded onto a flatbed truck and hauled off to the impound yard for investigation. It seemed the auto-theft detective thought the motorcycle was stolen. Over the next month, I argued with the detective about the legality of the parts on my seized bike. I had receipts for all the parts, but there was still the fact that there were no serial numbers on the engine cases; all Harley engine cases were supposed to have serial numbers.

I stuck to my story that I had bought the engine cases that way. In the end, the tests that were performed on the cases to locate the serial numbers came back negative. The detective was beside himself, for the actual report he had received stated that there never had been a serial number on either of the engine case halves. He knew that this was impossible, unless the engine cases had been stolen from the Harley factory before the serial numbers had been punched into them. In the end, we made a deal: the detective would sign a release allowing me to take possession of the entire bike, less the engine cases.

I agreed to disassemble the bike engine at the impound yard, using my field-truck tools to do so. He told me he wanted to use the cases for an exhibit, showing what someone could do to remove the serial numbers if they had the knowledge. I made that kind of hard for him, however, because when I took the engine apart, I smashed the cases into about thirty pieces, put them all in a large plastic bag, and left them at the salvage yard for him to pick up. I never heard from him again, but I bet he wasn't too happy when he got the bag full of broken metal.

As I pondered what to do with all the bike parts I now had scattered all over my apartment, my childhood buddy from Connecticut, Pete Hansen, arrived for a visit while on leave from the U.S. Navy. He was excited to find that I still had my other stroker chopper and talked me into letting him take it for a ride. I figured that he could do no harm to the old bike, and even if he laid it down, the paint job could be easily touched up; after all, it was from a Krylon spray paint can to begin with. As fate would have it, Pete lost control of the bike and wrecked it, putting himself in the hospital in the process.

Fortunately, he soon recovered from his physical injuries, but it took him quite a while to recover his pride. One good thing came out of Pete wrecking the bike: I now knew exactly what to do with all of my parts. I took the legal engine cases and legal Harley title from the bike Pete had wrecked, used all the parts left from the impounded Superglide, and built a totally legal, brand-new Harley in my apartment living room. The only real difference was in the style of engine cases: instead of having a set of stolen 1970 up-alternator cases holding the engine together, the engine was surrounded by a set of 1958 generator cases.

Shortly after I got the bike rebuilt and back on the road, I was able to change jobs and go to work for the local Caterpillar construction equipment dealer. Ever since I had worked on heavy equipment back at Cooke's, it had been my dream to work for Caterpillar. But it seemed that I always lacked the required experience. Now that I had enough experience, I had finally found someone at Richmond Caterpillar willing to give me a chance. Caterpillar was the Cadillac of the heavy construction equipment world, and it was a giant step up in prestige as well as pay. I worked mainly in the shop but occasionally would get to go out in the field to do simple repairs. I started getting particularly interested in their line of large bulldozers and developed a fairly good knowledge of them in a very short time.

One day, I was welding a bulldozer blade in the shop when the chain holding the blade broke. This caused the thousand-pound blade to fall on my foot and break some bones, in spite of the steel-toed boots I was wearing. As a result, I was forced to take leave from work so the foot could heal properly.

While convalescing, I hung around Departure Bike Works on Hull Street, getting to know the employees there. Most of them had been involved with a motorcycle club a few years earlier known as the Confederate Angels. Apparently, the Confederate Angels had disbanded when some of the club decided to become Hells Angels in North Carolina, and the rest refused to make the change. To keep the peace, the club disbanded in name only, and the remaining members in the Richmond area maintained the club camaraderie and organizational structure.

It took a while, but by the end of summer they were letting me hang around socially on a regular basis. I took part in my first club run with them, and even though they didn't wear colors, they still acted just like a motorcycle club. Around this time I also attended my first biker funeral. One of the ex-Confederate Angels, who was living in Florida, had been killed in a bar fight by a member of the Outlaws Motorcycle Club. I was invited to attend his interment, which was to be held in Virginia. The actual burial was very different from everything I had experienced up to this point, and I was extremely impressed at the way it was handled. After the deceased's casket was lowered into the ground, his brothers personally shoveled in the dirt on top of it until the grave was full. They piled all of the flowers on the grave and then had a few beers there before leaving the cemetery. We finally left in a large convoy of motorcycles, which had earlier escorted the body from the church to the gravesite.

Because of the injury to my foot and the amount of time that would be needed for it to heal, the Caterpillar dealership decided to cut me loose. I received a small settlement from them, and we parted on good terms. Toni, who in the meantime had come back into my life, now said she was homesick, and I decided to move back to Connecticut with her. I had mixed feelings about the move, but we loaded up our possessions in the fall of 1977 and returned home. All I could do was hope that the change would be for the best.

Within a few days, I located a magnificent townhouse on top of a mountain just north of New Haven, on the Hamden–New Haven town line. It was three stories tall and had a large garage that took up the entire ground floor: it was an ideal place to work on my motorcycles and store my treasure-trove of parts. As an added bonus, my buddy Pete was willing to rent a room from me to help pay the bills. Pete had been discharged from the Navy and had bought his first new Harley, a 1978 gray Low Rider.

A few weeks later, after we got settled in, I was surprised to find myself happy to be in Connecticut again. It was good to be home, but once again it didn't take long for Toni and me to start fighting. This time she took off for California; so much for being homesick!

In July, I took off on my bike for a vacation ride to Bowling Green, Kentucky, where there was a major biker rally held every year. I had made plans to meet the Tulsa crew there and was glad to see my old friend Lee McArdle was among them. He had made the journey with some new friends of his who were members of a California motorcycle club called the Mongols. I had never heard of the Mongols before and was surprised to hear they were living in Tulsa.

I was even more surprised to see the Mongols not wearing their colors; all of the motorcycle club members I knew of wore their patches everywhere they went. Many years later, I learned that the Mongols were in the middle of a war with the Hells Angels at that time, and the Mongols were not sure if the Hells Angels would be attending the event at Bowling Green. If the Angels were in attendance, the Mongols didn't want to identify themselves by displaying their colors, as it surely would have led to a confrontation. Although, on the surface, this appeared like the prudent thing to do, not wearing your colors in order to remain anonymous seemed strange to me.

While in Bowling Green, I ran into the Outlaws Motorcycle Club for the first time in my life; it proved to be an encounter that would have a dramatic impact on me. I was wearing a T-shirt, and the crossed pistons and skull tattoo on my arm were clearly visible. Lee had earlier kidded with me about the tattoo looking a lot like the Outlaws center patch, which in club circles is commonly referred to as "Charlie." I guess I should not have been surprised when I was suddenly surrounded by a group of Outlaws looking for trouble. They were very annoyed about my tattoo, and their leader, a guy called Wildman, demanded that it be removed immediately.

Before getting into an altercation that I knew I would surely lose, I figured I would try to talk my way out of the situation. I explained I had seen the image up on the wall of a tattoo shop in Rhode Island and just happened to like it. I had no idea at the time that the Outlaws Motorcycle Club even existed. From the expression on Outlaw Wildman's face, my story didn't seem to carry much weight. Ready to go down fighting, I said to him that if he thought he needed to, he should cut off the skin displaying the tattoo or let me go about my business.

The look in Outlaw Wildman's eyes told me that I had made a grievous mistake; he whipped out his knife, and before I knew it, three of the other Outlaws grabbed me. Before Wildman could perform the impromptu tattoo-removal surgery, however, a stranger appeared from nowhere, asking the Outlaws what they thought they were doing. The stranger just happened to be a member of the Rogues Motorcycle Club from Oklahoma City; his name was John "Little Wolf" Killip. I remembered him from when I was a prospect in the Rogues Tulsa chapter two years earlier. It turned out that Rogue Little Wolf knew most of the Outlaws who had surrounded me, and he seemed to know Outlaw Wildman better than the rest. While I silently thanked God, Outlaw Wildman explained the situation to Rogue Little Wolf. Little Wolf told Wildman that he knew me well and that I was a stand-up guy who regularly crisscrossed the country on my bike. He requested some sort of compromise to rectify the situation, and the Outlaws spokesman complied.

Outlaw Wildman ordered me to get the tattoo covered up within thirty days and told me to come to the Dayton, Ohio, Outlaws clubhouse as soon as I could to prove to him that the tattoo had indeed been removed. The pack of Outlaws dispersed, and I thanked Little Wolf for intervening. I learned that Rogue Little Wolf was a frequent visitor to the Outlaws clubhouse in Dayton. He told me they were a great bunch of guys. Little Wolf also told me that these guys were the real deal and a whole lot more serious about clubbing than the Rogues were. He told me to not be surprised if he became an Outlaw someday. Before we parted, Little Wolf asked me to come back to Oklahoma and rejoin the Rogues. I told him I would seriously consider it.

When I got back to Connecticut, I immediately had the offending tattoo covered up. I arranged some time off from work and left for a whirlwind trip to Oklahoma, where I planned to buy a load of Harley parts from Lee McArdle's bike shop for resale in Connecticut. I spent one night in Tulsa, where I ran into Rogue T-Chuck, one of the guys I had met when I first was first invited to the Tulsa chapter clubhouse. I told him all about the Outlaws and Rogue Little Wolf and that I was thinking about moving back to Oklahoma. T-Chuck told me he would love to see me come back and that I would be more than welcome to pick up with the Rogues where I had left off.

On the way back from Oklahoma to Connecticut, I stopped to see the Outlaws at their Dayton clubhouse. This time, I was prepared and carried a Colt .45 automatic for protection. I figured if things didn't go well, I could at least take a few of the Outlaws with me. When I arrived at the clubhouse, it was nearly dark. I knocked on the heavy door, which was answered by a mountain of a man who introduced himself as Outlaw Sampson; his real name, I learned later, was James Marr. I explained to him that I needed to see his brother, Outlaw Wildman, but refused to tell him why. Outlaw Sampson told me that Wildman was not there and I would just have to come back another time. He was ready to throw the door shut in my face, but I blocked it and explained that I was on my way home from Oklahoma to Connecticut and that coming back another time was not an option.

Like a total idiot, I demanded to speak with the chapter president. Sampson snickered at my audacity and motioned for me to wait just inside the door. He sent another member to get their president, who appeared to be upstairs. I knew that if the guy was sleeping, he wasn't going to be too happy about being woken up by some upstart stranger. I noticed there were about ten other Outlaws in the room; if things went bad, there was no way I could shoot them all. I resigned myself to the fact that there was a good possibility I could be dead within the next ten minutes.

The president of the Dayton Outlaws at the time was Kenneth "Hambone" Hammond, who was about thirty-two years old. It didn't take long for him to come downstairs, and it was obvious I had gotten him out of bed — this was not a good way to start things off. To my surprise, Outlaw Hambone didn't tear into me for waking him up. But rather than invite me to come and sit down at the bar, where he dropped himself on a stool, he ordered me to.

"You wanna drink, kid?" he said to me, as I joined him on one of the stools.

"Sure — whatever you're drinking. Thanks," I replied, figuring it was time to show a bit of politeness.

Outlaw Hambone nodded to the prospect tending bar, who retrieved two Pepsis out of a fridge that contained a lot more beer than soft drinks. I was surprised to learn that Hambone didn't drink alcohol, although I did find out that he apparently liked his Valiums.

"So, to what do I owe the pleasure of your company?" he said without a hint of sarcasm in his voice. Before I could answer, he said in an even tone, "You better have one hell of a good reason for being here. I don't particularly like it when some asshole wakes me up, especially some asshole I don't even know."

I proceeded to explain about the tattoo and what had transpired between me and Outlaw Wildman in Bowling Green a few weeks earlier. The rest of the guys were all hanging around the bar — mostly surrounding me — listening to my tale with detached interest and keeping an eye on their chapter president as if waiting for him to react, to give some kind of signal to pounce on me and beat me to kingdom come. I rolled up my sleeve and showed Hambone my arm, now minus the imitation "Charlie" tattoo. He glanced at my arm and nodded.

"Well, listen, thanks for your time. I better hit the road," I said. "Sorry to drop by unannounced like this, but your brother Wildman told me to get my ass down here within thirty days and prove I got rid of the tat. I told him I would, and I'm a man of my word."

"Yeah, yeah, that's fine. No problem," Hambone said with a dismissive gesture of the hand, eyeing me as if sizing me up.

That's when an already tense atmosphere got tenser, because he told me that there was no way he could allow me to leave. All the Outlaws in the room were on edge, waiting for the least excuse to beat my brains in. I didn't know what to do. I was debating whether to go for my Colt, but I knew if I did, I would cross the point of no return.

"Relax, man. Take a load off," Hambone said, a faint smile crossing his face. "You've come a long way; no need to run off. Let's get to know each other a bit."

This at once took the edge off things, and everyone in the room went back to whatever they were doing before I had arrived. While Outlaw Hambone and I sat at the bar, he revealed that he had spoken with both Little Wolf and Wildman about me, and knew that I would show up at the clubhouse before long.

"You kinda have lousy timing, but you're alright. You're 1%er material, man. Isn't that right, guys?" he said to his brothers.

The other men in the room readily agreed, which gave me a real boost in confidence. I was still an independent biker, but I knew that would soon change. Before we parted, Outlaw Hambone made me promise that every time I passed through Dayton, I would stop in and see him. He promised me that when and if I moved back to Oklahoma, he would visit me if he were in the neighborhood.

As I walked out the clubhouse door, I took a deep breath of fresh air and wondered how I had made it out of there alive. I had no idea of the relationship I had just forged or the significance of our meeting. It would take years for me to realize that the incident at Bowling Green had been another major turning point in my life.

Years later, Hambone told me he had been impressed that I had walked into their clubhouse by myself that night, and he knew right then and there we were going to be friends for life. Unfortunately, the Vietnam veteran was not going to live to a ripe old age — he was fatally shot in an Ohio bar on January 20, 1989; he was forty-two years old.

CHAPTER SIX

LIVING ON
BORROWED TIME

For most of the sad Monday after our return from Sturgis, Bandidos Canada Presidente Alain and I moped around my house and dealt with our grief, doing what we could to come to grips with the tragedy that had befallen us. We talked a lot about the life and death of Bandido Tout, a brother of whom we had both shared a high opinion. Alain had known Tout since before they became involved with the Rock Machine. Recalling his first meeting with Tout, Alain told me he had heard about him in the biker world as being a top Harley mechanic.

"It was in 1991. I had a Harley that I had bought three years earlier. It was my first Harley, and it really needed some repairs," Alain said. "So when I heard about Tout being one of the best Harley guys around, I went to his motorcycle shop near Montreal. From that day we became really good friends. And, well, you know . . . we were in the Rock Machine together."

I asked Alain what prospecting for the Rock Machine was

like back then. By now, he had experienced firsthand the way American Bandidos treated their prospects, which was not pretty. Alain explained that to be a prospect for the Rock Machine you needed to be there regularly and just hang out with the guys. You weren't considered a doormat, and the club valued new members.

"The regular guys treated prospects with respect and class — very similar to how the European Bandidos treat their prospects," Alain said.

Although I knew quite a bit about the Rock Machine's history, I didn't interrupt Alain when he proceeded to tell me about the club's beginnings and subsequent entanglement with the Hells Angels. He explained that the Rock Machine first saw the light of day in 1986, more or less as a direct result of the infamous Lennoxville Purge. The club was founded by Salvatore Cazzetta, who, with his friend Mom Boucher, had been members of a small biker club known as the SS. They were obviously Hells Angels material, but an incident in Lennoxville, Quebec, where five members of the Hells Angels North chapter were murdered by their own brothers, propelled Boucher and Cazzetta in opposite directions.

Cazzetta found what had happened in Lennoxville disturbing. He called it an unforgivable breach of the outlaw code. Rather than join the Hells Angels, he decided to form the Rock Machine with his brother Giovanni. Unlike the Angels and other outlaw clubs, Rock Machine members didn't identify themselves with colors or patches; instead, they wore a gold ring with an eagle insignia. The original purpose of the Rock Machine wasn't so much about riding motorcycles as it was about protection against the aggressive Hells Angels who were bent on taking over their territory.

Meanwhile, Boucher, not averse to the Hells Angels' modus operandi, joined the club and rapidly rose through the ranks.

For several years, the Hells Angels and the Rock Machine coexisted peacefully enough, reportedly because of Boucher's respect for the charismatic, Quebec Mafia–connected Cazzetta. But in 1994, after Cazzetta had been arrested and incarcerated on drug charges, Boucher, who had been installed as president of the Hells Angels Montreal chapter, began to pressure the temporarily leaderless Rock Machine.

At the time, the Rock Machine was estimated to have about sixty members and associates in its two chapters, Montreal and Quebec City, which made it about half the size of the Hells Angels. And the Rock Machine had nowhere near as many support clubs. For Boucher and the highly organized Hells Angels, taking on and crushing the highly disorganized Rock Machine must have had the attraction of shooting ducks in a pond. It should have been easy to assimilate or wipe out the outnumbered Rock Machine. But as history would eventually confirm, the Rock Machine proved to be formidable opponents. In fact, nobody before ever stood up to the mighty Angels the way the Rock Machine did, and it is highly unlikely anybody ever will again.

Boucher began his takeover bid by targeting Rock Machine–controlled bars and attempting to persuade the owners and resident drug dealers to turn over their business. When these overtures met with resistance, the inevitable bloodletting began. After the slaying of a Rock Machine associate in Montreal and the subsequent killing of Rock Machine member Normand Baker in Mexico, the war was officially on.

By 1997, now with both Cazzetta brothers behind bars, the Rock Machine were considered by many to be on their last gasp. The Hells Angels, like vultures circling a dying animal, continued to put pressure on the club, convinced the end was near and their biggest rivals would be no more. But one ambitious young member, Fred Faucher, who had been arrested three years earlier for plotting to kill members of a Hells Angels puppet club, the Evil Ones, began a series of maneuvers that would ensure the survival of the Rock Machine in one form or another and place the destiny of the club in his hands.

Faucher, accompanied by fellow Rock Machine members Tout Leger and Johnny Plescio, flew to Sweden on June 18, 1997, with the intention of attending the Bandidos Helsingborg Memory Run for fallen brothers. Swedish authorities had different plans for the trio, however. They detained the Quebecers for twenty-four hours and promptly deported them back to Canada.

Faucher remained unfazed and determined to integrate himself and the Rock Machine into the Bandidos Nation. On July 14, 1997, with Plescio and Paul "Sasquatch" Porter, another Rock Machine, Faucher went to a Luxembourg motorcycle show where they met with members of the European Bandidos.

In direct contrast to Tout's experience with the Houston Bandidos a few years earlier, the Rock Machine members were received with open arms. Because the turf war with the Hells Angels was still raging in Scandinavia at this time, the Bandidos and Rock Machine had a common enemy. At once, a friendship was formed, and this would ultimately lead to the Rock Machine being designated a hangaround club by the European Bandidos.

Not long after returning from Luxembourg, Faucher became the police's prime suspect in the July 24, 1997, attempted murder of Hells Angels Nomad member Louis "Melou" Roy. But there was no proof linking Faucher to the crime, and no one was brought up on charges. On September 11, Faucher took over the presidency of the Rock Machine's Quebec City chapter from Claude "Ti-Loup" Vézina, who had been arrested for drug trafficking.

From this point on, Faucher, already well respected in the

club, became a major spokesman for the Rock Machine. Buoyed by the inroads he had made with the European Bandidos in Luxembourg, Faucher invited George Wegers — then one of two Vice Presidentes for the American Bandidos — to come to Quebec City for a meeting. Faucher hoped that Wegers would seize the opportunity to expand the Bandidos into Canada and patch over the Rock Machine. In his mind, the merger would serve as the perfect antidote to the Rock Machine's problems with the Angels.

"The Hells Angels, which is a worldwide organization and well organized, will never sit down with such a small group of people as the Rock Machine," Faucher stated to the press prior to Wegers' visit. "The main goal was to be a part of an international club so one of these days they will agree to sit down to talk with us."

In October 1977, Faucher hosted a lavish dinner party for Wegers at the swanky Quebec City restaurant L'Astral. The gathering came to an abrupt end, however, when police raided the restaurant and arrested Faucher and twenty-two fellow Rock Machine members. Wegers was detained and immediately deported. Eventually, only three Rock Machine members present at the L'Astral raid were convicted in court for possession of firearms.

Not surprisingly, the Hells Angels took Wegers' visit to Canadian Hells Angels territory as a sign of bad faith, especially in light of the Scandinavian truce, which had recently gone into effect. When they realized that the Bandidos were in contact with the Rock Machine, the Angels called a meeting with Wegers and made it clear to him that his club should not take in their enemies. Wegers, always trying to appease everybody he dealt with, gave his assurance that the Rock Machine would not become Bandidos.

I was curious about how and when Alain got involved with

the club. Although he didn't want to talk much about it, he mentioned that he met his first Rock Machine member in the early 1990s and that he became a patch holder in 1995, when he was in his mid-thirties.

"You know, maybe if I hadn't joined the club, Tout wouldn't have either, and he would still be . . ." Alain's voice trailed off, and he sank into his own thoughts. When he emerged from his reverie, he went on to explain that Tout had a lot of reasons to hate the Quebec Hells Angels: he had been there at the very start of the biker war, and a close friend of his had been one of their first targets. In August 1994, Tout and Rock Machine Normand Baker had taken their wives on a vacation to Mexico. When they got on the plane in Canada, they had noticed a few members of the Hells Angels among the passengers but didn't think too much about it.

Although a Hells Angels sympathizer, Pierre Daoust, had been murdered on July 13, and a Rock Machine associate the following day, the lid had not entirely blown off the Montreal biker pressure cooker that would lead to the tit-for-tat killings that would eventually take more than 160 lives. The same day as the Rock Machine associate's murder on July 14, Fred Faucher and four fellow members of the Quebec City chapter of the Rock Machine were arrested in a hotel room as they planned a revenge attack on the Evil Ones, a Hells Angels puppet club. According to police, two pistols, three radio-detonated bombs, and twelve pounds of dynamite were confiscated. Faucher, who had joined the Rock Machine in the early 1990s, was convicted but received only a short jail sentence. Then twenty-four years old and one of the youngest members of the Rock Machine, Faucher would be destined to play a major role in the club.

A few days into their Mexican holiday, Baker and his wife went out for dinner. At the last minute, Tout and his wife had decided to stay at the hotel so both couples could have a private dinner. While Normand and his wife were enjoying their meal, a Hells Angels prospect suddenly walked into the restaurant and shot Baker point blank in the back of the head, killing him instantly. His horrified wife was splattered with pieces of his skull and brains. Normand Baker became the first fullpatch Rock Machine to die at the hands of the Angels . . . and the Montreal biker war had started.

The prospect who killed Baker was caught but only spent one year in jail. The Canadian Hells Angels came to his rescue, paying off the corrupt Mexican justice system to get him released and the charges dismissed. Tout was convinced that he would have died along with Baker if he had joined his friend for dinner. Little did he know that he was living on borrowed time.

CHAPTER SEVEN

FOOLS MASQUERADING
AS MASTERMINDS

On August 14, 2001, I took Alain to the Tulsa airport for his return trip home. Slowly, over the next few days, my life returned to a semblance of normalcy. I settled into my usual routines with my family, my business endeavors, and the Oklahoma Bandidos.

But in Canada it would be anything but normal for the Bandidos. On August 17, while on the way to the funeral for Bandido El Secretario Tout, William Ferguson, a Kingston Bandido, was arrested by the Quebec police for having a gun in his possession. It didn't end there. Less than two weeks later, on August 24, another Canadian Bandidos national chapter officer was murdered. This time it was Sargento de Armas Sylvain "Sly" Gregoire. Bandido Sly was murdered at the used-car lot he owned in downtown Montreal. While dealing with two men he thought were potential buyers, he was shot in the head as he turned around to retrieve some documents from a filing cabinet.

Bandido Sly was only thirty-three years old; just like

Bandido Tout, he left behind a wife and family. Once again, the Canadian Bandidos were in the middle of a war zone. It seemed like the only alternative was for the Bandidos in Canada to start fighting back, just like they had done when they had been the Rock Machine. Bandidos Canada was now surrounded by four enemies: Hells Angels to the rear, law enforcement to the front, public resentment to the left, and the media to the right.

No one was surprised when, as individuals, some members of the Bandidos, either through their associates, hangarounds, or friends, did start fighting back. Everyone took care of business in their own way and on their own terms. In September 2001, many of the bars that did business with the Hells Angels were burned to the ground. Some of the bar owners lied about the fact that they were doing drug business with the Hells Angels, and some probably did not know their employees were selling drugs for the Hells Angels.

Other bar owners and building owners jumped on the bandwagon and burned their own places down just to collect the insurance. The arsons continued into October, and sixteen people were eventually arrested. As usual, newspaper articles explained that the arsons were part of a struggle for control of the illicit drug trade. The truth was that the only thing the Bandidos wanted was peace, but to get the Hells Angels to agree, their illegal business endeavors had to be impacted.

In mid-October 2001, I decided I did not want to return to Canada to attend my upcoming immigration hearing, which was scheduled for October 22. This decision was made as a direct result of two major events: the tragic destruction of the World Trade Center in New York City on September 11, and the biological contamination of the U.S. Senate building with anthrax.

In early October, airplanes were still not considered to be a safe means of transportation; travel was extremely difficult because of a general state of heightened security. Day and night the government, and a melodramatic media, stoked the fires of our fear-based society by exposing the American public to the premise that more attacks on the United States were imminent. This resulted in a tangible climate of trepidation, which seemed to permeate everyone and everything.

My eight-year-old daughter, Taylor, did not want me to leave her, understandably so. Taylor was afraid that if I went to Canada, I might not be allowed to return. I made the only decision I could possibly make — stay home. I was not going to leave her, no matter what the cost to me: the $20,000 bond I had paid to secure my release, the lawyer fees, and future inability to travel freely to Canada. Although losing a ton of money over something as ridiculous as this immigration case was not a pleasant proposition, not being able to travel to Canada in the future bothered me immensely.

On October 18, my Canadian attorney, Josh Zambrowsky, wrote a letter to the adjudicator assigned to my immigration case, Rolland Ladouceur, advising him that I would not be attending the next scheduled hearing for the reasons cited above. Ladouceur had always been an extremely fair and impartial judge and was well respected by all the attorneys on both sides of my immigration hearings. He was the same adjudicator who had allowed me to return to Oklahoma after my time-wasting hearing of January 17.

In my humble opinion, this whole immigration case was ludicrous, a waste of government time, and an even bigger waste of taxpayers' money. I had always believed that Ladouceur shared my view, so it came as no surprise to me when, on October 19, he dismissed my case. Josh was surprised, however, that the judge had the audacity to stand up to the halfwits at Immigration Canada. He readily admitted that the adjudicator's logical way of thinking was profound, brilliant, and an act of pure common sense. Ladouceur dismissed my case based solely upon the fact that I was already in the United States. To continue the charade by bringing me back to Canada just to be "officially" deported to the United States was, in Ladouceur's opinion, an exercise in futility that only an idiot would consider.

In a letter addressed to my attorney, adjudicator Rolland Ladouceur clearly wanted to put the folly of Immigration Canada behind him.

Edward Warren Winterhalder File No: AI-00022

Following your letter of October 18th, 2001, I understand that your client is still outside Canada and will not be present for the continuation of his inquiry, scheduled to continue on October 22nd.

Considering that the allegations made against your client were pursuant to paragraph 27(2)(a) of the Immigration Act of Canada, and that your client is no longer ". . . a person that is in Canada . . ." I thereby consider the inquiry of Mr. Edward Warren Winterhalder to be concluded.

Concerning the documentation presented by the parties, since they were not yet introduced as evidence, it has been destroyed.

Concerning the $20,000 bond, your client's passport and his Bandido Vest, I recommend that he contact Immigration Canada for restitution.

Please inform your client accordingly.

Rolland Ladouceur — Adjudicator

Immigration Canada prosecution attorneys went ballistic! They sent a letter back to Mr. Ladouceur requesting clarification of his order, as if it wasn't spelled out clearly enough. They asked inane questions like *What do you mean by concluded?* and *Is the inquiry still adjourned?* It must have been a trying task for Ladouceur to respond in the polite manner he did. Perhaps he was so used to dealing with fools masquerading as masterminds, that to him it was business as usual.

Adjudicator Ladouceur wrote this lengthy letter, in which he did not mince words, to Immigration Canada after they demanded to know why he dismissed their case.

October 31, 2001

Ms Lynn Leblanc and Mr Toby Hoffman
Citizenship and Immigration Canada

BY FAX : (613) 952-4770

Subject: Edward Warren Winterhalder File No: A1-00022
On October 19th 2001, after receiving confirmation that Mr. Winterhalder would not be present for the continuation of his inquiry, I informed the parties that the inquiry was concluded. Here are the reasons.

The inquiry was opened on January 17th 2001. At the request of Citizenship and Immigration Canada, the case was adjourned until May 2001. A second adjournment was granted, as requested by the Minister, until October 22nd 2001. In the meantime, Mr. Winterhalder had returned to his country of citizenship (U.S.A.) and was expected to return by October 22nd 2001, to attend his inquiry.

On January 17th 2001, Citizenship and Immigration Canada presented a direction for inquiry and a report pursuant to paragraph 27(2)a) of the Immigration Act.

"An immigration officer or a peace officer shall, unless the person has been arrested pursuant to subsection 103(2), forward a written report to the Deputy Minister setting out the details of any information in the possession of the immigration officer or peace officer indicating **that a person in Canada**, other than a Canadian citizen or permanent resident, is a person who

a) is a member of an inadmissible class, other than an inadmissible class described in paragraph 19(1)(h) or 19(2)(c)."

On October 19th, 2001, Mr. Zambrowsky, Mr. Winterhalder's counsel, informed the tribunal that his client would not come back to Canada for his inquiry.

Considering that the *Immigation Act* is silent with respect to the conclusion of an inquiry in such cases;

Considering that the objective of the inquiry was to determine if Mr. Winterhalder should be removed from the Canadian territory;

Considering that the Mr. Winterhalder is no longer on the Canadian territory;

The tribunal decided to conclude the inquiry because the question has become moot.

Should Mr. Winterhalder return one day to Canada, Citizenship and Immigration Canada can seek his removal from Canada by causing another inquiry to be held as provided by section 34 of the *Immigration Act*.

Furthermore, at a pre-hearing conference held on October 5th 2001, Citizenship and Immigration Canada presented over 100 documents that they wished to introduce as evidence. Considering that these documents had not been disclosed to Mr. Winterhalder's counsel, they were not introduced into the record. The Board reserved its decision in that respect, which was to be taken at the continuation of the inquiry, scheduled for October 22nd.

Considering that these documents had not been entered into evidence, they have been destroyed upon the conclusion of the inquiry.

Rolland Ladouceur

Adjudicator

C.C.: Mr. Josh Zambrowsky,

I was thoroughly elated with Ladouceur's stance, and the fine folks at Immigration Canada were thoroughly pissed. The only remaining issue was the return of my bond money and personal property, which included my passport and Bandidos colors. Josh Zambrowsky wrote Immigration Canada a number of letters demanding the return of my money and property, but the vindictive officials basically told him to "screw off." I should have expected no less from these inept, sore losers. David Olsen, an Immigration Canada manager, claimed on November 29, 2001, that my cash bond was being estreated (forfeited) pursuant to section 94 (1) (e) and (f) of the Immigration Act. The peg they were hanging their hat on was that I failed to appear for the hearing; the only problem with that reasoning was that my case was dismissed for being moot.

Over the years I engaged four Canadian attorneys to pursue the return of my money. More than three years after I posted the bond, and more than two years after my case was dismissed, Immigration Canada's final position was that I never posted the bail money because Jean "Charley" Duquaire had. In the end, I did the smart thing and wrote the entire issue off to a lost cause. It was going to cost me a fortune to argue this in the Canadian Appeals Courts. I knew it was pointless. I would have thrown good money after bad. The deck was stacked against me, and more than likely I would never win the case.

Meanwhile, for Bandidos Canada everything remained in a state of flux as 2001 drew to a close; it had been an eventful year, and it ended with a bang. There was a mixed bag of news coming my way in Oklahoma. On November 12, 2001, at Beaver Lake on Mount Royal just north of downtown Montreal, some of our own guys got into a heated argument. The basis of the altercation was never made clear. One of the Bandidos involved, Stephane Lalonde, was shot and killed.

As difficult as it was to accept that Bandido Stephane's life was cut short by one of his own, it reminded me of the Old Testament story of Cain and Abel: brothers killing brothers is, sadly enough, as old as time itself.

A few weeks later, on November 27, Alain Chenier, a friend of some Bandidos members, was charged with murder. It was alleged that he had shot to death a Hells Angels associate, Steve Purdy, during an argument on August 11 in Buckingham, Quebec, a small community near the Quebec–Ontario border. It was said Chenier shot Purdy just to impress his Bandidos friends — none of his friends were impressed! Not surprisingly, newspapers identified Chenier as a member of the Bandidos.

There was some good news from north of the border, however. On the first day of December, 2001, forty-five Canadian Bandidos became fullpatch members. Everyone who had completed one year of probationary status received their 1% patch and their new "Canada" bottom rockers. With the attainment of full membership status, the Canadians were now free to chart their own course and no longer had to answer to the U.S. Bandidos.

A fullpatch party was held in Kingston again, this time at a hotel rather than the clubhouse. The police, vigilant as ever, camped out around the hotel's perimeter hoping to make their day by laying whatever charges they could, but none were laid and no arrests were made. Immigration Canada had vowed to arrest and deport any visiting U.S. Bandidos, but that didn't happen either. Some one hundred guests, including new probationary recruits, were in attendance to celebrate with the new fullpatch members. I would have liked nothing better than to have attended the party, but I knew there was no point in even entertaining the thought. As a matter of fact, nobody from the U.S. Bandidos entertained the thought — everybody stayed home.

The Canadian authorities were, needless to say, far from thrilled by their failure to keep the Bandidos from setting up shop in their country. On the evening of the fullpatch party, the police issued their usual cookie-cutter media statements such as *"they feared the new members would try to prove themselves by wresting control of the drug market from the Hells Angels."*

. And, of course, they sang the same old song that the Bandidos, like all 1%ers, *"made money any way they could, including money laundering, drug distribution, loan sharking, and prostitution."* I would be the last one to argue that there are Bandidos who do make money that way, but to paint all Bandidos and other 1%ers with such broad strokes is tantamount to saying that because some human beings are criminals, all human beings are criminals.

At the patch party, in a statement that accurately reflected our club's worldwide sentiment, Bandidos Canada sent out a message that they still desired peace despite all that had occurred in recent years. In an article written by the *Ottawa Citizen's* Gary Dimmock, who covered the party in Kingston, one of the national officers was quoted as saying: *"It's a great day, and we are all really proud to be part of the best motorcycle club in the world. We work hard, and the public has nothing to fear. We do our best to bring something to the community. We don't have to party (with Hells Angels) together, but there's no reason we can't all behave together."*

Unfortunately, not everyone seemed to have gotten the message. Early morning, December 5, Bandido Eric "Eric the Red" McMillan — who by now was a Sargento de Armas in the Bandidos Canada National chapter — had his abdomen sliced open during a fight with three men in downtown Oshawa. Eric had left a nightclub around 2:15 a.m. when he was ambushed while walking toward a friend's waiting car. Despite being severely wounded and shot at as he took flight, Eric managed to make it to the car of his friend who then sped away toward the Oshawa General Hospital. Three local Hells Angels members were later taken into custody as a result of the attack.

This incident, like the death of Tout and the attempted murder of Alain, really hit me hard. Bandido Eric was an upstanding guy and at twenty-five years of age part of a vanguard of younger members who I thought were the future of the club. I had a lot of confidence in him and believed he would be instrumental in charting a positive and progressive course for Bandidos Canada. Eric recovered from his wounds and was ordered by the Toronto Bandidos chapter not to seek revenge. I had no more contact with Eric after his recovery, but it seems he became disillusioned with the Bandidos, who in turn had become disillusioned with him. He apparently got on the bad side of El Presidente George for undisclosed reasons, and a few months after the stabbing, he left the club.

Despite his friendship with prominent Outlaws member

James "Big James" Williams, who had been a member of the original Bandidos Toronto North chapter, Eric was rejected by the Outlaws when he lobbied the club for probationary membership after leaving the Bandidos. He disappeared from the Canadian biker scene by the end of 2002 and presumably went on to devote his energies full-time to his dog-breeding business.

A former Toronto Bandido who knew Eric quite well told me some years later that Eric was never really a "biker" per se, claiming he was a "lifestyle" patch holder as opposed to a bike rider with a patch. Perhaps I had overestimated Bandido Eric the Red; I had only known him for a brief period. Perhaps he changed after his brush with death at the hands of the Hells Angels. Personally, I have good memories of the tough kid from Oshawa, but ultimately it makes me wonder if we really ever get to know anyone.

According to police, the attack on Eric the Red was the first solid indication that Quebec's biker war had spilled into Ontario, something they had been predicting for over a year. Gary Dimmock reported in the *Ottawa Citizen* that he had been told by members of both the Angels and the Bandidos that *"the fight ban remained in effect."* Dimmock further wrote that *"this left some outlaw bikers wondering if the recent attacks were launched to settle old, personal scores."* When taking into consideration Eric the Red's history with the original Toronto Bandidos, most of whom had defected to the Hells Angels, this assessment was probably much closer to the truth.

On December 12, 2001, Bandidos Presidente Alain once again went to the media to try to explain our intentions. *"We're holding out our hands. We just want to live in peace and be able to work and have fun. We want the situation to stay quiet for a long time,"* Alain said, clearly echoing what Bandidos and Hells Angels leaders from all over the world wanted.

His efforts, not surprisingly, fell on deaf ears. A newspaper article published worldwide played on the public's fear and ignorance of bikers in general and the Canadian "biker wars" in particular. The headline screamed GREED, NOT PEACE, IS BEHIND BIKER'S BID FOR PEACE WITH THE QUEBEC HELLS. In the article, the reporter wrote that *"a quest for money and good publicity, not peace, is behind the bid by the biker Bandidos to make nice with the Hells Angels."* We obviously were extremely disappointed that the truth had once again been sacrificed in the name of sensationalism.

We were serious about ending the violence and willing to try anything to get it to stop, but our intentions and comments had been misrepresented to keep up the ruthless, bloodthirsty biker image portrayed by the media, television, and Hollywood. Then again, that image has become so embedded in the public's perception, anything positive about bikers would be discounted by the majority. In a society driven by negativity, anything positive is perceived with suspicion. Nobody wants to read about "good" bikers, any good intentions they may have, or good deeds they may do. When good intentions are put forth and good deeds performed by bikers, it is automatically assumed that ulterior motives are behind them.

Ironically, if you ask any citizen who personally knows a biker — whether he'd be a neighbor or co-worker — nine times out of ten you'll get a favorable response. A lot of people even like the idea of having a biker or biker clubhouse on their street or in their neighborhood because it actually makes them feel safer. In a neighborhood that is home to a biker or biker clubhouse, crimes such as break-and-enter, car theft, and so forth, are usually nonexistent. Most regular people, however, only know bikers by what they read in newspapers or see on television.

The New Year started off on an ominous note for all motorcycle clubs in Canada. On January 7, 2002, the Canadian government's federal anti-gang legislation C-24 went into effect. According to C-24, *"those offenders found to be associated with a criminal organization are subject to fourteen years over and above any substantive charges. Those who are found to be directing a criminal organization could face life in prison."* C-24 also made it illegal for a criminal organization to recruit new members.

This only strengthened the resolve of Bandidos Canada members to become totally legitimate. Those who weren't already were urged to clean up their acts — those who were legitimate were urged to stay legitimate. Every member knew by now that this was the only way the club would survive long-term. Unfortunately for all of Bandidos Canada members in Quebec, their futures had already been carved in stone, and the passage of C-24 just set the stage for what was coming. By this time, no matter what Bandidos Canada members in Quebec did or tried to do, their world was destined to soon come crashing down. The one enemy they had in front of them that they could plainly see — law enforcement — was finally ready to terminate the biker war and the clubs once and for all.

The beginning of the end for the Bandidos organization in Quebec might have been imminent, but the hammer dropped first on the Outlaws Motorcycle Club that, ironically enough, wasn't even involved in the biker war. The sweep of Outlaws members nationwide, which had started in 2001, continued in London, Ontario, on January 8, with the arrest of my friend Thomas "Holmes" Hughes. Outlaw Holmes was the president of the club's London chapter and a prominent leader in the Outlaws hierarchy. He was charged with attempting to murder four members of a Hells Angels support club in an altercation the night before: the shootout was the culmination of a tumultuous winter in which most of the London Outlaws had switched sides and become members of the Hells Angels.

In late January, as a result of the decimation of the Outlaws London chapter, Bandidos Canada and the Outlaws formed an informal alliance and hung out together as much as possible in a show of unity against the Hells Angels and the authorities. At a motorcycle swap-meet organized by the Hells Angels in London on the first weekend in February, a group of twenty Bandidos and thirty Outlaws arrived unexpectedly to "take in the exhibits."

This demonstration of solidarity took everyone — from the public to law enforcement, and especially the Hells Angels — by surprise. Surrounded by police and members of the Hells Angels, the Bandidos and Outlaws walked through the swap-meet as if they were taking a Sunday afternoon stroll through the park. Bandidos Presidente Alain mentioned later that the tension in the building was at fever pitch — everybody watching everybody in anticipation, wondering what to do, and hoping not to be the ones to set off the powder keg.

To defuse the situation, law enforcement personnel, acting very diplomatically, persuaded the Bandidos and Outlaws to leave and then escorted them out of the building. "Sure it was crazy, but it was well worth it because I think we sent a strong message that we were going to even up the playing field a little bit," Alain told me. "Besides, it also showed the cops that we're reasonable people . . . that we only wanted to make a statement."

Whether or not the next headline-making incident was a response from the Hells Angels to the Bandidos and Outlaws for their audacity showing up at the London motorcycle swap-meet is a topic of speculation. But in the middle of March, a huge explosion was set off in front of a social club in Woodbridge, a large suburban community just north of Toronto. The club was connected to the new Toronto chapter of

Bandidos Canada. Rumors that the biker war had definitely arrived in Ontario were flying everywhere, and they were fueled by the inane media versions of the event. Fortunately, no one was injured in the bomb blast, and it was never determined who was responsible or why it occurred.

Meanwhile, in Quebec, things were still bad and fixing to get worse. There seemed to be no stopping the violence — it was like a runaway train. Despite the fact that most of the Quebec Hells Angels as well as most of the members of their support clubs were in jail, there were still individuals and teams of killers hunting for Bandidos.

On March 11, 2002, the Ontario Provincial Police shot and killed a man during a gun battle in the middle of Highway 401 between Montreal and Kingston. The deceased turned out to be Daniel Lamer, a career criminal and hitman working for the Hells Angels through one of their puppet clubs, the Rockers. Lamer was reportedly on his way to Kingston, where he was supposed to kill Bandidos Presidente Alain.

It seemed that my friend's life had been spared simply because the police had stopped Lamer for speeding. Lamer, obviously under the impression that he had "been made" by the authorities, had decided to shoot his way out of his predicament — although ultimately none of the five police officers involved were hurt in the gun battle. If an officer had been killed, the consequences would surely have resulted in an even more zealous crackdown on the biker world by the authorities.

Three days later, the biker-related killings continued. This one had no happy ending and unfortunately involved an innocent citizen who was just minding his own business. The victim, thirty-four-year-old Yves Albert, was fueling up his car at a gas bar near his Montreal home when a minivan pulled up beside him. A passenger in the van slid open the side door and, in classic overkill, pumped nine slugs into the hapless victim.

Not only was Albert at the wrong place at the wrong time, he had the distinct misfortune of resembling the actual intended target, Bandido Normand "Norm" Whissell. Whissell, president of the Montreal chapter of Bandidos Canada at the time, had survived an attempt on his life just a few months earlier. Once again, providence seemed to have spared him.

While the slaying of Albert can only be attributed to a case of mistaken identity, the similarity between him and Bandido Norm was truly bizarre. Albert drove the same type of Chrysler Intrepid as Bandido Norm; the license plate on Albert's Intrepid was nearly identical to Bandido Norm's Intrepid; both Intrepids were green; and neither car had its hubcaps installed.

Bandidos Canada, not to mention the public, was outraged by the senseless death of Albert, a devoted family man who left behind a wife and two children. *"If they want to kill each other, that is fine. But to get the wrong person, it's ridiculous. There are men who deserve this. Yves Albert was not one of them,"* an acquaintance of the victim said.

The next shooting was March 19, 2002. There was no case of mistaken identity when Steven "Bull" Bertrand, a Hells Angels Quebec Nomads associate, was shot in the middle of the day while eating lunch at a sushi bar in Montreal. Eager to make a connection, police claimed the shooting was payback for the botched assassination of Bandido Norm. The truth of the matter was much less dramatic. A young associate of Bandidos Canada, Patrick Hénault, by chance happened upon Bull Bertrand sitting in the sushi bar and made a spur-of-the-moment decision to shoot him. Bertrand survived the attack, and Hénault was later convicted of attempted murder.

Like everyone else, I was dismayed and shocked by the death of

Albert and the other biker-related incidents that were plaguing Canada. Although the biker violence in Scandinavia had been appalling, it paled in comparison to the reign of terror perpetrated by the bikers of Quebec. Their reputation as the most violent in the world was definitely not misplaced. I couldn't help but think back to a conversation I had with then–Bandidos Vice Presidente George, after he had returned from his ill-fated dinner meeting with Rock Machine Fred Faucher in Quebec City. "Who in his right mind would want anything to do with these guys?" George said. "They're fucking insane!"

At this time, I was starting to do a lot of soul-searching and wondering if I really could make a difference in the Canadian outlaw biker community. I was part of a milieu where violence was not unusual. But like most bikers, I am not a violent man and am very much in favor of peaceful coexistence with everyone. Like the majority of 1%ers, I was a biker because I loved motorcycles and the concept of a motorcycle brotherhood, not because I wanted to go on a mad killing rampage or be the target for someone's bullet. I was no saint by any stretch of the imagination, but I was not a killer, drug dealer, money launderer, loan shark, extortionist, or pimp. In my youth I committed the kind of crimes that only ended up costing insurance companies money. Eventually, I paid my debt to society for my indiscretions, and the whole experience ultimately made me a better person. I never made a lot of money through stealing, and whatever I did make didn't give me much of a sense of accomplishment or satisfaction. Making money legally, through working hard and working smart, has.

I spent quite a bit of time wondering if the killings in Canada would ever end. The gravity of the situation was reflected in a Canadian government report detailing the staggering cost of dealing with the *"biker problem."* In Quebec alone, the province had spent more than $100 million by the spring of 2002 — staggering! And still bikers kept dying; more than 150 people, including 6 innocent bystanders, had met their ends by this time. In addition to the death toll, there had been 124 attempted murders, 9 persons reported missing, 84 bombings, and 130 reports of arson.

I was happy to be living in Oklahoma, where, for the most part, motorcycle clubs got along. The Bandidos, Outlaws, Mongols, and Rogues not only coexisted, but they hung out together on a regular basis. Without question, an innate rivalry between clubs prevailed, and silly sentiments like "My club is better than your club" abounded, but effectively, they amounted to saying, "My dog is bigger than your dog." In the end, it is nothing more than a lot of bravado and posturing.

With the fullpatch membership party in Kingston, my official involvement with Bandidos Canada came to an end, but I knew I would not be able to just cut them loose. I had every intention of keeping up the relationships I had built during my visit almost one year earlier through regular phone calls and e-mail correspondence. If nothing else, I would make myself available as a consultant and offer advice when asked for it.

CHAPTER EIGHT

ON THE
ROAD AGAIN

By May 2002, I had convinced Bandidos Presidente Alain to come to Tulsa again and join me and the Oklahoma Bandidos at the annual Pawhuska Biker Rally, then take a road trip to New Mexico for the Memorial Day Run at Red River. The Memorial Day Run was one of four mandatory runs for Bandidos USA. Also included on the list of mandatory runs was the Birthday Run in March, which was in celebration of the founding of the club by Donald Chambers in 1966; the Labor Day Run at the beginning of September; and the Thanksgiving Day Run in November.

If a member missed any of these runs, he was levied a $500 fine, payable to the national chapter. In many cases, especially for the less well-heeled members or those who had to take time off from work, it was cheaper to pay the fine because going on a run could end up costing you as much as $1,500. Although at times I would have preferred just to pay the fine, I attended nearly every run while I was a Bandido. But for me these events were usually more about work duties than just having fun, because of my position in the organization.

The Pawhuska Biker Rally, which takes place at Biker Park USA, deep in the verdant Osage Hills of northeast Oklahoma, actually comprises two biker meets. The first one, known as the Mayfit, is held on the third weekend of May; the second one, called Biker Days in the Osage, takes place on the third weekend of September. Fliers and posters advertising the events make it clear that *No Dogs, No Glass, and No Firearms will be tolerated, No One Under 18 Years of Age will be admitted,* and to *Leave Your Attitude Elsewhere.*

The rallies take place on land owned by the Osage Indian Nation, meaning the police have no authority on the premises. It is interesting to note that since its inception in the late 1970s, there have never been any major incidents at Pawhuska. The annual Mayfit is one of the biggest biker parties in the state of Oklahoma and attracts up to seven thousand people. Compared to Sturgis and other major American rallies, this figure is a drop in the bucket, as Pawhuska has basically remained a regional affair since day one. When I attended, the rallies attracted independent bikers and members of motorcycle clubs from within a four-hundred-mile radius of Pawhuska, including Outlaws, Sons of Silence, Mongols, and Bandidos.

Bandido Alain and his girlfriend, Dawn, arrived at Tulsa International Airport a few days before Mayfit, which was kicking off May 15, 2002. At the time, I was in the middle of managing a "sound mitigation" project for the Tulsa International Airport Authority, so it was just a short jaunt to the airport where I met my guests at the Arrivals Terminal. Alain looked happy to be back in Oklahoma, and Dawn was obviously excited to be with him, thanking me for talking him into bringing her along. I had decided to take the rest of the day off from work, and the three of us headed the short distance to my home where we enjoyed a home-cooked meal with Caroline and Taylor. The next day, I left early for work while Alain and Dawn hung around the house, relaxing and gearing up for what would be a full agenda of traveling and partying, first at Pawhuska and then at Red River.

On Friday the 17th, Bandido Alain and Dawn rode the sixty miles of winding, tree-lined roads through Skiatook and Barnsdall up State Highway 11 to Pawhuska. This time around, because I would not be riding my bike, I loaned Alain my 1999 Harley FXDL for the duration of his stay and told him he could use it as he saw fit. Caroline and I followed in our pickup truck, which was loaded with souvenir T-shirts and supplies for the Bandidos party site. When we arrived in Pawhuska, we at once staked out a prime two-acre piece of real estate on a hill overlooking the entire rally grounds.

This would be the private compound of the Oklahoma Bandidos and our support club, the OK Riders, for the duration of the Mayfit. To leave no doubt in anyone's mind that admittance was by "invitation only," we surrounded the entire perimeter with orange construction fencing; there was only one way into the compound, and club underlings performed security duty at the entrance gate the entire weekend to keep out party crashers.

Within our compound, we designated an area for motorcycle parking and campsites, all clustered around a thirty-by-fifty-foot circus tent, which was "party central." Our site, resplendent with Bandidos Oklahoma and OK Riders banners and regalia, was one of the main attractions for anyone who was attending the Mayfit.

Although there was plenty to do and see at the rally, including rock bands and vendors of every description, for club members and their guests, numbering about 250 in total, the compound was *the* place to be at Mayfit. We served ice-cold beverages ranging from beer to soft drinks and bottled water. And instead of the usual hot dogs and burgers, delicious meals, catered by a local restaurant, were on the menu.

To cover expenses, every Oklahoma Bandidos member was assessed $100 to $200 each, while the OK Riders were assessed $40 to $60 each. For this fee, members and their friends and families could party, eat, and drink all they wanted all weekend long. Some years we ran over budget, and the deficit would be paid out of the Oklahoma Bandidos treasury. And if we happened to make a few bucks, the money went back into the treasury.

Either way, it was a win-win situation: Mayfit was not about financial gain, but about throwing a professionally organized party that was the envy of the outsiders looking in. It was almost like a show that we all put on for the enjoyment of all the other Pawhuska partygoers. On Saturday night, just after dark, the entire contingent of red and gold would take a ceremonial walk together. From our campsite down to the stage area, as the crowds parted to make room for us, our pride could be felt by all of those that stood by watching us.

Even though the main focus of the rally was to live it up and have fun, for me it was nonstop work and a logistical nightmare. Thanks to my organizational skills, which were being put to good use as secretary of the Oklahoma Bandidos, I was in charge of coordinating the Bandidos' party site. I was responsible for everything from staking out the compound, renting the circus tent, collecting power generators, and installing the perimeter fencing to ordering all the food and beverages. In addition, I also coordinated the purchase of ice and disposable dinnerware, the running of the Bandidos T-shirt booth, and making sure security was in place at all times.

During the festivities at Mayfit 2002, our chapter would see the acceptance of a new member. OK Rider Ian Wilhelm stepped up to the plate and decided he wanted to become an Oklahoma Bandido. I had known Ian since early spring of 1997 and had watched him with pride as he evolved from an independent biker into a well-respected member of the OK Riders. At twenty-eight, his youth was a real asset to us, and we hoped his presence would inspire others his age into hanging around with us. Statistically, it was becoming evident that being a member of a motorcycle club was a dying concept; almost everyone around us seemed to be in their forties or fifties; some had even crossed the sixty barrier. We had to attract younger members or we would eventually fade out due to attrition. Bandido Ian was one of the keys to our future, and by voting him into our chapter, we started out the summer on a high note. The Bandidos Oklahoma chapter was now eleven strong, with one member almost out of prison and ten on the street.

Meanwhile, Alain and Dawn had the time of their lives taking in the carnival-like atmosphere that permeated the entire rally site and, of course, partying down Oklahoma-style. To escape the sheer lunacy, which continued on into the wee hours of the morning, Caroline and I, along with Alain and Dawn, left before midnight each night for the Black Gold Hotel in Pawhuska. I had reserved ten rooms at the Black Gold for the occasion — it is biker protocol to always have rooms available for the comfort of visiting biker dignitaries.

Finally, after three wild days and nights at the rally, we returned to Tulsa. Alain and Dawn, other than doing a bit of local sightseeing aboard my Harley, stayed around the house for a few days just taking it easy, a luxury I could ill afford. Due to my heavy workload, I was unable to devote much time to my guests. While I was at work, Alain occupied his time with some of the Oklahoma Bandidos while Dawn socialized with Caroline and Taylor. Because of my connection to the world-wide biker community, Taylor was exposed to many interesting people who were frequently guests at our home. Alain and Dawn certainly fell into that category, and I was pleased that they introduced Taylor to Canadian culture — or as Alain would correct me, French-Canadian culture.

My position as independent, on-site project manager and superintendent for a major construction company out of Boston required me to oversee the "quieting" of existing homes that were located in the flight path of the Tulsa Airport runways. Each home required the replacement of all the doors and windows, upgrading the electrical systems, installing new heating, ventilation and air-conditioning systems, new insulation, new double-thickness drywall in the bedrooms, and painting everything upon completion. Because all the work had to be carried out while the owners occupied their homes, it was a daunting task and real challenge to do everything on time and within budget.

Complicating my life even more at this particular time was that I was speculating on real estate, something I had actually started doing in the late 1980s. I was in the process of purchasing seventy acres of prime land just three miles northwest of downtown Tulsa, behind the Gilcrease Museum. On the property stood a 2,400 square-foot house and two good-sized barns. I bought the property from an old friend and his two sisters. It had been the family farm for many years, and now that their parents had passed away, they wanted to sell the land, and they had given me the first chance to buy the property.

Although, as usual, I had way too much on my plate dealing with the sound mitigation project, the Pawhuska Rally, getting ready for Red River, and making sure Alain and Dawn were well looked after, I couldn't pass up their offer to sell me the land.

"I'd rather sell the farm to somebody I know, rather than somebody I don't," my friend had told me. "I know you're in this to make money, but I'm sure you'll do the right thing."

In keeping with my word to my friend and his sisters that I wouldn't turn the property into a major subdivision, over the summer I proceeded to divide the property into four different-sized parcels. One such parcel, a twenty-acre tract, was bought by ex-NBA basketball star Wayman Tisdale, who eventually built a million-dollar home on the property. I sold a thirty-acre tract to a gentleman who wanted to establish a horse ranch, and ten acres to a young couple who wanted to build a new home on it in the future. I leased the old farmhouse and remaining ten acres to Oxford House, calling it the Oxford Ranch.

Some years earlier, I had leased a four-story house I owned in Tulsa's south end to the people who run Oxford House, a nationwide chain of more than nine hundred rehabilitation homes for recovering male drug and alcohol addicts. They reside in an Oxford House home for as long as they want, after they complete an intense drug and/or alcohol treatment program. The Oxford Houses are run independently of one another, with each home being governed by an elected board of residents who actually reside in the home. All residents of the Oxford House facilities are required to have a job and must refrain from the use of mind-altering substances. If they fail to comply, they are expelled from the home. Each resident of the home contributes about $75 per week to a general fund that is used to pay the rent, utilities, and household staples.

On May 23, Caroline left in our pickup truck for Albuquerque, New Mexico, where we planned to meet the following day. From Albuquerque we planned to drive together to Red River, a small winter resort community located in a valley in the southern Rocky Mountains. Once again, our truck was loaded with T-shirts; we also carried all the supplies for the two condos we had rented in Red River. The condos were going to be the home away from home for the twenty-five people in the Oklahoma Bandidos entourage. Shortly after Caroline left Tulsa, Bandido Alain and Dawn, riding my Harley, hit the road with Bandidos Oklahoma chapter president Lee McArdle and a crew of other Oklahoma Bandidos.

On Friday, I left my second in command, Louis "Bill Wolf" Rackley, a longtime friend and fellow member of the Oklahoma Bandidos, in charge of the sound mitigation project. I caught a sunrise flight to Albuquerque, where I was met by Caroline at the airport. From there, we traveled through breathtaking mountain passes up to Red River, which got its start in the nineteenth century as a mining town. Today it is known for — in addition to the Red River Motorcycle Rally — winter sports, and is aptly called the "Ski Town of the Southwest."

According to plan, Caroline and I were the first of the Oklahoma crew to arrive. Alain, Dawn, the Oklahoma Bandidos, and their significant others arrived just after dark on Friday night. By then, Red River was rocking. The small town's residents, normally totaling about five hundred, always welcome with open arms the bikers who attend the rally. Even the local law enforcement treats the bikers who flood into their district with respect. It was a rare occasion when a Bandido got arrested in Red River.

There were only two things we kept an eye open for in Red River. The first was snow, since it sometimes snows there even in May; the second was the thin air. At an altitude of 8,750 feet, it is very difficult to breathe if you're not acclimatized to the height. Alain, who lived closer to sea level than any of us, had an especially hard time breathing. The big man was huffing and puffing the whole time he was there, much to the amusement of the heartier types among us.

Just east of Red River on the other side of Bobcat Pass,

Bandidos USA had a huge campground right in the middle of a town called Eagle Nest. At the campsite, which covers about eighty acres, you could always get a bite to eat or something to drink. The entire Oklahoma delegation also had plenty of food and beverages, and a place to sleep, at the condos we rented in Red River. Between the camp in Eagle Nest and the condos in Red River, no Oklahoma Bandido had to spend a dime unless he chose to. It was an ideal setting for a perfect weekend. Between selling T-shirts, visiting with Bandidos from all over the world, and hanging out at the condos with the guys from Oklahoma, Bandido Alain and I kept very busy.

In order to show him a real slice of biker life, Alain and I had invited the *Ottawa Citizen*'s Gary Dimmock — one of the few reporters we had any kind of respect for — to join us at the rally, which is officially called the Red River/Enchanted Circle Motorcycle Rally. What had started as a small event that attracted about forty bikers to its inauguration in 1981 grew to one with well over ten thousand attendees twenty years later. This would be the first time Gary had ever gone to a major biker rally in the United States, and it was also the first time he had ever been around the American Bandidos. For Gary, this was something akin to a working holiday, as he intended to write an in-depth article for his newspaper on the rally from the outlaw bikers' perspective.

Bandido Alain, Gary, and I spent most of the day hanging out on Main Street in Red River, which had been blocked off to all vehicular traffic except thousands of motorcycles — an estimated fifteen thousand bikers from across the States were in attendance. On Saturday night, I took Caroline, Alain, Dawn, and Gary out for dinner to a local steakhouse called Timbers, where we had a great time and enjoyed some fine Midwest steaks. After dinner, we headed to the Bull of the Woods bar and there continued the festivities for the rest of the evening.

May 26 was a mandatory "meeting day" at the Bandidos USA camp over the mountain in Eagle Nest. Club officers from across the United States addressed the four hundred Bandidos and two hundred support club members in attendance, bringing them up to speed on anything from new chapters that had or were being established to guys who may have been arrested or involved in an accident on their way to the rally. Because rank-and-file members were not privy to internally sensitive club information, what was shared by the hierarchy centered mostly on issues of a basic nature.

Other items on the agenda included recognizing members who had achieved twenty-year status in the club and the raffling and auctioning of crafts and artwork created by Bandidos who were in prison. I was always amazed by the artistic talent in the club and never left without buying something to take back home with me.

There were also sidebars between national chapter officers and regional chapter officers during which each chapter had to account for the presence of their members. If anyone was not present at the rally, a $500 fine would be levied unless the member had been arrested or involved in an accident on the way to Red River. This was also a time of catching up on dues; if a chapter was behind on their dues to the national chapter, an explanation had to be given as to why the dues were not forthcoming. Lastly, issues like grievances could be aired or at least expressed, in the hope that they would be resolved at a later date.

By Sunday night, we were all worn out; I felt like I had walked a hundred miles and couldn't wait to hit the sack back at the condos. After wolfing down my dinner, I went to bed early so I'd have a good night's sleep before tackling the ten-hour drive back to Tulsa. I got up early to pack the pickup truck with the help of Alain and a few other brothers, and after breakfast we were on the road heading east. Dawn and Bandido

Ian's girlfriend, Shelly, opting for a more comfortable ride than the back of a motorcycle, joined Caroline and me in our five-seat pickup.

Bandido Alain and the rest of the Oklahoma crew took off on their bikes shortly after we left. By 11:00 p.m. that night, we had all arrived back in Tulsa safe and sound. Alain and Dawn spent the following day resting up before returning to Canada. Once again, obviously prone to sunburn, Alain was a nasty shade of red in the face, and by now everyone was calling him "Tête Tomate," the nickname I had given him on the Sturgis road trip nearly one year earlier.

When, around 7:15 a.m., I got to my warehouse a few miles from the sound mitigation jobsite, I was quite surprised to find a crew of subcontractors waiting for me, and everything still locked up tight. There was no sign of my right-hand man, Bandido Bill Wolf, whose job was to open the warehouse doors by 7:00 a.m. This was totally out of character for him, so I assumed that the public bus system had failed him. When I had not heard from him by nine o'clock, however, I got worried and called the halfway house where he was staying as part of a parole condition.

I was quite distraught when I was told by one of the halfway house officers that Bill Wolf was extremely ill, laid up in bed, and unable to move around without experiencing pain. I asked him to have Bill call me immediately, but it took more than two hours for him to get back to me. I knew that something was very wrong, for Bill did not sound good at all. After profusely apologizing for not showing up at work, he told me he was experiencing extreme abdominal pain and that he could barely move.

"I'll see you at work tomorrow, okay? I'll probably feel better if I just take it easy today and stay in bed," Bill said.

"Don't worry about coming to work tomorrow or the next day if you're not feeling one hundred percent. You just look after yourself. I'll check in with you later," I told him, hoping he wasn't as ill as he sounded.

I tried to focus on my responsibilities at work the best I could without Bill around to assist me and was very grateful to see quitting time roll around that evening. I was totally exhausted from the weekend in Red River, the long drive home, and the trials and tribulations of my extended workload that day. We all went to bed early, and the next day Alain and Dawn grabbed a ride with me to Tulsa Airport. We spent our last few hours together visiting my sound mitigation project site near the airport. While for me it was just another workday, Alain was quite taken aback by the fact that his Bandido brother was overseeing such a major project. After giving Alain and Dawn a tour of the neighborhood I was working in, and explaining what the job entailed, I escorted them to the airport for their flight home.

Although for me it had been a hectic and very demanding couple of weeks, it had been a great holiday too. It was the kind of stuff dreams are made of: real in content, surreal in context. The best part of the Mayfit and Red River Rallies — two events that were old hat to me — had been the company of Bandido Alain: one hell of a man and one hell of a biker. Alain's courage, good nature, and lust for life made such an impact on me, I knew it would stay with me for the rest of my life. I hated to see him go, and I know he hated to leave.

As we were saying our good-byes at the airport, I found the mood somewhat reserved, with Alain appearing pensive and preoccupied. I knew that if I had been him, I probably wouldn't have been looking forward to returning to Canada, where who knows what was in store. When I thought of Canada, the image that came to mind was bikers killing bikers: it was about the only point of reference I had. Just before he and Dawn headed to the departures terminal, Alain mentioned that the past few weeks had been the best vacation of his life.

"You really know how to do things right. You have a lot of class, brother," he said, giving me a hearty slap on the back. "Someday I will have to take you for a bike trip around Quebec. It is the most beautiful province in Canada. You will be my guest, and then I will show you a good time."

As good as it sounded, I wondered if that would ever actually come to pass. As I watched the Toronto-bound plane soar into the air and disappear into the clouds, I wondered if I would ever see Alain again. He was returning to a place that, while no longer considered a battle zone, could still prove hazardous to one's life.

Meanwhile, Bill Wolf had still not returned to work. Over the next few days, I monitored his health situation the best I could, calling the halfway house twice a day. After a week, I got very concerned, for Bill was not getting any better; if anything, he was getting worse by the day. He had seen a Department of Corrections doctor, but she told him the pain, excruciating as it was, was a "figment" of his imagination and that there was nothing to be worried about. It would go away if he stopped dwelling on it.

Perhaps this indifferent attitude could be attributed to the fact that Bill was not only an ex-con, but an outlaw biker as well. Maybe she was just plain incompetent, and that's why she worked for the prison system. When all was said and done, the good doctor sent him on his way with a bottle of Aspirin. By this time, Bill had not eaten any food in more than a week. I was very concerned for his life, but no one at the halfway house seemed to care if he died or lived.

I finally threatened the facility with legal action unless Bill received immediate health care, and that afternoon he was finally transferred to an area hospital. In Emergency, he was quickly diagnosed as having appendicitis. Apparently, he had suffered an appendicitis attack over the Memorial Day Weekend. The infection had spread into the lining that surrounds the internal organs, and he was knocking at death's door.

Bill was immediately rushed into emergency surgery, where his appendix and as much of the infection as they could see was removed. His stomach was not sewn back up but left open for about a week to allow the infection to be treated properly. When I saw him for the first time after surgery, I was in a state of shock; he had lost about thirty pounds and looked like death warmed over. I assumed he would remain in the hospital for quite some time. When I learned that the Department of Corrections intended to let him "recuperate" in his dormitory bed at the halfway house as soon as his stomach was sewn back up, I blew a gasket.

I instructed my attorney, Jonathan Sutton, to have one of his staff lawyers file an emergency Motion for Post-Conviction Relief with the Tulsa County Court, which had sentenced Bandido Bill Wolf to prison two years earlier for methamphetamine possession. I assisted the staff attorney in drafting most of the actual petition myself, and we got it filed at the courthouse the day Bill was released from the hospital. He was terrified that he was going to die in the care of the Oklahoma Department of Corrections. I assured him I would do everything within my power to prevent that.

On June 20, 2002, the judge who had originally sentenced Bill Wolf to prison heard our Emergency Motion for Post-

Conviction Relief. Judge Gillert, who had never intended for Bill to die while incarcerated, ordered his prison sentence vacated and then immediately re-sentenced him to time served. Two hours later, I was able to pick Bill up and bring him home to my house.

It took two weeks of care by Caroline, Taylor, and me before Bill could get up and actually move around the house without being in pain. Everyone was convinced my actions had saved his life, but to me this was about friendship — being there for people when they needed you. Bill and I had been friends for almost thirty years, and there was no way I was going to stand by and do nothing while the Oklahoma Department of Corrections threw him to the dogs. As soon as he felt well enough, Bill returned to work, supervising the warehouse for my sound-mitigation construction project. I even hired a temporary hand to work only for Bill, doing all his heavy lifting and physical labor until he was completely well and back to normal.

CHAPTER NINE

THE HAMMER DROPS ON
THE QUEBEC BANDIDOS

Shortly after Alain and Dawn returned to Canada, law enforcement authorities dropped the hammer on all of the Bandidos in Quebec. No one was spared, and it was hailed by the police and media as the first time in the history of a Quebec crime investigation that an *"entire gang was taken off the streets."* In an exercise dubbed "Operation Amigo," some sixty-five members of the Bandidos were arrested on various charges ranging from drug trafficking to gangsterism to conspiracy to kill rival Hells Angels members. While no doubt some members were guilty as charged, most of the Bandidos were victims of circumstance. Operation Amigo, a project that had been launched in 2001, involved nearly two hundred police officers from Quebec and Ontario.

One of those taken into custody was Bandido Alain. As the club's national president, he was proudly proclaimed by the cops as the *"biggest fish"* to be caught in their dragnet. On June 5, 2002, just after 6:00 a.m. — a favorite time of day to bust down doors — police raided Alain and Dawn's apartment in Kingston. It was reported in the media that he surrendered *"peacefully,"* as the majority of his fellow Bandidos had done. After being taken into custody, he was transported to a Montreal jail by the Royal Canadian Mounted Police (RCMP), the equivalent of the Federal Bureau of Investigation (FBI) in the United States. Amazingly, Alain was the only Bandido in Ontario — at the time, there were estimated to be about two dozen — to be affected by the sweep. It was clear that the authorities' agenda was to take out the Quebec Bandidos. Ironically, considering Alain's efforts to maintain peace between the Bandidos and Hells Angels, he was accused along with nine other fullpatch Bandidos in Quebec of plotting to kill Hells Angels members.

According to the authorities, Operation Amigo was a pre-emptive strike against *"the gang"* out of fear it would eventually fill the void left by the Hells Angels after the lion's share of the Angels' membership in Ontario and Quebec was put behind bars in March 2001. The arrest of the Quebec Bandidos made headlines around the world. Canadian authorities wanted everyone to know they were on the job protecting their citizens from the *"biker menace;"* it was sweet revenge for their earlier failure to keep the Bandidos out of Canada in the first place.

The decimation of Bandidos Quebec was played to the max by the police and media, but it is interesting to note that despite their claim that the *"gang"* was a criminal organization whose members engaged in all kinds of illegal activities, of which drug dealing was the most profitable and predominant, only seventeen and a half pounds of cocaine and four hundred and forty pounds of hashish were seized. Next to no illegal substances were found in the homes or on the person of any actual members of the Bandidos.

Most of the contraband seized was taken from property

belonging to a female associate of the club. Conversely, when the Quebec Hells Angels were arrested fifteen months earlier, approximately $10 million in cash and nearly $10 million worth of drugs were seized.

When the Bandidos were arrested — after deducting what was seized from the home of the female associate — the police ended up with less than $100,000 in cash and illegal contraband.

This would lead any reasonably intelligent person to question the veracity of the premise that "all" bikers — in this case, the Bandidos — are involved in drug dealing. The other alternative is to assume that the Bandidos are insignificant players in the criminal world, a direct contradiction to what the authorities would have the public believe. All this was a moot point on June 5, 2002; it didn't change the fact that the Quebec Bandidos were up the creek without a paddle.

The crackdown on Canadian bikers, which had begun in earnest with the Quebec Hells Angels in March 2001, continued on September 25, 2002, when the entire Outlaws Canada Motorcycle Club was mothballed. Almost fifty members or ex-members were arrested on charges that were based upon the testimony of an undercover police officer who had become a fullpatch member of their Windsor chapter. The undercover law enforcement agent, whose street name was Finn, had been gathering intelligence on the Outlaws for more than two years, and he had done his job very well. Even the international president of the Outlaws, James "Frank" Wheeler, who lived in Indianapolis, Indiana, was arrested as a result of Finn's testimony. It was a major coup for the authorities in Canada; almost everyone arrested was charged under the new C-24 gangsterism law.

When it became known that Finn was an undercover agent, it was easy enough for me to put two and two together and come up with the source of the leak that had brought me to the attention of Immigration Canada nearly two years earlier. After I had crossed the border into Windsor, I had called Outlaw Holmes to see if he could arrange a ride for me to come and see him in London. When Holmes called their Windsor clubhouse to arrange a lift for me, Finn happened to be there, and he readily volunteered to drive me, despite the bad weather that made driving conditions treacherous.

Despite the distance separating me from Canada — a country where I was persona non grata — the time had come to do whatever I could for what was left of the Bandidos there. I am an eternal optimist and wanted to believe that not all was lost, that somehow I could still make a difference. The first order of business was to appoint an acting national president (Presidente) and a new national secretary (El Secretario). Prior to Operation Amigo, that position had been held by Eric "Ratkiller" Nadeau. To everyone's shock and disbelief, Ratkiller, who more aptly should have been nicknamed "Rat," was exposed as an informant after the ax had fallen on the Quebec Bandidos.

Nadeau had started his life as a biker with the Rockers Motorcycle Club, a puppet club of the Hells Angels' Montreal chapter. He appeared to be a standup guy and was recruited by the Bandidos sometime after the Rock Machine patchover. Unbeknownst to anyone in the Bandidos, Nadeau had been a career informant from day one, going all the way back to the time he had spent with the Rockers. Like everyone else, Presidente Alain had been duped by Nadeau when he appointed him El Secretario shortly after Bandidos Canada received fullpatch status in December 2001. Alain had based his decision upon Nadeau's computer skills and obvious enthusiasm for the Bandidos.

The true extent of Nadeau's deceit and machinations surfaced after Operation Amigo wrapped up. Many of the charges lodged against the Quebec Bandidos were based solely upon the word of Nadeau, who in the end, like so many informants and turncoats before him, proved to be a pathological liar. It even became apparent to the authorities that Nadeau was an unreliable source of information. Many of the Bandidos sitting in jail awaiting trial, with as many as six or seven charges against them, suddenly found all charges dismissed or had to answer to only one or two.

In many cases, those charges proved to be relatively minor, such as possession of a weapon or small amounts of hashish or marijuana. With freedom just around the corner, they readily pleaded guilty to those charges and received a sentence of time already served while awaiting their day in court. Only a dozen Bandidos did not enter guilty pleas — among them Alain Brunette — because they were innocent of the more serious charges they were still facing. They were assured a trial date would soon be set, but for one reason or another, things would drag on for two more years before any progress would be made.

Earlier in the spring of 2002 — after Ontario Bandidos Vice Presidente Peter "Peppi" Barilla had been placed under arrest for alleged drug dealing — Presidente Alain, with my approval, appointed Bandido John "Boxer" Muscedere to take over that position. A few months later, after Alain and the entire Quebec Bandidos membership were arrested, the only logical choice for the job of Presidente proved to be Bandido Boxer. The forty-four-year-old Italian Canadian was the only Bandidos national officer not in jail or in trouble with the law.

Before becoming a Bandido, Boxer had been a senior figure

in the Annihilators, a nondescript regional motorcycle club, and later led the St. Thomas Loners chapter. At the end of June, Bandido Boxer — an avid amateur boxer, hence the nickname — took over as acting Presidente of what was left of Bandidos Canada. At this time, there were nearly sixty-five Bandidos in prison or out on bond awaiting trial. There were another half dozen who had gone underground in a bid to avoid arrest. Left on the streets and not in trouble with the law were fewer than fifteen Bandidos in Ontario — and none in Quebec!

Shortly after taking over as national leader of Bandidos Canada, Presidente Boxer and Bandido Luis Manny "Porkchop" Raposo, whom I had been introduced to at the 1999 Sturgis Rally, came all the way to see me in Oklahoma. They had tried to meet with Bandidos USA El Presidente George Wegers and other national officers, but had been unsuccessful. There was still a lot of dissention in the club, and the majority of the American Bandidos wanted nothing to do with the Canadians.

"You're the only brother who's even remotely interested in our fate," Boxer told me when he and Porkchop arrived on my doorstep. "We want nothing more than to keep the club afloat because our only other alternative is to join the Angels, and we definitely don't want to do that."

"Yeah, we definitely don't want to do that," Porkchop chimed in. "We're Bandidos and we're proud to be Bandidos, and we're gonna do whatever we have to do to stay Bandidos."

I admired Presidente Boxer's and Bandido Porkchop's tenacity and told them they could count on me to do whatever I could. I welcomed them into my home, and we spent an entire day discussing how we could resurrect what was left of Bandidos Canada. I knew that in order to do that, it was imperative to recruit new members and start new chapters, not just in Ontario, but in Western Canada as well.

The first thing on the agenda was to appoint a new El Secretario. Boxer wanted to appoint a new Bandido he liked by the name of Jeff "Burrito" Murray, but I persuaded him that Bandido Glen "Wrongway" Atkinson would be a better choice. Thirty-three-year-old Glen had joined the Toronto Loners chapter in 1997 and became a Bandido in May 2001 when the club patched over. He was extremely intelligent, well respected, articulate, and knew his way around computers. Furthermore, he was a college graduate, a clever businessperson, and devoted family man. I had exchanged regular correspondence with Bandido Wrongway for about a year and was impressed by his positive attitude and understanding that legitimacy was crucial for the future of Bandidos Canada. Although Boxer gave in reluctantly, he had to admit that Bandido Burrito could not match Glen's credentials.

Throughout July 2002, El Secretario Wrongway and I stayed in almost daily contact. As I was looked upon by many of the younger Canadian Bandidos as an elder statesman in the biker world — I had been an outlaw biker for more than twenty-five years and was well into my forties — I found it imperative to offer not only my expertise, but moral support as well. This was a troublesome time for anyone who was a Bandido in Canada, whether they were still enjoying their freedom or locked up behind bars.

The authorities — enemy number one — had all but eradicated the club and made it clear they had every intention of finishing the job; the Hells Angels — enemy number two — were lurking in the shadows, equally determined to wipe out what was left of the Bandidos. While the police were harassing and intimidating the Ontario Bandidos, hinting it was only a matter of time before they were served with arrest warrants, the Angels were harassing and intimidating them with death threats and presenting them with two options: retire or patch over.

In the aftermath of Operation Amigo, Bandidos Canada issued a statement to the media confirming that the three Quebec chapters — Montreal East, Montreal West, and Quebec City — were indeed history. They insisted, however, that the club would survive by focusing on Ontario and Western Canada. As good as this sounded, there were doubts in the minds of all but the most stalwart and optimistic members that there was any kind of future for the Bandidos in Canada. In this climate of uncertainty, El Secretario Wrongway and I did our best to keep a flicker of hope alive. We had a lot to do in the way of organizing and keeping a lid on the situation in Ontario.

The first task we faced was to attempt to verify the identities of all the Bandidos who were incarcerated. This turned out to be a monumental task, for the prison authorities would not allow us to make contact with any club members. If a letter sent to them had even a remote Bandidos reference, it was confiscated. And because all the club records had been turned over to the authorities by Nadeau — who, thanks to his position as national El Secretario, had a wealth of information at his disposal — we had no idea who was in the club and who wasn't. All we had to work with initially was an old list I had compiled during the Rock Machine patchover days, a list that had not been updated because it was no longer my concern. It took months for El Secretario Wrongway and me to configure accurate membership, corresponding phone numbers and e-mail addresses, and jail lists.

Our second objective was to figure out how to preserve Bandidos Canada long-term. But ultimately, that was a project for Presidente Boxer and El Secretario Wrongway; my input and influence from more than a thousand miles away in Oklahoma was limited.

Once the Operation Amigo dust had settled, everything remained fairly calm. There wasn't any biker news of note until the middle of September 2002, when the Toronto media zeroed in on a rather insignificant story and blew it up into headline-making news. A young member of the Kingston chapter of Bandidos Canada, Carl "CB" Bursey, had violated parole by leaving his area of designation to go fishing with his girlfriend for a few days longer than he should have. After he failed to report to his parole officer on the scheduled date, a warrant was issued for his arrest. As soon as the warrant was issued, the press ran with it, quoting police sources that a *"blood bath"* was anticipated because Bandido CB had vowed *"not to be taken alive."*

It was during this time that I became aware of the incident, and I didn't really know what to make of it. Unbeknownst to me and pretty well the entire Canadian Bandidos membership, CB had become a Bandido while he was in jail serving a three-year federal sentence. In the summer of 2000, he had become a member of the Rock Machine and thus became a Bandido by default after the patchover. When he was released from prison, everyone who knew him was either still incarcerated or had just been arrested in the massive sweep of Operation Amigo.

When the first newspaper articles surfaced about CB, nobody on the streets even knew if he truly was a Bandido. Initially, no one in Bandidos Ontario was aware of who he was. It took El Secretario Wrongway and me a few days to determine his identity and how he got into the club. Even after we figured that out, we learned that only one or two of the Kingston members were in contact with him. The more we learned about Bandido CB — like the fact that he had never even ridden a motorcycle — the more we realized how very little he knew about us and that he could only be called a biker by definition.

In addition to the incredible stories the newspapers fabricated, what amazed us so much was that Bandido CB would only have to serve ten days in jail — the time remaining on his original sentence — if he surrendered. None of this made any sense, and one has to wonder if CB didn't relish his fifteen minutes of fame as a *"notorious escape artist"* who was an *"extreme danger to the public,"* according to the newspapers. In reality, all the media hoopla and statements made by the police concerned a minor parole violator. If he hadn't been a Bandido, he would undoubtedly have received very little media attention. It was another flagrant example of how the authorities glommed onto anything they could when it came to promoting their outlaw biker agenda and how the media loved to play along.

As things heated up, the press characterized twenty-seven-year-old CB as a prominent Bandido with a lengthy rap sheet that included obstruction of justice, narcotics trafficking, weapons possession, possession of stolen property, threats, assaults, robberies, dangerous driving, breaking probation, and four jailbreaks — in other words, their favorite portrait of a 1%er. Although no one could dispute CB was anything but a model citizen, one thing he wasn't was a prominent Bandido. He shouldn't even have been a Bandido in the first place, and he was on a fast track out of the club.

To help defuse the situation, we asked Gary Dimmock from the *Ottawa Citizen* to act as an intermediary for Bandido CB and the police so CB could surrender peacefully as per his actual intentions. Even though CB may have been considered something of a loose cannon, he didn't have a death wish and certainly didn't want to die in a hail of bullets over what amounted to a mere ten more days in prison.

Under the terms of the surrender negotiations, which Dimmock helped to orchestrate, Bandido CB was not going to have to serve additional time for his parole violation. *"I just want to go back to jail and get the time over with and then get on with my life,"* Bandido CB had told Dimmock. *"I don't intend to hurt anyone, and I certainly don't want to get shot when I turn myself in."*

Around 4:30 p.m. on September 24, 2002, Bandido CB, who had eluded police for two months, arrived at a Kingston coffee shop for a prearranged rendezvous with Detectives Neil Finn and Brian Fleming and surrendered without a hitch. So much for the *"bloody last stand"* expounded by the authorities and promoted by the press. Detective Greg Sullivan was quoted by Dimmock in a September 25, 2002, *Ottawa Citizen* article detailing the arrest that *"we're just glad he turned himself in and that it went down peacefully."* We all concurred.

By this time, the Kingston chapter of Bandidos Canada — to which CB officially belonged — had come to the realization that he was not a biker at all and had no business being in a motorcycle club. As a result, he was told to leave the club. Upon expulsion from the Bandidos, CB joined forces with his old friends, the Hells Angels. According to a newspaper article, the Angels had aided him while he was on the lam from the police. He would again make the news in late February 2003 when he was arrested again — this time for possession of drugs and firearms. I was not at all surprised. As recently as the summer of 2007, CB made more headlines when once more he was on the lam from police and portrayed by the media as a dangerous outlaw biker.

All the media hoopla was basically about a parole violator who, when caught, would only have to serve ten more days in prison. In this article, which appeared in the Toronto Sun, *it states that Bursey had one month left to serve. Another newspaper mentioned the actual ten days. It is just one more example of discrepancies in newspaper*

reports. It makes one wonder: if they can't get a simple fact straight, what do they get straight?

Bandido vows to not be taken alive

By Alan Cairns

September 17, 2002

A fugitive Bandido has "numerous handguns and a grenade launcher" and threatens to "shoot it out with police," police said yesterday.

The grenade launcher is believed to be a rocket-propelled grenade (rpg) system, similar to Russian-made models that bring down U.S. helicopters in the hit movie, Black Hawk Down.

And in a strange twist to the case, Carl Thomas Bursey, 27, is apparently being hidden by rival Hells Angels.

"A dangerous weapon like an rpg in the hands of a person who is as volatile and as violent as Bursey makes this an extremely scary situation," said Det. Greg Sullivan of the provincial repeat offender parole enforcement (rope) unit. "We have credible information that Bursey is in the Toronto area . . . and he says he won't be taken alive and will get into a shootout with police."

Bursey, whose 55 prior criminal convictions include narcotics trafficking, weapons possession, threats, assaults, robberies and four jailbreaks, went on the lam in July and has since avoided an Ontario-wide dragnet. Bursey, who was once a Rock Machine member, was serving a two-year, 10-month prison term for escaping from an Ontario jail in December 1999.

Bursey had only one month left to serve in his sentence when he went underground, started doing drugs and began hoarding weapons and making threats to kill his police pursuers, Sullivan said.

Prior to his latest release, Bursey twice had his early release revoked — once in August 2001 after police seized 45 kilos of homegrown marijuana from where he was staying at his uncle's home, and again in May when police found a loaded handgun when Bursey and two other biker associates were stopped in a stolen car in Milton.

National Parole Board documents also reveal that Bursey was "implicated in a weapons-related investigation in a homicide matter" in Quebec.

Sullivan said police have received information that Bursey is being aided by Hells Angels in Toronto. Bursey, who was raised in Guelph and was allowed to live with his mom upon his latest release, is 6-feet tall, about 220 pounds, with hazel eyes.

He has several jailhouse tattoos, including one of a loaded gun, the motto "sworn to kill" on his right wrist and the word "anarchy" across his belly.

June 12, 2003, will be remembered as a dark day for Bandidos Canada. On that day, Bandido Andre Desormeaux officially pled guilty to arson, drug trafficking, and attempted murder charges. In addition, he pled guilty to a gangsterism charge. Up until his time, no member of the Bandidos had pled guilty to gangsterism, and it was a big setback for the club all across Canada and would present a serious hurdle in the future. Ultimately, Bandido Andre received a total of sixteen years in prison. Andre's sentence was the longest prison term ever given to a Bandidos member in Canada at that time. It surpassed by four years the sentence given to my old friend, Bandido Jean "Charley" Duquaire, the brother who had lent me the money to post bail after being arrested by Immigration Canada.

This time, the media actually got it right when they branded a Bandido an important club member. In the following Montreal Gazette *article, they correctly noted that Desormeaux was a Sargento de Armas in the Bandidos Canada national chapter at the time of his arrest.*

Key Bandido gets 16 years in jail

Involved in botched hit at Sushi bar. Desormeaux offered gang underlings $1,500 to torch clubs used by Hells drug dealers

By George Kalogerakis

Saturday, June 14, 2003

André Desormeaux brandished $15,000 in cash before underlings in the Bandidos gang.

"I want it to burn in my area," he said of his Hochelaga-Maisonneuve drug territory.

Anyone who set fire to bars frequented by competing dealers for the Hells Angels would get $1,500 for each.

Thirty-five places burned down that summer of 2001, until police officers contacted high-ranking members of the Bandidos.

Police said they were not that interested in investigating the Bandidos at the moment, but that could change unless the fires stopped. The fires stopped.

Police had lied. They were actively following the gang and arrested 65 one year later.

One of the top members was Desormeaux, who yesterday was slapped with the severest sentence so far.

A judge at the Montreal courthouse gave him 16 years in prison after he pleaded guilty to drug trafficking, pot growing, gangsterism, attempted murder and plotting arson.

Prosecutor Denis Gallant said the Bandidos were setting fires in 2001 to take advantage of the huge police sweep that jailed more than 100 people connected to the Hells drug network. "The Bandidos wanted to take over the market," he told the judge.

Desormeaux was a full-patch member of the Bandidos and had his own marijuana plantation in a Rivières des Prairies home. When police raided the 71st Ave. place, they found 400 plants as well as the shirt and badge of a Montreal police officer that had been stolen in a break-and-enter.

The 36-year-old Joliette man was also involved in trying to kill rivals in the Hells, including the failed March 2002 attempted slaying of Steven (Bull) Bertrand at a Bernard Ave. sushi bar.

Bertrand, now doing seven years in jail for cocaine importation, has close ties to Hells leader Maurice Boucher.

When Bertrand was shot, Desormeaux acted as lookout and gave the signal — taking off his baseball cap — for the shooter to fire away. "Desormeaux would say he was ready to pay to have Steven Bertrand killed and he would pay even if it failed," Gallant told the court.

Quebec Superior Court Justice Kevin Downs confiscated the home where Desormeaux had his pot plantation as well as $117,000 in Canadian cash and $11,000 in U.S. funds.

Desormeaux's wife, Nancy Paquette, also pleaded guilty yesterday, but only to helping her husband sell hashish to other inmates in prison. The inmates would deposit payment in a bank account, and she would collect the money from the outside.

The 27-year-old mother of four young children was sentenced to house arrest for one year.

So far, 49 Bandidos or associates out of the original 65 have pleaded guilty. The stiffest sentence before yesterday was 12 years for another top leader, Jean Duquaire.

A megatrial is expected as early as this fall for the remaining 16 accused. A large room is being renovated at Laval's courthouse for the case because the special biker courthouse near Bordeaux Jail is busy with two Hells trials.

In July 2003, the demise of Bandidos Canada in Quebec came without so much as a gunshot — no bombs, no killing, not even a whimper. Only a small article in a Montreal newspaper was devoted to this milestone occasion. The article correctly stated that all members of the Quebec Bandidos, in a deal with the Hells Angels, agreed to immediately quit the club and not resurrect Bandidos Quebec after their release from prison. In return, Hells Angels Quebec guaranteed their safety while they were serving their time in prison and subsequently after their release.

The agreement also specified that if any of the former Quebec Bandidos had a desire to continue being Bandidos after their release from prison, they could transfer to Bandidos Ontario. Complying with this agreement meant that there would never again be Bandidos in Quebec. More important, the agreement meant that the biker killings were definitely over in "La Belle Province." For all intents and purposes, the Hells Angels had won the so-called biker war. Ironically, it was a war won with the assistance of the authorities. By taking the Bandidos off the streets of Montreal, law enforcement actually contributed to the Hells Angels rising to the top of the biker pyramid in Canada.

It had been a difficult decision for all the Bandidos involved to disband the club in Quebec, but in the end their instincts for self-preservation and common sense prevailed. The killings had gone on long enough; everyone was tired of looking over their shoulders. Initially, I was confused by their acceptance of the Hells Angels' terms, but after a few days of deliberation, I understood the reasoning behind their decision. It neither diminished my respect for them nor did it change any aspect of my relationship with them. Even though the patch was gone, I continued to be their friend and brother — they would still be mine as well.

Shortly after the collapse of Bandidos Quebec, I came across an old Christmas card I had received from them in December 1999. It is now, I believe, an important and significant piece of history. It is a testament to the legacy of men who are now considered biker heroes, held in high regard as men of respect by bikers worldwide. The Quebec Bandidos are indicative of a fearless and principled group of men who refused to be told what to do, refused to be controlled, and who ultimately refused to sacrifice their integrity, no matter what it took.

Of course, there were some who lacked dignity, honor, integrity, or even the most basic of human values like honesty, compassion, and respect. They belong to a criminal element that finds its way into all 1%er motorcycle clubs, men who see motorcycle clubs as a vehicle to further their own illegitimate agenda. There were also those who would sell out their mothers to save their own skins, but of more than one hundred former and existing members and associates of the now ex–Rock Machine and Bandidos Quebec, only four had become informants. These were Pierre "Buddy" Paradis, Eric "Ratkiller" Nadeau, Sylvain "BF" Beaudry, and Patrick "Boul" Heneault. Turncoats and traitors are the lowest of the low — and not even the authorities have any use for them other than to exploit them for their own ends.

It came as no surprise to anyone when some of the incarcerated ex–Quebec Bandidos were charged with more crimes, including murder. Notwithstanding the fact that some of the informants had been charged with attempted murder themselves, and were liars to the core, as a group they were formidable foes, and their testimony provided enough evidence — both real and fabricated — to deliver convictions.

As all of these dire developments went down, I couldn't help but think about how important it had been to Robert "Tout" Leger and Alain Brunette to become Bandidos. While Tout, sadly, was no longer around to reflect on the situation, Alain was. If he was experiencing second thoughts about having become a Bandido, I certainly could relate to his feelings. As I tried to speculate on Alain's state of mind, I found myself taking a trip down memory lane, thinking about how I had become a member of the Bandidos Nation. It had been nothing short of an obsession for me and one that consumed me for more than a decade.

CHAPTER TEN

BE CAREFUL WHAT YOU WISH FOR

In August 1996, I traveled to Galveston, Texas, to speak with Bandido John "Big John" Lammons again about starting a Bandidos chapter in Oklahoma. Bandido Big John, who was originally from Oklahoma, had been one of my main supporters in my quest to get an Oklahoma chapter operational. I had first met him in Muskogee, Oklahoma, in 1980, when I was a member of the Rogues Motorcycle Club. Back then, John was a hangaround for a Muskogee-based motorcycle club called the Drifters. The Drifters wanted to become Rogues, and I was one of the Rogues who had been sent to Muskogee to check them out. I had thought at the time that John was the best of the bunch, better than all the Drifters put together. But at the age of sixteen, he was too young to be a patch holder. Years later, I ran into Big John again on Galveston Island. To my pleasant surprise, he had become a member of the Bandidos; seeing him again turned out to be one of the highlights of my trip. I was especially excited that he had really made the grade in the 1%er world.

It had been more than sixteen years since I had originally discussed the concept of founding an Oklahoma Bandidos chapter with Bandido Buddy in Mobile, Alabama. And I had never given up on my dream of becoming a Bandido. Actually, it was not just about becoming a Bandido — something I could have done during my earliest interactions with the club — but starting my own chapter. Over the years, I had been invited to join chapters in various cities, but that would have entailed moving out of state. My intentions were to stay in Oklahoma and bring the chapter to me, rather than going to a chapter somewhere else.

The constant delays I had encountered trying to start a new chapter are an indication that it's not only a difficult procedure, but a fair indication that 1%er outlaw motorcycle clubs are not hell-bent on staking out new territory to expand their so-called turf. The authorities and the media like to perpetuate the notion that outlaw biker clubs are always on the lookout to expand into new territory or somebody else's territory to take over its drug market, prostitution market, or what-have-you. If this was the case, I would have had an Oklahoma Bandidos chapter set up within a year of proposing the idea.

But in the summer of 1996, the timing finally seemed right; still, it wasn't going to be as simple as one-two-three! Even more patience would be required of me. Although I have never claimed to be a saint, I do, fortunately, have the patience of one. Bandido Big John suggested I bring up my proposal at the drag races in Ennis, Texas, which were scheduled for the first week of October at Texas Motorplex, one of the premier drag strips in the country.

Bandido Big John assured me he would talk on my behalf to the powers that be. I already knew that Bandido Jack "Jack-E" Tate from Louisiana was going to do the same. He had promised me as much when I visited him on my way to Texas. I felt more confident than ever and believed that I had set things in motion; I just had to make sure they would continue to pick up momentum. Having Bandido Big John in my corner meant a lot to me, and I knew his word was good as gold. Because Big John was originally from Oklahoma, he had been one of my main supporters to get an Oklahoma chapter operational.

I left, full of anticipation, for Ennis in early October to attend the drag races at Texas Motorplex and what I hoped would be an audience with the top-level Bandidos who would be in attendance. The first person I spoke with upon my arrival was then–Bandido El Presidente Craig Johnston. I told him about the long odyssey I had been on, trying to get permission to start the Oklahoma chapter. Craig was quite receptive, and he invited me to present the concept to a large contingent of national officers who were watching the drags from one of the press boxes above the racetrack.

There were Bandidos from all over the world at Motorplex, and they asked all sorts of questions after I made my pitch to them. When I was finished, their response was overwhelmingly positive; I was granted permission to officially start the process toward founding the chapter. The first step was to compile a list of prospective members. Although this sounds easy enough, choosing guys who had the right stuff — meaning that they would meet with approval from the national chapter — was a procedure that required quite a bit of thought and scrutiny. Not everyone who wanted to be a Bandido was cut out to be a Bandido, and some who would make perfect Bandidos had no interest in joining the club. It took me till the end of February 1997 to compose a list — it was quite impressive! The list included Lee McArdle, John "Turtle" Fisher, and Keith Vandervoort from Tulsa; Earl "Buddy" Kirkwood and Mark "Bones" Hathaway from Sapulpa; my childhood friend Harry "Skip" Hansen, Joseph "Popeye" Hannah, and Joseph "Little

Joe" Kincaid from Muskogee; and Lewis "Bill Wolf" Rackley from Broken Arrow.

In April, the Bandidos national chapter sent Vice Presidente Larry, one of two Vice Presidentes at the time — Larry was in charge of the southeastern USA while George Wegers looked after the northwestern region — to Tulsa to check us out and see if we were truly worthy of wearing the Bandidos patch. Bandido Big John came up from Galveston at the same time, and we all sat down together to work out the details. Larry, who wore his title like a crown, had a condescending attitude toward us, and in the final analysis told us it would be a long time before we would be allowed to become Bandidos.

"Until that happens, I'll see what I can do about getting permission for you guys to wear support shirts," Larry said, acting as if this was some magnanimous gesture on his part.

It was obvious that in Vice Presidente Larry's opinion, wearing support shirts was all we were worth. It was not only a letdown but an insult. Still, I wasn't going to let one man's opinion discourage me, especially knowing I had made such a positive impact on the Bandidos at Texas Motorplex. Big John wasn't too impressed with Vice Presidente Larry's assessment either, but other than give me further encouragement, there was nothing he could really do.

Any concerns we had over what might transpire after Larry's visit proved unfounded. A week after his visit, Bandidos El Presidente Craig assigned Bandidos Vice Presidente George to oversee the new Bandidos chapter in Tulsa, effectively saving us from the ax of Bandidos Vice Presidente Larry. I had met Bandido George a few months earlier when he had come to town with California AIM attorney Richard Lester for an Oklahoma Confederation of Clubs (COC) meeting. Richard Lester and Bandido George had stayed at my house, and we had gone over to the COC meeting together, despite the fact I was not a Bandido yet. For me, this had been a real vote of confidence, and I was sure I could count on the Vice Presidente to fast-track the process of getting a Bandidos probationary chapter operational in the near future.

As I had expected, Vice Presidente George's attitude was a whole lot different from Vice Presidente Larry's. George took us on with the full intention of getting the chapter off the ground. By now, John "Little Wolf" Killip, president of the Oklahoma Outlaws — whom we had been waiting on to be released from prison before he gave us the nod to start a Bandidos chapter in Okalahoma — had finally finished serving his lengthy sentence. I wasn't surprised when Little Wolf gave us a tentative go-ahead. I had a long history with him, as Little Wolf was in the Rogues when I was a prospect in 1975. He had also been my rescuer at Bowling Green in 1978, when I got into trouble with the Outlaws over my crossed pistons and skull tattoo.

Although Little Wolf would have to meet with the Outlaws national chapter to get their blessing, because Oklahoma was his territory and he had no problems with the Bandidos, the chances were at least 99 percent in our favor. To comply with 1%er protocol, an out-of-state club, seeking to set up a new chapter in a territory another 1%er club is already based in, needs approval from that club before launching the new chapter.

Unless there was a dramatic reversal of fortune, it would only be a formality before the Bandidos Oklahoma chapter became fact. Vice Presidente George told me and everyone on my list to head down to Hallsville, Texas, for the annual drag races and show ourselves "as a chapter" to the Bandidos who would be in attendance. While we were all at the racetrack, Bandidos national chapter officers congregated in Longview, Texas, for a meeting with members of the Outlaws' national chapter. At the meeting, the Outlaws officially gave their okay for the Oklahoma chapter startup. We later heard that some of the Oklahoma Outlaws were totally against it, but Outlaws national president Harry "Taco" Bowman told the Bandidos they could have the new chapter and that he couldn't care less about Oklahoma. The stage was now set, but we still had no idea when we would actually get our Bandidos patches. In early May, Vice Presidente George notified us that we all needed to go to the annual Gulfport Blowout in Biloxi, Mississippi, for the upcoming Memorial Day weekend. George told us he would drive to Tulsa and then personally make the ride down to Biloxi with us.

Six of the potential new Oklahoma Bandidos were scheduled to ride down to Biloxi with Vice Presidente George and two other Washington state Bandidos who had accompanied him to Tulsa. The four remaining members of the proposed Oklahoma chapter were unable to make the trip due to previous commitments. We were all brimming with excitement when we left for Biloxi on the Thursday evening of the long weekend at the end of May. Our first destination was Little Rock, where we spent the night at Bandido Leo "Murray" Murray's house. The next day, we rode from Little Rock to Biloxi, a distance of 350 miles. Because we had received no advance warning from George to go to Gulfport, we had not thought about reserving motel rooms in advance. By the time we rolled into town, the only rooms we could find were more than $150 per night. So we got two rooms, packed three of us into each room, and split the cost.

The Oklahoma contingent was over the moon when it was announced to the Bandidos who had gathered at Gulfport that there was going to be a new probationary chapter of Oklahoma Bandidos. To our chagrin, however, we weren't presented with our new probationary patches. We did meet plenty of Bandidos who were quite excited about the new chapter, but there were the inevitable ones who were not very happy about it at all.

The ride home was a long one because we all had expected

to get our patches while we were at Gulfport. To complicate the journey, John "Turtle" Fisher's bike broke down in southern Arkansas. John had apparently forgotten to check his battery water, and it had boiled dry. We were dead in the water, with Little Rock the closest place that had a battery. It did not take long before Vice Presidente George and I got into an argument about what course of action to take. I had traveled this stretch of road many times and knew the only thing to do was to call Little Rock for help. George, because of some discord between himself and the Little Rock Bandidos president, did not want to call for help and insisted we figure out some other way to rectify the situation.

We tried everything we could, but it was Memorial Day; there was no help available and no stores were open. I eventually called Bandido Murray for help, despite the fact that Vice Presidente George had specifically told me not to. But I'm the type of person who thinks for himself, and I knew that if I did not call Murray, we would be in the sticks for the rest of our lives, trying to fix something that could not be fixed. George was angry with me, but soon resigned to the fact that help was on the way and no doubt relieved it was coming. When Bandido Murray arrived, we loaded John's bike into the back of his Ford Ranchero and finally got into Little Rock just before 10:00 p.m. Once again, we spent the night at Murray's house. We got John a new battery in the morning, and finally we were back on the road to Tulsa.

After we arrived home, Vice Presidente George ordered us all to be at my house the next evening for a meeting. He stressed that it was an important meeting, and everyone on the potential member's list had to be there. Knowing how peeved he had been with me, we wondered if this was a good thing or a bad thing. On the morning of May 27, 1997, an overnight FedEx addressed to Vice Presidente George showed up at my house. By the shape, size, and feel of the box, I was convinced the day I had been waiting for had finally arrived — it had been a long sixteen years!

That night, all of us gathered at my house for our first formal weekly meeting. We had been told that from now on we had to act like we were a Bandidos chapter, even though we were not Bandidos yet. Acting like a Bandidos chapter meant we would have to have weekly meetings, which the Bandidos normally refer to as either "church" or "card games." When Vice Presidente George called the meeting to order, he told us he was in possession of our new patches. But before he handed them out, we first needed to choose our chapter officers.

By unanimous decision, I became the first Oklahoma Bandidos chapter president; Earl "Buddy" Kirkwood was chosen as the first vice president; Harry "Skip" Hansen, my old friend from Connecticut, was selected as the first sergeant-at-arms; Lee McArdle volunteered to be the first chapter secretary and treasurer. Vice Presidente George appointed John "Turtle" Fisher to be the first chapter road captain. As I was the new chapter's president, and because I had been around the Bandidos for so many years, I was given an "Oklahoma" bottom rocker to wear, despite the fact that I was a probationary member. All of the other probationary members got "Probationary" bottom rockers. The next day, we all went out and got our patches sewed on to our vests. We were on top of the world!

Less than a month after receiving our Bandidos patches, we made our first public appearance in Oklahoma. It was at the first annual Bikers Against Child Abuse (BACA) fundraiser and party at the Cimarron Bar in Tulsa. We had our own booth from which we sold T-shirts and ball caps emblazoned with Support Your Local Bandidos. Two Bandidos MC Oklahoma banners — made especially for the event — hung on the fence on either side of our booth. Our intention from the beginning was to provide the public with a positive perspective on the club. Some of us, who had previously been members of other motorcycle clubs, wanted to make sure we did not repeat mistakes we had made in our past.

Our presence at the BACA event was met with accolades and approval from everyone except the Rogues Motorcycle Club, the first and only outlaw club I had belonged to up until now. I had rejoined them upon moving back to Tulsa from Connecticut in 1978, and quickly rose up the ranks to national sergeant-at-arms. I had left the club in 1981, shortly before I entered the federal prison system, and had remained an independent biker for the next sixteen years.

The Rogues were upset with us because they claimed we had moved into "their territory" without their permission. But because the Rogues were not a 1%er club, no permission was needed from them. Some of their members tried to pick fights with us, but we had no intention to get caught up in skirmishes that would have been counterproductive to our purpose for being at BACA and a public relations disaster.

By the end of the summer of 1997, shortly after attaining my Bandidos dream, the old idiom "be careful what you wish for, because you might get it" was starting to nag at me like a bad toothache. I had finally gotten my Bandidos Oklahoma chapter off the ground, and now I was starting to have second thoughts about it all. Just being a member of a 1%er club is demanding enough. Being the president of a chapter magnifies your commitment tenfold.

Despite my desire to give the club all I had, I still had other obligations to meet, obligations that defined who I was in addition to being a biker. I was a businessman; I was a father to four-and-half-year-old Taylor; and I had just gotten divorced from her mother, Teresa. We had gotten married in 1988, but the marriage had unraveled due to Teresa's substance-abuse problems. Although Teresa and I shared custody of Taylor, Taylor lived with Teresa most of the time. But I was constantly worried that Teresa, who needed to remain drug-free while Taylor was with her, might relapse.

Workwise, it had been a demanding and exhausting year. In addition to a large demolition project in Wichita, Kansas, I had purchased an old abandoned house in Owasso, just outside of Tulsa, that I was renovating for myself. Late that summer, I had accepted a contract with a local property company to remodel nineteen residential properties simultaneously. To further complicate my life, the national chapter had decided we would benefit from the presence of a Bandidos Nomads member, Earthquake. (The four 1%er outlaw motorcycle clubs each have an elite Nomads chapter whose members are not confined to any one geographical area.) Their intention in sending us Nomad Earthquake was to make sure we understood the Bandidos way. Despite the fact he was a friend of mine, Earthquake's presence caused us more grief and discontent than we could ever have bargained for.

Even though he had no authority to tell me what to do, Earthquake was under the impression he did, and it came to a head within a few weeks. Earthquake and I got into one hell of an argument, and I had no choice but to call on El Presidente Craig for him to explain to Nomad Earthquake that he was here only to advise me, not to direct me. Earthquake was told as much by Craig, but the tension that had been created could not be undone, and Nomad Earthquake left soon thereafter. It took us more than a year before he was willing to acknowledge his mistake and apologize to me.

In October 1997, my ex-wife Teresa once again dove into the

deep sea of alcohol and methamphetamines. As a direct result, I petitioned the court for sole custody of our daughter, Taylor. By sheer coincidence, we encountered the same judge who had set the conditions for Teresa's visitation rights the last time this had happened, and he at once terminated those rights. I now had Taylor living with me full-time, and this added even more stress to my already busy life.

This time, I knew it would not be a temporary situation, as it had been on previous occasions; I also knew I had arrived at a major crossroads in my life. I had to figure out if Taylor was more important to me than being a Bandido, and I needed to make this decision fast. Although biker brotherhood was truly important to me, flesh and blood was even more so.

I started to seriously question my role in the Bandidos and the way the new Oklahoma chapter was progressing. By now, I already doubted my leadership abilities as a Bandidos president; I also came to the conclusion that Bandido Lee was not the best choice as chapter secretary as he did not have the required organizational skills. I placed a phone call to Vice Presidente George, explained my situation to him, and resigned my chapter presidency. I even attempted to quit the club, but George wouldn't hear of it.

"It's your chapter, and the only reason we sanctioned it was because of you, so you're not walking away from it now. You stepping down as president I can live with. You leaving the club right now, I can't. You get your shit together, brother, and we'll work things out," George said, more as a caring father would to a troubled son than a national vice president putting a subordinate in place.

In the interim, George appointed Bandido Lee to run the chapter while assuring me he would come to Tulsa within a few weeks to help sort out my problems. Upon his arrival, Vice Presidente George diplomatically helped us set the stage for a much better Bandidos chapter while simultaneously helping me get a better handle on my life. For the betterment of the club, Bandido Lee was asked to keep his position as the new chapter president, something he readily accepted. It was decided that I would take over the role of the chapter's secretary; this reversal in positions would reduce my responsibilities and require less road time of me. Everyone in the chapter agreed to do what they could so I had more time at home to take care of Taylor. I was impressed with the way George had handled the situation, and proud of the fact that everyone thought enough of me, and my daughter, to support this unconventional solution.

As I settled into being a single dad, I began attending the local Parent Child Center for much-needed guidance on how to be an effective parent. Being entrusted with major child-rearing responsibilities took me a while to adjust to, but I knew I had to be up to the task if Taylor was going to have a normal life. To give my mind and spirit some much-needed therapeutic distraction, I put the finishing touches on a new CD I simply called *The Best of Warren Winters — Forever & Always*. Warren Winters had been my alter ego and stage name since 1979, when I recorded my first album. The musician in me had never quite left, and over the years, I had written and recorded three albums of songs that covered a broad range of musical styles. Putting together the compilation CD marked the closing of an era for me, for I no longer possessed any desire to continue being a musician. I had enough on my plate being a dad, businessman, and a Bandido.

Although the Oklahoma Bandidos were slow in taking on new members, by the spring of 1999 we had established two chapters of a support club we called the OK Riders. One chapter was located in Chandler; the other in Claremore, which had been the home of the humorist Will Rogers. Even though we were a national 1%er motorcycle club and did not need anyone's permission to start up support clubs, we did the right thing and approached the three major Oklahoma-based outlaw clubs — Rogues, Outlaws, and Mongols — for their blessing. We were surprised by the initial opposition we received, but with perseverance we finally got all three to give their approval and live with their decision. But, like everyone else, motorcycle clubs are territorial and don't like seeing "others" on their turf. It is no different from a business owner wanting to keep the competition away from his doorstep.

The OK Riders' presence initially helped give the impression that we were much larger than we actually were. Most citizens did not notice the difference in the two clubs; to them, the patches were all the same because both had red and gold colors. We were also quite surprised when most law enforcement thought we were the same club. Upon closer examination, however, the OK Riders patch was a reversal of the Bandidos colors; it was gold on red instead of red on gold. Furthermore, the OK Riders patch featured a cow skull with snakes, set in a diamond. Presumably, bikers all look alike to the public, regardless of their colors.

Both OK Riders chapters grew like weeds. This was primarily because the club's members were not treated like lowly subordinates and because the chapters were under the leadership of seasoned motorcycle club veterans Charles "Snake" Rush and Raymond "Ray" Huffman. OK Rider Snake had been a member of the Rogues Motorcycle Club back in the 1970s when Bandido Bill Wolf and I had both been Rogues ourselves. OK Rider Ray had once been a member of the local Mongols chapter in the early 1990s.

From the outset, we intended the OK Riders to be a support

club for the Bandidos, yet different from all other Bandidos support clubs scattered across the United States. Support clubs are to 1%ers what a minor league baseball team is to a major league team: both a training and proving ground for prospective members. This process not only allows the wheat to be separated from the chaff, it is a fairly effective buffer against law enforcement infiltrators.

In the outlaw biker world, support clubs are traditionally called upon to do all of the dirty work, and its members are treated like personal slaves by the parent club. I was never big on treating other people like dirt, whether they were citizens or bikers, and didn't want to carry on the subordinate tradition of old with the OK Riders. We guaranteed the members of both chapters that they would not be treated like lackeys by members of the Bandidos Motorcycle Club, which made the OK Riders a much more attractive proposition to potential members.

Bandidos Oklahoma President Lee and I wanted the OK Riders to have a different focus. In essence, the bylaws we created and used were an extension of what we advocated across the board: (1) no methamphetamine addicts are allowed to be a member of the club; (2) to be a member you must have visible means of support, meaning that you either had to have a job, or a pension, or your wife or girlfriend needed to be employed in a capacity that obviously provided sufficient income to support your lifestyle; (3) your family and employment came first; the club came second; (4) you would not be treated like a slave by a member of the Bandidos Oklahoma chapter. This innovative approach sent shock waves throughout the Bandidos Nation and eventually changed the way most support club members were treated.

CHAPTER ELEVEN

QUEBEC
JUSTICE

In September 2003, another blow was dealt to what was left of Bandidos Canada. This time, a former fullpatch member of the Montreal chapter, Tony Duguay, who had also been a Rock Machine in Quebec City, was charged with the first-degree murder of Normand "Biff" Hamel. Hamel was a member of the Nomads and a close friend of Maurice "Mom" Boucher. He had been one of just a few Hells Angels members to be assassinated during the bloody biker war, but he had the distinction of being the highest-ranking one.

In a carefully planned ambush outside a medical office in Laval on April 17, 2000, Duguay and an accomplice allegedly shot Hamel, who, along with Boucher, had been a founding member of the Quebec Hells Angels elite Nomads chapter. Duguay was awaiting trial with the remaining ex-Quebec Bandidos still detained in the aftermath of Operation Amigo when he was charged with Hamel's murder. Sylvain Beaudry, an Alliance associate turned informant, implicated Duguay in the crime. According to Beaudry, who had already betrayed Duguay once, Duguay had boasted to him shortly after the killing that he had been Hamel's assassin. Before testifying against Duguay in the Hamel case, Beaudry had given evidence against his friend in another trial, which tied Duguay to the attempted murder in August 2001 of Gaetan Bradette. Consequently, Duguay was found guilty of attempted murder, conspiracy to commit murder, and drug trafficking, and received an eight-year sentence at the conclusion of his trial in 2004.

Duguay had to wait another two years, until December 2006, to go on trial for the murder of Hamel, at which time Beaudry delivered the coup de grâce. Whether or not Duguay had actually bragged to Beaudry about killing Hamel amounts to little more than hearsay, which under most circumstances would never be allowed as evidence in a court of law. To his credit, Justice Marc David told the jury, before they were sequestered to reach a verdict in the trial, that they should carefully weigh Beaudry's testimony; he said Beaudry had a personal interest in seeing Duguay convicted.

The judge went on to explain that Duguay posed a threat to the informant, as Duguay could implicate him in a murder committed on Christmas Eve 2000 in Toronto. Furthermore, Justice David deemed the testimony of one eyewitness at the murder scene as untrustworthy and noted that another witness clearly suffered from memory problems. Despite the dubious testimony presented by the prosecution, the jury found Duguay guilty as charged. He received a life sentence with no chance of parole for twenty-five years.

After Duguay's conviction, Denis Boivin, who at the time spearheaded an association of informant witnesses seeking reform in the way the Quebec government handled informants, further fueled the question of whether Duguay was railroaded into a conviction because of the high-profile nature of the case.

Boivin suggested that Beaudry had testified under duress. After obtaining an informant's contract in the wake of Operation Amigo, Beaudry had been released from prison after serving only one-sixth of his fifteen-year sentence. Refusing to testify against his former friend was not really an option for him if he wanted to remain a free man. Beaudry had confessed to carrying out the murder in Toronto, but he had never been charged with the crime. As far as the authorities were concerned, the murder in question was considered under ongoing investigation. This could easily be construed as holding Beaudry's confession over him so he would do the prosecution's bidding.

Boivin, dismayed with the way the case had been handled, called the verdict a *"huge surprise and a defeat for justice"* in the province of Quebec. Conversely, in a separate trial, Duguay's co-accused, Tony Marault, a former member of the Rock Machine who had been fingered in 2005 by yet another informant, found his first-degree murder charge dropped. According to defense attorney Patrick Davis, the prosecution's case held no merit because the informant, Christian Dumont-Lambert, lacked any credibility whatsoever as a witness. Did Duguay actually kill Normand "Biff" Hamel? The only person who really knows the answer to that is Duguay himself.

In mid-January 2004, trials finally started getting underway for the handful of remaining now ex–Quebec Bandidos who had been rounded up in the summer of 2002. Of the sixty or so Bandidos arrested, few actually ever went to trial. Forty-eight entered plea bargains, and charges were dropped against five members of the club due to insufficient evidence. Not included in this group, however, was my friend ex–Presidente Alain Brunette and ex–Sargento de Armas Serge "Merlin" Cyr. For various reasons, disposition of their cases was put off until June 2005, which was three years after their arrests.

No doubt, officials had kept putting off their trial in an attempt to force them to plead guilty, especially to the wide-reaching gangsterism charge. After many of the initial charges were dropped, the only ones Alain and Merlin faced were minor drug charges, possession of a gun, and gangsterism. They both received eight-year sentences, minus the time they had already served, and were released at the end of June 2007.

While the wheels of justice were slowly turning in Quebec, and the province's Bandidos were slowly becoming a memory except for the odd bit of post–Operation Amigo trial and sentencing news, the Bandidos in Toronto were locked in a desperate struggle for survival. They were getting no support from the American Bandidos, financially or morally, no matter how much they pleaded with El Presidente George and other national officers — when they managed to even get through to them. If anything, these so-called brothers were hoping for the total collapse of Bandidos Canada.

By this time, I was having my own problems with the American national chapter and becoming disillusioned with the motorcycle club that had meant so much to me. Although I stayed in regular contact with El Secretario Wrongway, there wasn't much I could do except offer advice and encouragement.

But not everybody in the Bandidos Nation turned their backs on the Toronto Bandidos. Help was extended from thousands of miles away in Australia and Europe: those national chapters of the Bandidos sent financial aid and moral support in a bid to keep hope alive for Bandidos Canada, which was all but broke. Still, not all was lost, and despite the desperate situation, there was hope on the horizon.

In the fall of 2003, like the mythological phoenix rising from its own ashes, a new chapter of Bandidos Canada rose in Edmonton, Alberta, from the ashes of Bandidos Quebec. The startup of the chapter had been in the making for quite some time. But nothing came of the proposition until early 2003, when a Toronto Bandido, visiting family members in Edmonton, ran into an independent biker at a local bar. That initial contact led directly to a meeting with a group of mostly ex-members of the Rebels Motorcycle Club who were disillusioned with the Alberta Hells Angels, by now pretty much the only game in town. They expressed interest in forming an alternative club with enough clout to stand up to the Angels, and the prospect of becoming Bandidos appealed to them. One of those, Joey "Crazy Horse" Campbell, a former Rebel who had been a Hells Angels member for a short time, believed that becoming a Bandido and setting up a chapter for the club in Edmonton was the answer.

In late spring of 2003, Crazy Horse traveled to Toronto, where he met with El Secretario Wrongway to set things in motion for the founding of the Edmonton chapter. It was decided that the first step toward that goal was to make Crazy Horse a probationary member of the Toronto Bandidos. On May 25, 2003, Crazy Horse became the first actual Bandido to live in Edmonton, home of the largest shopping and entertainment center in the world.

Five months after joining the Bandidos, Crazy Horse, with the assistance of the Toronto chapter, formed the first probationary chapter of Bandidos Canada in Alberta. More than a dozen ex-Rebels became members, and things were finally looking up. But the hope for a new Bandidos Canada era started to unravel on January 30, 2004, when Bandido Crazy Horse was gunned down outside an Edmonton nightclub. Also killed was Robert Simpson, a friend and club supporter, who had the misfortune of being in the wrong place at the wrong time.

Like most men who are attracted to the outlaw biker lifestyle, Bandido Crazy Horse would never have been nominated for sainthood, but his good side far outweighed his bad. He was thirty-four when he died needlessly and left behind a wife and family. In one of the Edmonton newspaper articles after the shooting, there was a footnote worth noting, since it gives an accurate picture of the man's character: *Joey Morin (now Campbell) received a medal of bravery from the Governor General in 1991 for his role in the rescue of three people from a burning truck in October 1989 in Edmonton. Morin (now Campbell) and a friend noticed the back of a truck was on fire as they were driving by. When they stopped and approached on foot, they saw someone in the smoke-filled cab. With the help of his friend, Morin (now Campbell) grabbed the man and pulled him to safety. The man told them his son was also in the truck, so Morin (now Campbell) and his friend returned to rescue the son, who said his friend was also in the truck. The flames had reached under the cab, but Morin (now Campbell) went back a third time and was able to pull the friend from the flaming vehicle.*

The death of Bandido Crazy Horse and Robert Simpson inspired local newspapers to run the usual sensational front-page headlines, which included banners such as GANG MAY SEEK REVENGE FOR DOUBLE SLAYING and GANGLAND-STYLE KILLINGS PART OF A TURF WAR BETWEEN HELLS ANGELS AND BANDIDOS. As is the norm when bikers are involved in controversy, so-called "biker experts" crawl out of the woodwork with all kinds of clichéd analyses and dire predictions. One such expert, retired Sûreté du Québec police officer Guy Ouellette — deemed more credible than most and often consulted by the Canadian media — was not at a loss for words. *"You're going to have more shootings in the next couple of weeks,"* he was quoted as saying in one article. *"It will create some kind of turmoil there. The Hells Angels won't let the Bandidos organize. They don't want to share territory with them. It's going to be interesting to see what will be the next move, if there is going to be some retaliation."* Another so-called biker authority, Yves Lavigne, author of a number of books on the Hells Angels, didn't jump to the same conclusions as Ouellette. *"The police owe it to the public to say whether or not this was an isolated incident, whether it was a targeted shooting, whether these people were just victims of circumstance and whether people should stay away from that area or not,"* he was quoted in the same newspaper article.

Lavigne should have left it at that, but he went on to explain that Bandidos Canada was on its way to becoming extinct saying *"that there were only five Bandidos members in Canada, all in Ontario."* It made me wonder which hat he pulled that figure out of, for at the time there were actually almost a dozen Bandidos in Ontario and a dozen Bandidos in Edmonton. Most of the Bandidos, like El Secretario Wrongway, were low-key, low-profile guys who stayed clear of criminal activities; nearly all were family men and gainfully employed. When there is no criminal activity, there is no justification for continued police surveillance; hence the police, the media, and most biker experts have no idea what is really going on with the majority of motorcycle club members. They like to scratch the surface and focus on the criminal element — it's the criminal element that keeps law enforcement in business and newspaper sales flowing.

Contrary to the predictions of Guy Ouellette and Yves Lavigne, no more Bandidos died in Edmonton after the slaying of Joey Campbell. The new chapter, however, would unfortunately last less than a year. In the fall of 2004, all of the remaining Edmonton Bandidos became Hells Angels, proving once again that all was not what it seemed to be in the Canadian outlaw motorcycle world. By the summer of 2005, all that remained of the Bandidos Motorcycle Club in Canada was the Toronto chapter, which by then had less than a dozen members.

I was not surprised when an Edmonton newspaper announced the arrival of Bandidos Canada in their city and once again quoted Yves Lavigne, who now jumped back on the "bikers are badass people" bandwagon. Doug Beazley, the reporter who quoted Mr. Lavigne, mentions that Lavigne has made a "study" of the Hells Angels and their biker rivals in Canada. It would have been more appropriate to state that he has made a mini-industry of writing books about them and playing the role of "biker expert."

Death predicted for Bandidos bikers

By Doug Beazley

February 8, 2004

Edmonton has had its own probationary chapter of the Bandidos outlaw biker club since November — and their public debut at Joey Campbell's funeral Friday might mark the start of a bloody year in Alberta, says gang expert Yves Lavigne. "That funeral was the first time these guys appeared in public in Edmonton in their colours," said author Lavigne, who has made a study of the Hells Angels and their biker rivals in Canada. He said the Bandidos Canada organization in Ontario confirmed to him recently they were responsible for giving the Edmonton chapter its charter.

"We're talking six to 10 members in Edmonton, a probationary chapter that's got a year or so to prove itself. That generally means setting up a drug network of their own.

"But every one that pulled on a Bandidos vest last week is committing public suicide. Alberta is Angels territory. Setting up a Bandidos chapter there is stupid, just stupid.

"These guys are all gonna die. My big concern is civilians getting caught in the crossfire."

Word of a probationary Edmonton chapter is backed up by the fact that several Bandidos mourners at Campbell's funeral were spotted wearing Alberta patches on their vests in gang colours — red and gold. But news of a Bandidos chapter in Edmonton may have caught city police by surprise.

Lavigne's grim assessment comes from a comparison of the two gangs' relative strengths in Canada. The Angels are the dominant criminal biker gang in the nation and are, according to the last report of the Criminal Intelligence Service Alberta, the only one with chapters in Edmonton, Calgary and Red Deer.

"There's a treaty between the Bandidos and the Angels that says whoever gets into a territory first, owns it," he said. "Well, the Angels own Alberta. So what happens next in Edmonton is going to end there — it won't spread further."

CHAPTER TWELVE

PAINTING CANADA RED & WHITE
FROM COAST TO COAST

Pondering everything that had happened with the Rock Machine and the Bandidos, I couldn't help but think about the victors of the biker war: the Hells Angels. They were definitely survivors, and I was reminded why they were the ultimate 1%er outlaw motorcycle club in the world. It had been more than twenty years since they had established a chapter in Canada, and they had come a long way.

It was in December 1977 that the Hells Angels first established a presence in Canada when the Montreal-based Popeyes officially traded their colors for the American club's winged death's head. It had been a banner year for Hells Angels expansion. Two chapters were established in England earlier in 1977: one in Wessex in January and another called South Coast a month later. But these were not the first chapters to be created outside of the United States. Previous to the 1977 expansion, the Angels had launched chapters in Auckland, New Zealand (July 1961); London, England (July 1969); Zurich, Switzerland (December

1970); Hamburg, Germany (March 1973); the west coast of England (August 1974); Melbourne and Sydney, Australia (August 1975); Vorarlberg, Austria (November 1975); Essex, England (August 1976); and Kent, England (December 1976).

A feverish worldwide wave of expansion would see the presence of Hells Angels chapters in thirty countries on five continents by 2007. At present, there are more than 230 Hells Angels chapters and twenty-eight elite Hells Angels Nomads chapters worldwide. In total, it has been estimated that the Hells Angels have in excess of three thousand members. In Canada alone, there are more than five hundred Hells Angels members in thirty-two chapters stretching from coast to coast; this accounts for one of the highest concentration of Hells Angels members in any one country in the world.

Unlike the other "big four" outlaw clubs, each chapter, once it has received fullpatch status, is run autonomously but based on the same ideologies and guidelines set forth by the Hells Angels worldwide. Each chapter reserves the right to pass bylaws, recruit hangarounds, associates, and prospects, as well as create puppet and support clubs. Patching over an existing 1%er club, or starting up new chapters, however, still needs the approval of the indigenous Hells Angels Nomads chapter.

Since Montreal joined the fold in 1977, the Hells Angels would evolve, city by city, province by province, into the premier Canadian outlaw motorcycle club. Despite this distinction, the Hells Angels weren't the first American 1%er club to set up shop in Canada. That honor belongs to the Florida-based Outlaws; they had established a presence in the Niagara Region town of St. Catharines, Ontario, five months earlier. In July 1977, the forward-looking Outlaws patched over the local Satan's Choice chapter, one of the most powerful of more than a dozen motorcycle clubs in Ontario at that time. The Satan's Choice Windsor and Ottawa chapters patched over simultaneously —

and a chapter was created in Montreal shortly after. Eventually, the club spread throughout Southwestern Ontario and all the way to the northern reaches of the province.

Not all Satan's Choice chapters in Ontario were as eager to follow suit. The majority of chapters and their members were opposed to burying their colors. Unlike the patchover of the Popeyes, the assimilation of the first three Satan's Choice chapters came about in a clandestine manner. A deal to convert the St. Catharines chapter into an Outlaws chapter had been brokered by its president, Garnet "Mother" McEwen. The charismatic former hippy had convinced his own membership and the Windsor and Ottawa chapters to patch over to the Outlaws without the knowledge of Satan's Choice founder and national president Bernie Guindon. Guindon, who was serving a seventeen-year prison term at the time, had entrusted McEwen with the club's presidency but had not empowered him to make any substantial decisions that would change the path of the organization.

McEwen's duplicity, and alleged pocketing of a large amount of the club's funds, earned him a contract on his life. In the ensuing years, the three-hundred-pound giant survived two assassination attempts: one a brutal beating in which his own wooden leg was used against him; the second, a shooting that left him with five gaping holes in his body. The near-death experience made McEwen see the light: he changed his name, became a reborn Christian, and took on the role of preacher.

It is interesting to note that more than twenty years later, Guindon and the remaining Satan's Choice chapters did bury their colors — not to join the Outlaws, however, but the Hells Angels.

Although the Outlaws became a force to be reckoned with, they were never able to enjoy the same degree of success in Canada as the Hells Angels. By the early years of the twenty-first century, the club had become next to extinct there — not because they were absorbed by the Hells Angels, but because the authorities all but crushed them. Today they have mostly been relegated to memory; what tomorrow may bring is anybody's guess. Like the other "big four," the skull-and-crossed-pistons club's intention is to be around "forever."

In the ensuing seven years after they absorbed the Popeyes, the Hells Angels added two more chapters to their sphere of influence in the Montreal area. In 1979, the Montreal chapter, which had grown too large, was split to create the North chapter. Five years later, the Gitanes — an existing motorcycle club, based eighty-two miles south of Montreal in Sherbrooke — patched over.

The Angels also spread their wings westward to British Columbia in 1983 and eastward to Nova Scotia in 1984 without drawing too much attention. In June 1985, all that changed when police divers found four bodies — tucked in sleeping bags and weighed down with concrete blocks — at the bottom of the St. Lawrence River. Another body, which had become partially dislodged, had been pulled to the surface by a local fisherman a few days earlier, revealing the watery grave. The five decomposing bodies were identified as Laurent "L'Anglais" Viau, Jean Guy "Brutus" Geoffrion, Michel "Willie" Mayrand, Guy-Louis "Chop" Adam, and Jean-Pierre "Matt le Crosseur" Mathieu, all members of the North chapter. The grisly discovery ignited not only heightened police interest in the Hells Angels, but a lot of media attention as well. The incident became known as the "Lennoxville Purge."

Two years after the slayings, thirty-nine Hells Angels, including Rejean "Zig-Zag" Lessard, Jacques Pelletier, Luc

"Sam" Michaud, Michel "Jinx" Genst, and Robert "Snake" Tremblay, were taken into custody. Later, at the trial of the Lennoxville shooters, evidence provided by some of those present at the murders revealed that out-of-control cocaine use and large sums of money owed to other Hells Angels members had cost the victims their lives. They had been lured to the Sherbrooke chapter's Lennoxville clubhouse where they were systematically shot in the head.

This was not the first internal cleansing: four other Hells Angels had met their doom in 1982. Others would follow. Some would end up in the St. Lawrence River, a favorite dumping ground for unwanted Angels. The Quebec Hells Angels rapidly gained a reputation for being the most brutal and ruthless bikers on the planet. A decade later, they would live up to this image again under the reign of Maurice "Mom" Boucher.

Around the time of the Lennoxville Purge, Boucher, who would become a key player in reshaping the Quebec Hells Angels into what the authorities branded a "criminal organization," was establishing a reputation for himself as a member of the SS, a small motorcycle club based on the eastern tip of Montreal Island. In the SS, which he had joined in 1983 when he was thirty years old, Boucher would meet two people who would feature prominently in his future: Normand "Biff" Hamel and Salvatore Cazzetta. Hamel would become a confederate — Cazzetta a sworn rival!

After the SS disbanded, Boucher and Hamel joined the Hells Angels Montreal chapter in 1987, where they rapidly rose through the ranks. Salvatore Cazzetta and his younger brother Giovanni founded the Rock Machine. To further their own agenda, Boucher and Hamel created the Rockers, a Hells Angels puppet club in 1992. In June 1995, during the early stages of the turf war with the Cazzetta brothers' Rock Machine, Boucher and Hamel, along with seven other hard-core Hells Angels recruited from the Montreal, Trois-Rivières, and Halifax chapters, founded the elite Nomads chapter. Unlike other Hells Angels chapters, the Nomads were not confined to any clubhouse or territory, making it more difficult to track their actions. Through the Nomads, Boucher would successfully take the Hells Angels into Ontario, where a number of longstanding clubs, including the Outlaws, had resisted their overtures and threats.

From the time Boucher and Hamel joined the Hells Angels, three more fullpatch chapters — in addition to a number of puppet and support clubs — would be created in Quebec by 1997. After the Gitanes' patchover in Sherbrooke, the Angels ventured 145 miles east of Montreal to Quebec City, one of the oldest towns in North America and the capital of "La Belle Province." In 1988, two existing clubs, the Vikings and Iron Coffins, were patched over to form the Quebec City chapter.

Next to join the Hells Angels' growing Quebec family was the Satan's Guards, formerly known as the Missiles; they patched over to form the Three Rivers (Trois-Rivières) chapter in 1991. Finally, in March 1997, the South chapter was founded by eight fullpatch members and two prospects who left the burgeoning Montreal chapter. While Quebec remained the premier province of the Hells Angels in Canada, the club was slowly spreading across the country with chapters in British Columbia, Nova Scotia, and New Brunswick. In July 1997, the Grim Reapers patched over to create two new chapters in Alberta: one in Calgary and one in Edmonton. Around the same time, the Alberta Rebels were designated as prospects; ditto the Saskatchewan Rebels who were based in Saskatoon, the capital of Saskatchewan. Three months later, the Manitoba Los Brovos, who were based in Winnipeg, became a hangaround club.

The Hells Angels ended 1997 on a triumphant note by throwing a huge party to celebrate their twentieth anniversary in Canada. Hundreds of members, prospects, associates, and friends from across the country attended the gathering in Sorel, located on the South Shore of the St. Lawrence River. Less than a one-hour drive from busy Montreal, Sorel had been the home of the original Montreal chapter since day one. It was a fitting choice for the party and one that impressed upon older and younger members alike a sense of longevity.

By the time of the anniversary bash, the turf war between the Hells Angels and Rock Machine was in full swing. Even though the authorities seemed powerless to do anything about it, and unable to make any significant arrests, slowly but surely the writing was beginning to appear on the wall, however faint, for the Hells Angels and Boucher. Funding in the millions, new legislation, and elite police squads would become the Hells Angels' worst nightmare.

Bill C-95 — passed by the Canadian Parliament in April 1997 as a direct result of the death of eleven-year-old Daniel Desrochers — had amended the Criminal Code of Canada to permit the prosecution of members of perceived organized criminal associations simply for being a member of the organization. In essence, it became illegal to belong to a criminal organization. For the police, the legislation facilitated the use of electronic surveillance of suspected criminal organization members; it also made it easier for them to arrest suspects and detain them indefinitely. Bill C-95's broad-stroke wording was left open to interpretation, however, and many Canadian civil rights groups challenged the legislation, saying it violated the federal Charter of Rights.

What wasn't open to interpretation was the formation in August 1995 of a special anti-biker taskforce dubbed the Wolverines. It was assembled for only one reason: to combat the Hells Angels. The multidisciplinary force, which totaled close to sixty outlaw biker investigation experts, was recruited from the Quebec detachment of the RCMP, the Montreal Urban Community Police, and the Quebec Provincial Police. It proved to be the largest special law enforcement unit to see the light of day in Quebec since 1970, when the government faced off against the FLQ, a radical organization seeking to separate the province from Canada.

Over the next four years, the diligent work carried out by the Wolverines would result in the biggest bust in Canadian history; one that would deal a serious blow to the Hells Angels iron-fisted rule in Quebec.

CHAPTER THIRTEEN

TROUBLE IN
HELLS' PARADISE

The beginning of the end for Maurice "Mom" Boucher came when he was charged with ordering the murders of two Quebec prison guards in 1997. The first guard, Diane Lavigne, was shot on June 26 from a passing motorcycle as she drove home from her place of employment at a Montreal jail. The second guard, Pierre Rondeau, died when an empty prison bus he was driving was ambushed. Rondeau's partner, Robert Corriveau, also targeted for assassination, escaped with his life. The guards, who had no connection to the biker world, were, according to police, marked for death for no other reason than to intimidate and destabilize the province's security personnel.

Although Boucher was found not guilty during a trial in 1998, the murders would prove to be his Achilles' heel. Two days after he met with the Rock Machine's Fred Faucher on October 8, 2000, to call for a truce in the biker wars, Boucher was arrested again for ordering the hit on the two prison guards. Only hours earlier, the Quebec Court of Appeal came to a unanimous decision to order a new trial for Boucher. At the Appeal Court hearing, Crown Counsel argued that the judge presiding over Boucher's original trial had given the jurors flawed instructions, essentially directing them to a not guilty verdict.

Boucher would have to wait one and a half years for his day in court, but on May 5, 2002, he was convicted of the murders of Lavigne and Rondeau, largely based on the testimony of Serge Boutin and one of the assassins, Stephane Gagne. Although there was no direct evidence that Boucher ordered the slayings, the Crown successfully argued that in the Hells Angels' hierarchy, only he could have sanctioned such extreme action. The guilty verdict was by no means a shoo-in: it took an eight-man and four-woman jury eleven days of deliberation to break an impasse that nearly derailed the trial.

Boucher, who had also been charged with additional murders committed during the biker war, was sentenced to a life term with no possibility of parole for twenty-five years. Up until the time he was sentenced for the prison guards' murders, Boucher had only been convicted of thirteen minor charges, the first one dating back to 1976. These charges included sexual assault with a weapon, theft, and weapons possession. Amazingly, he never spent more than two years behind bars for any of those crimes.

But with his conviction for ordering the prison guard murders, the forty-nine-year-old president of the Nomads finally discovered he was not above the law. Boucher wasn't the only Hells Angel to be dealt a reality check. Just before his arrest, Quebec Justice Minister Linda Goupil had announced that her ministry would spend an extra $1.6 million a year on thirteen new prosecutors. Their primary focus would be to bring organized crime bosses and their underlings before the courts and to their knees. Putting Mom Boucher away was just the beginning.

A few months after Boucher's arrest in October 2000, another party was held at the Hells Angels' heavily fortified clubhouse in Sorel. It is one Mom surely would have wanted to attend, and more than three hundred invited guests actually did. In an unprecedented move that bypassed the usual hangaround or prospect protocol, 168 members of the Ontario-based Satan's Choice, ParaDice Riders, Last Chance, and Lobos became official Hells Angels, literally overnight. This fast-track maneuver finally gave the Hells Angels a serious foothold in Canada's most populous province. Their empire now stretched uninterrupted from coast to coast.

But the celebratory mood would not last long. Canadian authorities were getting ready to start dealing out debilitating blows to the world's most notorious bikers. It all started with what, on the surface, looked to be a rather insignificant affair, especially to the public, and no doubt, to the Angels themselves. In January 2001, two members of the British Columbia Hells Angels were found guilty in a Vancouver courtroom for cocaine trafficking. It proved to be the first ever successful prosecution of Hells Angels in Canada's most westerly province.

Compared to the dramatic actions that followed a few months later in Quebec, the conviction of the two British Columbia Angels proved to have been a mere prologue. In the early morning hours of March 28, close to two thousand law enforcement officers comprised of members of the RCMP, Quebec Provincial Police, Montreal Urban Community Police, and twenty-three other municipal police forces pounced on members of the Hells Angels and affiliated clubs in Quebec, Ontario, and British Columbia. More than seventy-seven locations were targeted, including homes, clubhouses, and biker hangouts. The action, dubbed "Operation Springtime 2001," was the culmination of two major police investigations: "Project Rush" and "Project Ocean."

The cornerstone of Project Rush was Bill C-95, the anti-gang legislation introduced in April 1997, which allowed investigators and prosecutors to build cases against gang members for the murder of rivals, no matter what role they played in the gang's affairs. In real terms, this enabled prosecutors to prove guilt by association. It also meant anyone convicted of committing a crime as a member of an organized criminal organization could receive up to an additional fourteen years in jail on top of the sentence received for the actual crime they were convicted of. Project Ocean, which was an offshoot of Project Rush, delved into the dynamics of the Hells Angels organizational methods and their money-laundering schemes.

Some four years of investigative work, which included wiretaps, surveillance, and handling informants, led to the arrest of as many as 130 fullpatch Hells Angels and associates — more than one hundred in Quebec alone! Not a single shot was fired; no resistance was encountered during the round-up. In addition to actual persons, some twenty buildings, twenty-eight vehicles, seventy firearms, 265 pounds of hashish, twenty-two pounds of cocaine, and $8.6 million (CDN) and $2.7 million (U.S.) were seized.

Within days of Operation Springtime, two hundred Calgary police officers and members of the RCMP raided twenty-seven locations in and around the oil-patch city. Eight of the eighteen-member Calgary Hells Angels and more than thirty club prospects and associates were arrested. The raid was the culmination of an eleven-month undercover investigation dubbed "Project Shadow." Twenty-four pounds of cocaine and nine pounds of hashish were seized.

For the next six months, things were relatively quiet. Then, in September 2001, two Hells Angels prospects and an associate were arrested in London, Ontario. Another lull followed until the early morning hours of December 3, when police raided homes and businesses connected to the Hells Angels in Halifax, Nova Scotia. Twenty people were arrested this time, of whom three were fullpatch Angels. Finally, the long-awaited crackdown on the Hells Angels was underway, in a big way.

To process the huge volume of accused bikers and associates, mega-trials were planned to be held at a new, specially built $16.5 million state-of-the-art courthouse close to Bordeaux Jail, where most of the accused were incarcerated. For security reasons, a 365-foot long tunnel was constructed to link the courthouse and Bordeaux Jail, the second-oldest detention center in Quebec and chief prison of the judicial district of Montreal. To protect the anonymity of jurors, a one-way mirror was put in place to shield them from view. Not all of those arrested during Operation Springtime would go to trial, however.

By the end of 2001, twenty-four of the accused had entered plea-bargains. Sentences handed down ranged from fifteen months to four and a half years for drug trafficking and conspiracy. More plea-bargains would follow before the inaugural mega-trial got underway on April 19, 2002. By the time the aftermath of Operation Springtime 2001 drew to a conclusion in April 2004, less than ten percent of the 130 charged had gone all the way to a jury verdict.

One of the earliest pieces of evidence submitted at the trial of the first seventeen Hells Angels who had elected not to enter into plea-bargain negotiations was a list of people slated for assassination by the club. It was a daunting list that took the court clerk almost ten minutes to read. It contained 132 names — some on the list were already dead. Most of those targeted for assassination were Rock Machine members — Bandidos after the year 2000 — or associates. A Hells Angels associate testified that there was a standard price put on the head of anyone on the list successfully eliminated: $100,000 for a fullpatch member, the highest level in the Rock Machine or Bandidos; $50,000 for a prospect, a middle-level member; $25,000 for a hangaround, the lowest level.

A great deal of the evidence presented during the early stages of the trial had been gathered by Dany Kane, a member of the Rockers who acted as an informant for the RCMP and later for the Quebec Provincial Police. Kane, who had become an informant in the fall of 1994, allegedly committed suicide in August 2000. Much of the evidence he had accumulated consisted of tape-recorded conversations, which held up in court despite his demise and subsequent absence from the trials.

The first mega-trial hit an unusual snag on July 22, 2002, when the judge in the case, Justice Jean-Guy Boilard of the Quebec Superior Court, stepped down following a reprimand from the Canadian Judicial Council (CJC). The reprimand concerned a complaint by defence lawyer Gilles Dore, who was representing one of the defendants, Daniel Lanthier. Dore had complained to the CJC about comments Boilard made to him following a bail hearing for Lanthier on June 21, 2001. Boilard had not only denied bail; apparently, he had been verbally abusive to the lawyer.

Quebec Superior Court Justice Pierre Beliveau, who replaced Justice Boilard, ordered a hearing for September 3 to prepare for a new trial. The original jury, which had heard evidence from 113 witnesses, examined 1,114 exhibits, and sat through 56 CD-ROMs of police surveillance audio and video, was dismissed. Selection of a new jury was fraught with controversy and delays, and it wasn't until October 21 that the trial resumed.

On November 18, another twist developed in the circuslike proceedings when six of the seventeen on trial suddenly decided to enter plea-bargain negotiations. The six, who were either members of the Nomads or Rockers, pled guilty to conspiracy to commit murder, drug trafficking, and participation in a criminal organization. One of those to walk away from the main group and enter a plea was fullpatch Rocker, Francis Boucher, the twenty-seven-year-old son of Maurice "Mom" Boucher. With the approval of Quebec's Justice Department, they received sentences ranging from three to eleven years. There was one stipulation: each had to serve at least half of his sentence before being eligible for parole.

The remaining ten, who decided to stick it out and take their chances with the jury, wouldn't return to court until 2003. This trial, under Justice Réjean Paul, also ended before going to the jury. In September, nine of the group — one of them had been dropped from the trial due to a terminal illness — entered guilty pleas to drug trafficking, participation in a criminal organization, and conspiracy to commit murder. The first-degree murder charges they had faced were dropped in plea-bargain negotiations. Four of the accused, who were members of the Nomads chapter, received twenty years each; the other five were sentenced to fifteen years. Because the Crown had direct evidence linking them to the murders of thirteen victims, new trials were scheduled for the final three of what had originally been a group of thirteen. All would eventually be found guilty and receive lengthy jail sentences.

The cost of dealing with Quebec's outlaw motorcycle clubs didn't come cheap. More than $100M (CDN) in public funds had been spent to cover expenses incurred by the Ministries of Justice and Public Security, the RCMP, and municipal forces. The majority of this money was earmarked to fight the Hells Angels. The creation of special police squads, construction of the new courthouse in Montreal, prosecutors' salaries, and the cost of detaining more than one hundred Hells Angels members and associates between the time of their arrest and sentencing ate up most of the money that was spent.

It is interesting to note that, despite the expenditure of this staggering amount of money, little was done to eradicate the "biker problem" and the drugs put on the market by them. The reason for this is simple enough, but one that escapes the authorities: people want drugs and will go to the ends of the world to buy them, legally or illegally. Pharmaceutical companies know this, and they peddle their drugs with the blessing of governments worldwide. The huge profits generated from psychotropic drugs alone (i.e., tranquilizers, sedatives, antidepressants) makes the illegal drug market look like a poor cousin. Alcohol and tobacco wreak much more havoc on society than illegal drugs, but they have been deemed legal anyway. Governments recognize the fact that their citizens need to have access to some kind of artificial stimulants to keep them in check. Legalizing drugs would not solve the problems of drug abuse in society, but it would, as in the case of booze, solve the problem of the crimes associated with their production and possession. Canada, which is one of the most liberal and forward-looking countries in the world, has come close to at least legalizing or decriminalizing marijuana on a number of occasions, but pressure from Uncle Sam, who no doubt would still like to see Prohibition in place, has thwarted this.

Despite the conviction of Maurice "Mom" Boucher, the collapse of the Montreal Nomads, the lengthy trials, plea-bargains, and sentencing of dozens of fullpatch members and associates, the Hells Angels did anything but roll over and play dead. In fact, they just got stronger and smarter. The Toronto chapter, which had close to thirty members, split to form an additional chapter in Richmond Hill, a Toronto suburb. At the same time, a Hells Angels affiliate club called the Foundation, which already had a chapter in Hamilton, Ontario, also formed a Richmond Hill chapter.

By the summer of 2005, Hamilton had its own Hells Angels chapter. It became the club's sixteenth Ontario chapter and was set up in a clubhouse that at one time belonged to Hamilton's Satan's Choice. A fullpatch chapter was created overnight in Welland, Ontario, bypassing the usual probationary stage. Another chapter was planned for Sudbury, a mining town in Northern Ontario. Alberta saw the creation of the Red Demons, a Hells Angels puppet club, in Grande Prairie. In Moncton, New Brunswick, an existing club called the Bacchus was being considered for probationary status.

While most of the expansion activity was outside of Quebec, for obvious reasons, the Sherbrooke Hells Angels chapter, which had kept its distance from Mom Boucher's biker war, split to form the Estrie chapter. Most of the older members remained with the Sherbrooke faction, while the newer recruits left for Estrie.

Although the Nomads chapter was wiped off the map of Quebec, five other Hells Angels chapters remained, with the Three Rivers (Trois Rivières) chapter more or less filling the void left by the Nomads. When Operation Springtime was carried out, the Angels reportedly had 106 fullpatch members in Quebec. According to police estimates, that number had risen to 124 by 2006. Without a doubt, the Hells Angels remain the largest and most powerful outlaw motorcycle club in Canada. In all probability, they will keep growing.

In the aftermath of Operation Springtime 2001, not all that much changed, except maybe the faces. Over the next ten years, a lot of those who went to jail will be back out on the street, either to return to the fold or to pursue a different lifestyle. But peace reigns in the Great White North — the biker war has become history. This, however, can mostly be attributed to the fact that there are no motorcycle clubs left in Canada that rival the Hells Angels. Still, the Hells Angels continue to face challenges that can be attributed to the results of Operation Springtime. Ongoing monitoring by law enforcement, occasional raids, arrests, and convictions dog the Angels as they go about their business.

CHAPTER FOURTEEN

DISILLUSIONMENT

It took me sixteen years to become an official member of the Bandidos Motorcycle Club, but only six to start becoming disillusioned with being one. Actually, the beginning of the end for me dawned in the spring of 2002, when El Presidente George and El Vice Presidente Jeff, as well as the majority of the American national chapter and some chapter presidents, started to condone the manufacture, distribution, and personal use of methamphetamine (meth) — the Oklahoma chapter notwithstanding. I was rapidly getting tired of all the methamphetamine-related problems affecting the Bandidos and was no longer able to tolerate the drug addicts who seemed to be crawling out of the woodwork.

In my estimation, some 20 percent of Bandidos members in the United States had become involved with this horrifying drug, although most of them were just occasional users. Despite my best efforts to keep it out of the Oklahoma chapter, there were a few members who were using and dealing methamphetamine. I had no absolute proof until the summer of 2003, and by then I had seriously started to question my desire to remain a member of the club.

By this time, the Oklahoma-based red and gold world, which had taken me so long to get off the ground, stretched about four hundred miles east to west and about two hundred miles north to south. It contained only eight Bandidos and one prospect, but those eight Bandidos and one prospect oversaw about fifteen Ozark Riders and twenty OK Riders, support clubs I had founded a few years earlier. Together with our recognized hangarounds, we were nearly fifty strong and a force to be reckoned with in the state of Oklahoma.

I should have been on top of the world, but I wasn't in the least. We were attracting major attention and jealousy within the Bandidos Nation, for the Oklahoma chapter was known for getting things done. As opposed to many other chapters whose members seemed to be adrift with no real aim or focus, our chapter was unique. Just like my business interests, it prospered because it benefited from my analytical mind and my organizational skills.

Still, I wasn't 100 percent happy with the way things were progressing, and I was especially dismayed that meth had become an issue, sometimes dividing the chapter I had founded. No matter how you roll the dice, when "meth logic" enters the equation, everything starts going to hell in a handbasket: squabbles, deceit, jealousy, pettiness, lying, and failure to honor financial commitments filter into all areas of club life, even if only one member succumbs to meth use, or worse, becomes involved in trafficking.

The Oklahoma chapter wasn't my only area of concern. There was a division occurring within the Bandidos nationwide, and this was no more evident than at the July 2002 Birthday Party Run in Houston, which I was unable to attend due to my Tulsa airport sound-mitigation project. For the first time in the club's history, there were two different party site camps: one was for those members who supported El Presidente George — the other for those who opposed him.

At this point, the club as a whole was in massive turmoil. There was a distinct crew of Bandidos, among them the entire Nomads chapter, who were not very fond of El Presidente George's new club policies. George was for any change required to successfully bring the club into the future, no matter what the cost, and there were those who supported his views. The other group, mostly the older members, wanted to return the club to its past and keep it that way forever. The positions of both sides were diametrically opposed, and the correct path was probably somewhere in between.

There were also problems brewing between the Hells Angels and Bandidos, which was especially troubling to me, considering my involvement with the Quebec Bandidos and the biker war they had inherited through the Rock Machine. Although things didn't really get out of hand in the United States, the tension between the two clubs remained palpable at all times and continues today.

Furthermore, bad blood had started to trickle between the Kansas Sons of Silence, with whom we were on good terms, and the Missouri-based Galloping Goose and El Forastero Motorcycle Clubs, which affected us in Oklahoma. Most of the El Forastero and Galloping Goose members were dinosaurs. Many of them were whacked out on methamphetamine and had no concept of reality in today's world. They were adamant that no member of a 1%er club was going to ever wear his colors in the state of Missouri, which the Galloping Goose and El Forastero considered their exclusive territory.

When dealing with the El Forastero or the Galloping Goose, it was for all practical purposes the same organization, even though the clubs wore completely different patches. Over the spring and summer that year, there had been frequent altercations between their members and Sons of Silence members, and there also had been threats made against Bandidos who were living in Missouri and members of the Hermanos Motorcycle Club, a Bandidos support club I had established in Kansas.

To defuse the situation, El Presidente George sent Sargento de Armas Danny "DJ" Johnson to join us for a sit down with the Galloping Goose and El Forastero in Springfield. Joining DJ for the trip was Bandido Chester from Texas, who had just become a fullpatch member of the club. Bandido DJ was chosen because he had known the El Forastero and Galloping Goose in Missouri twenty-five years earlier, when the Bandidos had a chapter in Springfield.

We met with an extremely unfriendly bunch of Galloping Goose and El Forastero members who outnumbered us three to one. Only Bandido DJ and Bandido Lee McArdle were allowed to attend the meeting with about ten El Forastero and Galloping Goose members. Despite the hostile atmosphere that hung over the meeting, a truce was established: the red and gold were allowed to have members living in Missouri, but would never be allowed to have a Missouri chapter. The Ozark Riders were also allowed to have members living in Missouri, but they could never have a chapter located in Missouri either.

Around Halloween of 2002, the Bandidos national chapter, the Sons of Silence national chapter, and representatives from El Forastero and the Galloping Goose agreed to discuss further the ongoing tensions in Missouri. The meeting was held in Sioux Falls, South Dakota, and most of the Oklahoma Bandidos chapter made the trip north in a rented fifteen-passenger van. At the meeting, El Secretario Christopher "Chris" Horlock represented the Bandidos, while Lyle Donkersloot represented the El Forastero. The situation was tense, but fortunately cool heads prevailed.

We made sure El Forastero and the Galloping Goose knew about all of our friends in the Kansas City area and the fact that there were now three Bandidos living in, or very near, the southwestern corner of Missouri. It was inevitable they would wear their colors when riding their bikes in Missouri, but this was not intended to be taken by El Forastero and Galloping Goose members as a message of disrespect. We all thought the meeting had gone well, but apparently some of the El Forastero did not feel the same way.

Unfortunately, we would not see the light until early spring of 2003, when two El Forastero members attacked one of our Tulsa hangarounds in the parking lot of Big Dog Cycles in Wichita, Kansas, as he was coming out of work. In self-defense, the hangaround shot both El Forastero members, killing one in the process. High-ranking members of the Bandidos were outraged that "we" had killed an El Forastero, rather than being outraged at the El Forastero for attacking one of our guys. I, obviously, fully supported the hangaround for making a split-second decision that saved his life. The hangaround would be acquitted in the fall of 2003 of the criminal charges that had been filed against him as a result of the shootings.

I hoped that things would get better, but I was losing faith in El Presidente George and his administration. I could not put my finger on the problem, but some of what the older Bandidos thought about our El Presidente was making more sense to me now. The saying "being hung out to dry" had crossed my mind more than once in the past year, and I had a bad feeling that I had been used by George in more ways than one. I was also hearing a lot of rumors that he would regularly tell one person one thing and then tell another just the opposite. There were even accusations that he was telling Bandidos members one thing and telling other 1%er motorcycle clubs just the opposite. By this time, I was wondering if all those rumors were true and was starting to believe that where there was smoke, there indeed had to be a fire.

One incident that fueled my thoughts along these lines was permanently etched in my brain. A year earlier, in the summer of 2002, George had called me from Oklahoma City. He was there visiting his mother-in-law and had asked me to come and pick him up. He wanted to spend the night in Tulsa and visit with Bandido Lee and me. On the way from Oklahoma City to Tulsa, George mentioned some things about fellow Bandidos member, Jack-E, which I knew were absolutely untrue. When Lee took the El Presidente back to Oklahoma City the next day, George told him the same malicious story about Jack-E. Later, when Lee and I compared notes, we both knew for sure El Presidente George had flagrantly lied. Lying to a fellow Bandido was, according to the club's bylaws, a patch-pulling offense; it was obvious there was a set of double standards present in the club's hierarchy. I knew that if George had lied to me once, it was very likely he had lied to me, and others, many times before.

Over the next year, various issues frequently crossed my mind, all concerning my life as a member of the Bandidos Motorcycle Club. I was sick and tired of being used by El Presidente George to complete his assignments and then being fed to the wolves when a Bandido complained to George about the project I had been assigned. I was annoyed that while I was getting every assignment done, most national officers sat on the couch and did nothing. I was also disenchanted with being asked to do national officer duties while not being officially recognized and treated as a national officer. I had actually been a member of the national chapter on three different occasions. Each time, after only a few days, I had been dismissed but was still expected to carry out and complete my duties and assignments. I had my fill of spending hundreds of hours a year working on behalf of the club for free and not even being appreciated for it.

But more than anything, I was appalled by the rampant use and sale of methamphetamine by a growing percentage of the American Bandidos. Even more disturbing to me was the fact that all this had become acceptable behavior, tolerated by El Presidente George. Last but not least, I had enough of the lying, jealousy, and deceit that had become ingrained in the Bandidos way of life. Somehow or other, the club had evolved from everything I stood for back in 1997 to everything I hated in the late summer of 2003.

You can imagine my state of mind as I rode from Tulsa to the annual Sturgis biker rally in South Dakota in August 2003. I wondered what internal political problems I would encounter while I was there. Being who I am, I had by this time, voiced my disapproval of current club policy to many Bandidos members all over the world. I also knew that El Presidente George was not very happy with me, and expected some type of confrontation with him while I was there.

Within a few hours of my arrival at the Bandidos clubhouse in Rapid City, South Dakota, quite a few prominent members advised me that El Presidente George and El Vice Presidente Jeff were out to get me, and it did not matter to them what they had to do to achieve their goal. Although not a surprise to me, their words echoed through my mind the next day when the entire Oklahoma chapter was summoned into the clubhouse for an interrogation by El Presidente George, El Vice Presidente Jeff, and their entire national chapter.

The subject of the meeting was to find out who was really running the Oklahoma chapter and how everyone in the chapter felt. Bandido Lee and I, as well as most in the chapter, were in a state of shock when three of our own chapter members sold us down the river. First, Bandido Steven "Steve" Buitron, who was everything but dead from pancreatic cancer, devastated us with his version of what our chapter was all about. While looking directly at Bandido Lee and me, Bandido Steve told everyone that I really ran the chapter and that Bandido Lee was just my puppet. I was amazed because this babbling idiot did not even own a motorcycle at the time and had not owned a motorcycle for years. Not owning a motorcycle was a valid reason for immediate expulsion and was a major violation of the Bandidos bylaws; but we had overlooked this fact since Steve discovered he had cancer.

I knew we were in trouble when I saw a look of joy come over El Presidente George's face. I was thinking that I wanted to wring Steve's neck on the spot. If it had not been for the Oklahoma chapter helping him since he transferred from a Texas chapter three years earlier, he would have been expelled from the club a long time ago, either for not owning a bike or for not paying his monthly chapter fees. Next up at bat was Bandido James "Smurf" Ragan, who concurred with what Bandido Steve had said. The third one to rub our faces in the dirt was our newest member, Bandido Michael "Mick" Barnett, who in reality didn't have a clue what was going on. But Bandido Mick also agreed with what Bandidos Steve and Smurf had said, and the damage was done.

After listening to the outlandish stories told by the three stooges, El Presidente George decided the Oklahoma chapter needed to be split into two chapters at the next Oklahoma Pawhuska Biker Rally in mid-September. Bandidos Oklahoma would then have a new chapter in western Oklahoma, which would include the current members who resided in Oklahoma City and Lawton. The eastern Oklahoma chapter, which would include the current members that resided in Tulsa, Joplin, Muskogee, and Springfield, would be run by Bandido Lee. That was not so much of a problem, as we had all planned on doing that anyway in the following six months. What surprised us was that El Presidente George suggested Bandido Steve would be the perfect candidate to run the new Oklahoma City–Lawton chapter, for we had all expected Bandido Charles "Snake" Rush to be the president of the new chapter.

Before we even got over the shock of that, Bandido Smurf announced he wanted to be president of his own chapter, and El Presidente George announced to all of us that Smurf would make a great president. And so it was also ordered that the new eastern Oklahoma chapter would be split again before the end of the year, and that Bandido Smurf would be the president of that new chapter. Bandido Smurf's new chapter would be headquartered out of the Joplin, Missouri, area and would contain all the Oklahoma members who lived in Missouri and northeastern Oklahoma. The notion was ludicrous, for Bandido Smurf was incapable of taking a dog for a walk, much less controlling a Bandidos chapter. Of all the members in our chapter most incapable of being leaders, all three of the whiners — Bandidos Steve, Smurf, and Mick — were now somehow at the top of the list. As the rest of us came out of the meeting in the clubhouse, we knew we were all screwed and that Bandidos Steve, Smurf, and Mick were two-faced, lying traitors. Bandido Lee and I realized it was just a matter of time before Bandido George got what he wanted, which was for me to be forced out of the club. It surprised us, though, that he was willing to destroy the Oklahoma chapter in the process.

By the time I got back to Tulsa, I knew my days were numbered. A little more than a month later, on September 20, 2003, I finally decided I had had enough. I knew I had reached the proverbial fork in the road, and I needed to make a major change in my life to avoid what appeared to be an inevitable dead end. Although I felt relieved, it was still with a heavy heart that I quit the club. I turned in my club colors to chapter president Bandido Lee, a man who had been such a good friend for such a long time. Accepting my resignation with regret, Lee told me I would be out of the club "in good standings," and if I ever wanted to come back, I was more than welcome. I felt as if an eight-hundred-pound gorilla had been taken off my back, and I knew that I had made the right decision.

A week later, El Presidente George, in a vindictive act designed to prevent me from joining another American-based 1%er organization and fraternizing with Bandidos members, declared me "out in bad standings." This effectively mandated, under penalty of expulsion from the club, all current Bandidos, worldwide, from communicating with me. No valid reason was even given to me for being ostracized from the world of 1%er outlaw biker clubs. Even though it hit me hard, I soon learned to live with it.

CHAPTER FIFTEEN

THE

SHEDDEN MASSACRE

After I had been declared "out in bad standings," a few of the Canadian Bandidos kept in touch with me, despite the fact they had been ordered by the American national chapter to have nothing to do with me. Many other ex-Bandidos, who were "out in good standings," also stayed in contact with me. This in itself was vindication enough that I had received a raw deal from El Presidente George. Even though I was no longer a Bandido, I kept abreast of what was going on with the club worldwide. I was especially interested in what was happening in Canada and followed the stories through the media, which provided a broad, if not always accurate, picture of what was going on. Whenever new tidbits of information appeared, I would verify their accuracy by getting in touch with some of the current and former Canadian Bandidos who ignored the boycott imposed on me.

But other than the Toronto chapter, which seemed to be on a fairly strong footing, things were relatively quiet. The proposed expansion of the Bandidos into British Columbia did not occur. Other than probationary chapters in Edmonton, Alberta, and Winnipeg, Manitoba, which didn't really materialize into anything significant, the Bandidos more or less became an afterthought in Canada's biker world. That is until April 8, 2006, when the country woke up to the news of a grisly, multiple murder in Shedden, Ontario, a small village not far from London.

Initial media reports cited that eight bodies had been found in a field off Stafford Line, two miles north of Shedden. Four vehicles, including a Volkswagen Golf, an Infiniti suv, a Pontiac Grand Prix, and a Chevrolet Silverado tow truck, with bodies stuffed inside, had been discovered by a farmer. According to police, the victims were probably shot at several nearby locations before being brought to the field in the various vehicles, meaning the slayings were the work of more than one individual. What appeared to be a gangland-style slaying flared into the headlines as Ontario's worst mass murder and Canada's worst biker massacre.

When I saw the first news article about the Shedden incident, I immediately contacted some of my old friends in Canada. I at once suspected that a murder of this scale could very well involve members of the outlaw biker world. The reaction I was met with over the phone confirmed my suspicion: the victims were those of members and close associates of the Bandidos. By 6:00 p.m. on Saturday night, I was 99 percent certain that some or all of the bodies belonged to patched members of the Bandidos Motorcycle Club.

That evening, I also started fielding inquiries from members of the Canadian media. Ever since publication of my first book, *Out in Bad Standings: Inside the Bandidos Motorcycle Club — The Making of a Worldwide Dynasty*, Canadian journalists contacted me for comments whenever a new biker incident surfaced. This time, they wanted to know if I had any idea about what was transpiring in Shedden. One of the journalists, Jen Horsey, who was with Canadian Press, asked me if I thought the slain men were Bandidos or other outlaw bikers. I advised her that, in my opinion, it was highly probable that some would turn out to be members of the Bandidos or close associates. To qualify my statement, I mentioned I had spoken with insiders who had been able to identify some of the vehicles shown in television news footage, and that one of the bodies visible in an open hatchback looked familiar.

"I guess you're not going to tell me his name," Jen said, hoping to get a scoop. At that time, I did indeed refrain from giving up the name.

By 8:00 p.m. I had figured out the identities of two more of the victims. They were Bandidos who were not answering their cell phones, responding to messages, or answering their pagers. By mid-Sunday morning, I knew five of the victims' names and was shocked to learn, although not totally surprised, that some of the dead were members of the Bandidos national chapter.

On April 9 at 1:00 p.m., the authorities held a media conference at which time they confirmed that the bodies — all men, ranging in age from late twenties to early fifties — were members of the Bandidos Motorcycle Club. They included forty-eight-year-old John "Boxer" Muscedere — Canadian Bandidos national president — and forty-one-year-old Luis Manny "Porkchop" Raposo. This was not news to me, because I had already learned that they were among the victims the previous evening. Only four years earlier, Presidente Boxer and Bandido Porkchop had come to Oklahoma to see me regarding the salvaging of what was left of the Bandidos after Operation Amigo all but decimated the club. Now they were dead, along with four other fullpatch Bandidos that included George "Pony" Jesso, at fifty-two years of age the oldest of the victims;

Frank "Bam Bam" Salerno; Paul Sinopoli; and George "Crash" Kriarakis, at twenty-eight the youngest. The two other victims included Bandidos Prospects Jamie Flanz and Michael Trotta. According to media reports, Trotta was an associate, but this was erroneous.

Before various theories of the murders started to surface, the Ontario Provincial Police were quick to state that the killings were isolated incidents and that there was no fear for the safety of local residents. It was also reported that neither the Hells Angels nor other rival motorcycle gangs appeared to have had a role in the slayings. This came as no surprise, because the police wanted to quash rumors that the long-awaited and predicted Ontario biker war was finally getting underway.

"There's nothing to indicate that there's anything outside the Bandidos. This is simply an internal cleansing," said Detective Inspector Don Bell of the Ontario Provincial Police Biker Unit.

The media, however, jumped on the biker bandwagon with their usual glee and ran front-page headlines to the tune of MASSACRE SPARKS FEAR OF ALL-OUT BIKER WAR. The Hells Angels, for their part, distanced themselves from Shedden by stating on their Web site that *"The Hells Angels Motorcycle Club, or any of its members, are not involved in this crime in any way shape or form."* According to one source, the slain bikers had considered joining the Hells Angels, something I personally found hard to believe, as Presidente Boxer and the others had worked very hard to save the Canadian Bandidos. They had also been instrumental in establishing the ill-fated probationary chapter in Edmonton back in 2004 and had recently launched a new probationary chapter in Winnipeg.

Law enforcement authorities in Ontario wasted no time tracking down the people they believed to be responsible for, or at least involved in, the murders of the Bandidos members. On April 10, police arrested Wayne Kellestine, Frank Mather, Brett

Gardiner, Eric Niesson, and Kerry Morris. All five were charged with first-degree murder. For Niesson and Morris — the only woman arrested — those charges were later changed to eight counts of being accessories after the fact and obstruction of justice. By following a trail of evidence, which was not disclosed, police officers ended up at Kellestine's Iona Station farm, only a few miles from where the bodies had been discovered.

Kellestine, whom locals described as a dangerous man, had previously served a two-year prison sentence starting in 2000 for weapons offences and running a marijuana-growing operation. Not only did they find Kellestine at home, they found the others there as well. Fifty-six-year-old Kellestine was the only suspect identified as belonging to the Canadian Bandidos. The other men were labeled as associates, always a convenient term when police are in doubt of someone's actual status in the outlaw biker world.

Despite the arrests, no motives for the murders were immediately obvious, but speculations aplenty started circulating. Although Kellestine was considered to be a tough customer, few who knew him believed he would have broken the bikers' code by bringing a woman to a killing. Some said he was too smart, others that he was too stupid to be involved in the murders.

Conjectures broadened to include the possibility that the murders were sanctioned by the American national chapter, which supposedly had sent a four-man hit-squad from Chicago to Canada. Suggestions were also made that a Winnipeg Bandidos support club, Los Montoneros, was used to orchestrate the assassinations. It's no secret that the American Bandidos were unhappy with the way things had progressed north of the border. Current El Presidente Jeff Pike — George Wegers had given up the presidency by this time due to problems with the law that landed him in jail — had already revoked the charter of the Canadian Bandidos and no longer recognized them as part of the Bandidos Nation. This fact fueled the theory that the American Bandidos had indeed sent a hit-squad to Canada.

The Australian and European Bandidos, who had been the first to welcome the Canadians into the Bandidos Nation, and who supported them through thick and thin, were dismayed with Pike's stance. Nothing they said, however, changed his or the American Bandidos' attitude. There had already been major differences of opinion between Pike and the Australian and European Bandidos, who still believed in the true meaning of "brotherhood." Revoking the Canadian Bandidos' charter fueled rumors that the Americans did have something to do with the Shedden Massacre, and totally turning their backs on the Canadians after the massacre was the straw that broke the camel's back.

While the American Bandidos tried to put as much distance as possible between themselves and what remained of the Canadian Bandidos, four Bandidos from Australia and two from Germany arrived in Ontario within days of the slayings to comfort the dead men's families and conduct a fact-finding mission. They would be the only international Bandidos to venture into Canada to show support. Even the funerals of the eight victims were conspicuously non-biker events, as only close friends and family members attended each individual interment. Usually, when a Bandido is laid to rest, other Bandidos and bikers show up en masse to pay their respect; the victims of the Shedden Massacre received no such honor.

Another theory for the murders suggested that the eight victims had gone to Kellestine's farm to turn in their patches because they wanted to leave the club — hence the rumor they were going to join the Hells Angels. Yet another theory proposed that Kellestine was supposed to voluntarily turn his patch, bike, and club property over to Presidente Boxer.

Kellestine, like Boxer, had at one time belonged to the Annihilators and the Loners before becoming a member of the Bandidos. Kellestine's failed ventures and mounting debts had become such an embarrassment to the Bandidos that he had to be eliminated from the club one way or another.

The specter of drugs inevitably entered the equation: apparently local narcotics police had kept three of the Bandidos under surveillance for a number of weeks prior to the murders. Ironically, they had followed their targets to Kellestine's farm on the weekend of the massacre. Surveillance was called off when the police thought the bikers had gone there for a party. Eventually, the police officers were able to connect the dots, placing some of the victims at Kellestine's farm the day of the murders. After the fact, it was suggested that the three Bandidos were victims of a deadly drug rip-off instigated by Kellestine and the co-accused. The five other Bandidos supposedly arrived separately later that night and were systematically killed.

As things seemingly simmered down, the plot thickened: on June 16, police in Winnipeg, Manitoba, arrested three additional men in connection with the murders. These included Marcello Aravena, Michael "Tazz" Sandham, and Dwight Mushey. Sandham and Mushey were fullpatch members of the Bandidos, while Aravena was said to be a prospect. Like their counterparts in Ontario, the three Manitoba residents were charged with eight counts of first-degree murder. They were later taken to a jail in St. Thomas, Ontario, a town near Shedden, from where the police investigation and legal proceedings were being coordinated. *"We followed the evidence trail and it led us to Winnipeg, Manitoba,"* Ontario Provincial Police officer Paul Beesley said at a news conference.

How and why the trail led to Winnipeg also belonged in the realm of conjecture, but according to witnesses, the three men had been seen with Kellestine in a local Shedden-area restaurant before the slayings in April. One of their vehicles, a red SUV, matched the description of one seen in the weeks before the slayings. The SUV was promptly sent from Winnipeg to Ontario for forensic tests. As if the additional arrests — in a city nine hundred miles from where the actual crimes had been committed — didn't stir up all kinds of new waves, the fact that Sandham, the leader of the Winnipeg Bandidos chapter, was a former police officer certainly did!

In 2002, Sandham had been suspended from the East St. Paul police force, a community just north of Winnipeg. Shortly after being suspended, allegedly for doing security at a biker party, Sandham resigned from law enforcement to pursue life in the 1%er biker world, where he had connections to both the Outlaws and Bandidos. Just days before his arrest, Sandham had been in Texas to discuss the expansion of the Bandidos in Canada with members of the Bandidos national chapter. He had requested a meeting with El Presidente Jeff, but was ultimately rejected when it was learned he had been a police officer prior to becoming a Bandido.

And finally, there was the methamphetamine connection: in 2004, Dwight Mushey had been charged with conspiracy to produce the drug. Eric Niesson, although never charged with any drug-related offences, had come up in several major drug investigations. In the period leading up to the massacre, police linked Niesson to Dan McCool, who has been credited with bringing the "ephedrine-based" meth manufacturing process to Ontario from Texas; and to Eddie Thompson, who had a record of manufacturing the drug.

With arrests made and charges laid, it seemed like a clear road to the next chapter in the Shedden drama: bringing the accused to justice. But as in Quebec, the wheels of justice in Ontario turn rather slowly. The preliminary hearings that got underway in the spring of 2007 failed to establish an actual pre-trial date.

Lawyers for the eight also asked that the case be moved out of the immediate area to another location. The hearings of those applications weren't scheduled until the fall of 2007, with either side able to appeal to Ontario's highest court. An application for a venue change can be made if it is believed an accused is in danger of not receiving a fair trial. Among other reasons, pre-trial publicity could affect a jury pool where the charge was laid. The case had already officially moved from St. Thomas to London, where a three-month preliminary hearing had been held. As the crow flies, London isn't much farther from Shedden than St. Thomas, and eventually the trial is expected to take place well outside the area. Toronto has been suggested as a possible venue, although other towns in southern Ontario are being considered. As of May 2008, nothing had been resolved. In fact, the trial, which was scheduled and rescheduled a number of times, with the most recent date set for September 2008, was postponed in early April and rescheduled for the spring of 2009.

So what actually happened that night at Kellestine's farm? While the truth may never be fully known, in my opinion there was no grand conspiracy or plot. The murders were no doubt the result of a spontaneous act of madness, with meth likely the catalyst that fueled the madness.

According to my sources, at the time of the killings there was a deep division in the Bandidos organization all across Canada. On one side of the fence there were members and associates like Wayne Kellestine, Michael "Tazz" Sandham, Dwight Mushey, and Eric Niessen, who wanted to use, manufacture, and distribute meth. On the other side of the fence were members who were adamantly opposed to the whole venture, wanting nothing to do with the drug.

Bandido Wayne Kellestine also had personal views that could best be described as "neo-nazi." Kellestine hated Bandido prospect Jamie Flanz because Flanz just happened to be Jewish, but that on its own was no reason to run him off. So Kellestine lied and told everyone in the club that he thought Jamie was an informant. A chapter meeting was to be held in Kellestine's old barn the day of the murders, where members would talk about these allegations. The meeting, as per custom, was supposed to be over some time late that evening.

Everyone in the Bandidos Toronto chapter was ordered to attend the meeting, but some members, like Bandido Robert "Bob" Pammett Sr. and James "Rip" Fullager, were a no show; if they had, the number of dead would no doubt have been more than eight. Winnipeg Bandidos chapter member Sandham was present that day, no doubt whacked out of his mind on meth just like Kellestine. It is highly probable that Sandham was hiding somewhere in the barn to cover Kellestine's back, just in case the chapter turned on Kellestine and/or the meeting got out of hand.

Shortly after entering the barn, Bandido Luis Manny "Porkchop" Raposo saw or sensed movement somewhere in the shadows of the barn. Likely believing that they were all being attacked, or maybe thinking that it was just an animal, he drew his gun and shot at the movement. Sandham, being the target of the shots fired by Raposo and having avoided being shot, in a spontaneous reaction fired back at Raposo. Being an ex-police officer his aim was much better and he killed Bandido Raposo. As bizarre as it may sound, everyone else who died that night was no doubt murdered in a knee-jerk reaction to the first killing. And when all was said and done the perpetrators believed that maybe it was a blessing in disguise, because not only was the Jewish problem solved, so was the problem of any interference in their proposed meth business.

EPILOGUE

I have been out of the Bandidos Motorcycle Club for more than four and a half years and have never looked back. Still, in a strange way, I have retained some kind of spiritual connection with the club; one I believe can never be broken. Club issues, whether they occur in the United States, Europe, Australia, or Canada, still remain near and dear to me.

I'm amazed at how much I have accomplished, and how far I have come since leaving the Bandidos. I know there is no way I could have achieved the level of success I did in the construction and real estate business if I had still been a member of the Bandidos Motorcycle Club. It is with great honor that I dedicate this success to my late mother Dolly's memory. In the summer of 1995, three years before she passed away, Dolly went into the construction management business with me. It was a wise and timely move and a defining moment of her life. Although she was in her seventies and legally blind for most of her adult life, she was extremely proud to be in a business corporation with her only son. Besides the fact that I was able to totally trust her, which made her a perfect partner, she was a guiding light for me.

Over a ten-year period, the corporation Dolly and I set up, Blockhead City Construction, morphed into seven additional companies, including Blockhead City Motorcycles; Blockhead City Music; Blockhead City Real Estate; Blue Collar Financial Group of Oklahoma; Blue Collar Financial Group of Texas;

Blockhead City Press; and most recently Blockhead City Entertainment. Today, my main interest lies in the entertainment and publishing industry. In addition to producing the pilot for a television/DVD reality series entitled *Living on the Edge*, which focuses on the biker lifestyle, a number of book projects are in the works, both fictional and non-fictional.

These days, I consider myself a retired biker and a simple family man. I treasure the time I can spend with my daughter, Taylor, who is maturing into a beautiful and considerate young woman. I also value the time I can spend with my beautiful wife, Caroline, who definitely lives up to the adage "three's a charm."

Most of my time is still devoted to taking care of my business interests, which includes a lot of traveling. No matter what I get involved with, traveling seems to be part of it. It is in my nature to be continuously on the move, to do things, explore new avenues, and keep living a life of adventure. Once we reach the age of fifty, we tend to reflect much more on life, what has passed, and what may lie ahead. To be honest, I am quite surprised that I am still alive. I have always believed in fate, that we have a purpose in some kind of grand plan, and I am obviously fulfilling my own destiny by doing the things I do.

I am extremely proud of the fact that I have gone through life without sacrificing my integrity or principles, and that I have always been a "man of my word." There are a few things I regret having done, but nothing I regret not having done. The majority of what I do regret is with regards to the people I have hurt, usually as a direct result of my behavior, sometimes inadvertently. Despite the things I have done, I sleep with a clear conscience because I have found peace of mind. I have reached a level of maturity that has allowed me to address the wrongs of my past and, whenever possible, make atonements in the present.

I am pleasantly surprised that I do not miss the life of a Bandido. In fact, I am quite relieved that I'm no longer required to do things I have no more desire to do, like being someplace I do not want to be and being at someone's beck and call twenty-four hours a day. I realize I am blessed to have lived the life I have led and to live the life I have today. I know that I am quite fortunate to have been able to travel all over the world and meet so many fascinating people.

I am honored to have had the privilege of knowing most of the men I have written about in this book; I consider many of them to be lifelong friends. Many have been my mentors and taught me a lot. I only hope that I have had half the impact on them that they have had on me.

Alain Brunette was released from prison in June 2007; he has no intention of taking up where he left off as a 1%er biker and only wants to put the past behind him. Alain plans on living in the country, maybe on a farm, somewhere in Ontario with his girlfriend, Dawn, who remained faithfully at his side throughout his incarceration. I communicate with Alain on a regular basis, and we hope to see each other again some day in the future. Considering neither one of us can cross into each other's country, we'll have to get together on neutral territory, but that will make it easier to look back on where we came from.

Considering the toll the biker war took on all those concerned, it is ironic that Salvatore and Giovanni Cazzetta, founders of the Rock Machine, became members of the Montreal Hells Angels in January 2006. Even though the Cazzettas founded the Rock Machine — and one would assume they kept their connections with the club intact throughout their lengthy incarceration — they denied any involvement in the biker war with the Hells Angels, precisely because they were behind bars the entire time the war raged. The Cazzetta brothers weren't the only former Rock Machine/Bandidos members who crossed the line and donned the colors of the Hells Angels. Others who did the same included Fred Faucher, the man who negotiated the truce with Hells Angels Nomads president Mom Boucher back in November 2000. Perhaps the old adage "if you can't beat them, join them" rings true for some people.

In addition to the ups and downs of the Canadian Bandidos, which will be with me forever, the failure of Bandidos Canada to thrive has hit me hard. To some extent, I view the debacle that befell Bandidos Canada as a personal failure, although, ultimately, I know I had no control over what transpired and what continues to unfold today. Even after Project Amigo and the decimation of the Quebec Bandidos, I believed the club would recover. At the beginning of 2001, I had such high hopes for Bandidos Canada and did everything I could to make them a success story. I never imagined that the only story to come out of that cold, snowy country, for me, would be one of disappointment.

In the summer of 2007, the U.S. based Mongols Motorcycle Club took over the Loners Motorcycle Club in North America, establishing a short-lived foothold in Canada by patching over the remainder of the Loners chapter in Toronto. After establishing a new chapter in Calgary and doubling the size of their Winnipeg chapter, in the fall of 2007 Bandidos Canada ceased to be when all Bandidos members patched over to the Mongols organization. When all was not what it seemed with the Mongols, some of those disgruntled ex-Bandidos/Mongols members tried desperately to restore their relationship with the European and Australian Bandidos. After this attempt at reconciliation with the Bandidos fell on deaf ears, and the remainder of the Mongols in Canada quit, most of the ex-Bandidos, ex-Mongols, and ex-Loners finally got on the same page in April of 2008 when they established a new motorcycle club. Actually, what they did was reestablish the defunct Rock Machine in honor of the guys in Quebec who started it all back in the 1980s. To date, four chapters are up and running including Kingston (Ontario East), Toronto (Ontario West), Winnipeg (Central Canada), and Edmonton (Western Canada).

I suspect that the Bandidos Motorcycle Club in the United States will undergo major changes in the near future, as it is highly likely additional federal indictments will incarcerate many of its members. I often wondered when George and the house of cards he had built would come crashing down, and it finally did on June 9, 2005. Along with twenty-one other members of the Bandidos Motorcycle Club in Washington, Montana, and South Dakota, the fifty-two-year-old Bandidos world leader was arrested by federal authorities and charged with conspiracy to tamper with witnesses; conspiracy to traffic in certain motor vehicles and motor vehicle parts; conspiracy to commit racketeering; and trafficking in certain motor vehicles. The operation was the nation's most significant bust of the motorcycle club in twenty years. Caught up in the two-year-long federal investigation along with the then–El Presidente were three other members of the Bandidos American national chapter.

According to George's attorney, Jeffrey Lustick, the charges against his client were a case of guilt by association. Lustick also said that George didn't remember being in the places he was alleged to have been or making the statements he was alleged to have made. I had to laugh at this because the European Bandidos had told me in May 2003 that George seemed to be suffering from Alzheimer's disease. I wondered if having Alzheimer's was going to be his principal defense when he had his day in court. On October 6, 2006, George was sentenced to twenty months in

federal prison; he pled guilty to one single charge of his indict-
ment: conspiracy to commit racketeering. As set forth in his plea
agreement, George admitted that the Bandidos Motorcycle Club
was a racketeer-influenced, corrupt organization.

Many more members will no doubt quit rather than endure
the stigma of being involved with what is perceived to be a
criminal organization. I am sure the club will survive in some
shape, fashion, or form, but I am willing to bet that someday
soon, meth use and sale by its members will be prohibited and
no longer tolerated.

While I was a member, I did what I could to effect change
and organize the Bandidos, but I was just one man, and one
man cannot do much by himself. I did succeed in helping to
bring the Bandidos into the twenty-first century, teaching them
along the way to open lines of communication, both internally
and externally. I introduced the club as a whole to the concept
of the worldwide web and did what I could to get them to look
at themselves as a legal, worldwide business.

I, for one, hope that the right people will find their way into
the club's hierarchy and bring about the changes that will see
the Bandidos celebrate their hundredth anniversary in July
2066. Donald Eugene Chambers would be proud. If I were
around, I would be too.

El Presidente: The United States national president and international president of the Bandidos Motorcycle Club. The El Presidente is the boss of all members of the Bandidos worldwide. His corporate equivalent would be the chairman of the board. The El Presidente is the only Bandido that wears an El Presidente bottom rocker on the back of his club colors.

El Secretario: The secretary in charge of all other Secretarios in a particular area or country for the Bandidos Motorcycle Club. The area or country that the El Secretario is in charge of is signified by the country or area rocker he wears on his side under his arm or a small ribbon he wears on his chest. The El Secretario assigns all Secretarios their job assignments and is usually the keeper of the club treasury. His corporate equivalent would be the CFO.

El Vice Presidente: The United States national vice president of the Bandidos Motorcycle Club. The El Vice Presidente is the underboss to all the Bandidos in the United States. His corporate equivalent would be the CEO.

Presidente: The European, Australian, Canadian, or Asian president of the Bandidos Motorcycle Club. The Presidente is the boss to all members of the Bandidos in that particular country or area. The area or country that the Presidente is in charge of is signified by the country or area rocker he wears on his side under his arm or a small ribbon he wears on his chest. His corporate equivalent would be the president.

Vice Presidente: A vice president for the Bandidos Motorcycle Club. The area or country that the vice president is in charge of is signified by the country or area rocker he wears on his side under his arm or a small ribbon he wears on his chest. His corporate equivalent would be the vice president.

Secretario: A secretary or treasurer for the Bandidos Motorcycle Club. The area or country that the Secretario is in charge of is signified by the country or area rocker he wears on his side under his arm or a small ribbon he wears on his chest. His corporate equivalent would be the Secretary or Treasurer.

Sargento de Armas: An enforcer for the Bandidos Motorcycle Club. He is in charge of enforcing the club's rules and decisions, both internally and externally. The area or country that the Sargento de Armas is in charge of is signified by the country or area rocker he wears on his side under his arm or a small ribbon he wears on his chest. There is no corporate equivalent for this person.

Hangaround: In the normal process, an individual who wants to become a member will hang around for a year or many years, then become a "prospect" or "probate" (probationary), and then "fullpatch."

Probationary: In the Bandidos Motorcycle Club, if a potential member has previous motorcycle club experience, then that potential member is eligible to become a probationary member. His probationary period will last for a minimum of one year. While he is a probationary, he is retrained in the ways of the Bandidos Motorcycle Club. A probationary wears the Bandidos Fat Mexican center patch and Bandidos top rocker, but wears a bottom rocker that says "Probationary."

Prospect: Prospecting occurs when the prospect has no experience with the motorcycle club lifestyle. He undergoes an intensive six-month minimum period of learning before becoming a fullpatch member. While he is prospecting, the prospect only wears one rocker at the top of his back that says "Prospect."

Support Club: A support club is normally an existing motorcycle club or a motorcycle club specifically created by a larger, well-established motorcycle club. The support club supplies the larger established motorcycle club with basic moral and physical support, and supplies the larger, established motorcycle club with a selection pool to draw future members from. This is very similar to the situation in American baseball, where the major leagues get their new recruits from the minor leagues. Members of a support club have a different set of priorities than a traditional 1%er motorcycle club: their families and jobs come first. A support club operates on its own, under its own bylaws, and is free to operate as it sees fit.

Puppet Club: A puppet club, like a support club, is normally an existing motorcycle club or a motorcycle club specifically created by a larger, well-established motorcycle club. The puppet club also supplies the larger established motorcycle club with basic moral and physical support, and supplies the larger established motorcycle club with a selection pool to draw future members from. Once again, this is very similar to American baseball, where the major leagues get their new recruits from the minor leagues. Members of a puppet club have the same set of priorities as a traditional 1%er motorcycle club: their families and jobs come after the club. A puppet club operates under the direct control of a larger established motorcycle club and is not free to operate as it sees fit.

Hangaround Club: A hangaround club is normally an existing motorcycle club that wants to join a larger motorcycle club. The first stage of the process is for that smaller club to "hang around" with the larger club, hence the name "hangaround." The actual term puts everyone on notice, from clubs to the rest of the biker world, that the smaller club wants to join the larger, and the larger is considering the change. Usually, a hangaround club will hang around for a year or more, then the larger club will take a vote as to whether the members of the smaller club are worthy of the larger club's patch. If so, then there is a patchover, where the old club's patches are swapped for the new club's patches. In the Bandidos world, usually the members from the old club retain the old patches, though sometimes they are burned.

Patch: The club colors of any motorcycle club. A patch can be the entire vest with the club colors sewed on it, or it could refer to just the actual club colors by themselves.

Patchover: When the members of a smaller club change their patches and then start wearing the patches of a larger club. The actual assimilation of a smaller motorcycle club into a larger motorcycle club.

Property Patch: A patch worn by a female associated with a motorcycle club that denotes which member that female belongs to.

Hangaround & Prospect Information

The following document has been used over the years by various 1%er outlaw motorcycle clubs as an orientation document to inform the hangaround or prospect of what is in store for them if they choose to join a "traditional" 1%er motorcycle club that wears a three-piece patch on their back, either on a vest or jacket. A three-piece patch consists of a top rocker, bottom rocker, and center piece.

Introduction

This information has been put together to give you a better understanding of the new world you are entering and a better understanding of what is expected of you in your new role. Once you understand the scope of the task you are undertaking, you should examine your feelings and question your motives for wanting to become a member of a motorcycle brotherhood. There are many riding clubs that require only casual participation from its members. Others require a total commitment to the motorcycle club lifestyle. Your degree of interest will direct you towards an organization that you will fit into.

Be certain that you are both willing and able to commit yourself to the level that will be required. Be certain that your family understands the demands that the club will make of your time and that those demands will continue to an even greater extent once you become a patch holder. If after reading this packet you should have any reservations about being able to meet any of the requirements, it would be better not to consider moving forward at this time. Instead, either continue your present level of association with the club until you feel that you are ready and are confident of your success, or find a different organization that better suits your needs. Such a decision would be respected and would be to your credit.

Club

The intent of this section is to give you an overview of the structure and philosophy of the traditional motorcycle club (MC). This does not necessarily express the feelings or priorities of any particular club, as all motorcycle clubs differ on some points. Regardless of the basic philosophy of your club, it is important that you understand the perspectives of other clubs that you may be associating with from time to time. If your lifestyle is influenced by motorcycles, then you are part of the motorcycle community. Of all the types of organizations found within that community, the traditional motorcycle club stands apart and ranks highest in stature.

Respect

A serious club commands respect for one or both of two reasons. Those who are correctly informed recognize the deep level of personal commitment and self-discipline that a man has to demonstrate and sustain in order to wear a patch. They understand that it is akin to a religion or vocation to that man. They realize that a club's "Colors" are closely guarded and the membership process is long and difficult. Other factors notwithstanding, they respect patch holders for what they have accomplished by being able to earn and keep the patch they wear. This is respect born out of recognition of dedication and accomplishment.

Those who are less informed see only the surface. They see the vigilance of mutual support. They see the potential danger of invoking a response from a well-organized unit that travels in numbers and is always prepared for confrontation. They know that no one can provoke one club member without being answerable to the whole club, and that such an answer is a point of honor that must come, to the last man. The type of respect that this generates is one born out of fear. We strive for respect for reason #1, not reason #2! This is especially true as it pertains to those persons outside of the motorcycle community. This segment of society is by far the larger, and therefore represents a larger market for any fundraising activities that the club might undertake.

It stands to reason that cultivating a relationship with these people is important, and to be perceived by them as "biker scum" would not be advantageous to the club. We, therefore, will conduct ourselves as upstanding citizens in every way . . . "good neighbors," so to speak. The goal is to be admired and respected by the general public, rather than feared. The serious club, and its members and prospects, will always conduct themselves publicly in a highly professional manner. They will not go out of their way to cause trouble or to present themselves as an intimidating force without purpose or provocation.

Club Colors

The general public does not draw a distinction between different club colors. In many cases, they simply can't tell the difference: we're all "biker scum" to them. If one club causes a problem that touches the public sector, the offending club's identity is either confused or ignored, and the heat comes down on all clubs. The clubs tend to police themselves to avoid such incidents.

Officers

Within a club, officers are usually elected to the positions of president, vice president, secretary, treasurer, and Sergeant-at-Arms. Other less traditional posts are road captain and enforcer.

Process

In most cases, the patch holder was a hangaround with the club for about a year. Before that, he was a long-standing acquaintance, and his attitude and overall conduct were well known. He then prospected for the club for one to two years before he got his patch. Of all things in this man's life, his loyalty and commitment to the well-being of the club comes first above all else. There is never any doubt which comes first. Though most things in life can let him down, he knows that his club and his brothers will always be there because he is always committed to being there himself. To be sure that this ideal and attitude continues on with any new members, he participates in teaching, conditioning, and even testing the club's prospects.

The term "prospect" comes from the words "prospective member." Before he allows another man to wear his colors, he is sure that the prospect is as dedicated as he is! A patch holder has the attitude that there are only two types of people: those who are brothers and those who are not. For this reason, he will not discuss any club business, whether it's about membership numbers, club goings on, or any member's personal information, with anyone outside of the club.

He will keep his voice down when discussing club business, and he will be aware of anyone coming within listening distance. He understands that he is a patch holder twenty-four hours a day, whether or not he is wearing his colors. Everything he says or does in public can affect the club or the brothers. He also understands that if he gets out of line, he is subject to be counseled by his brothers for his own good and for that of the club.

Wearing a patch is more than getting together for good times. It also means getting together for the other times, too. It constitutes a lot of work. It's committing yourself to a lifestyle in which you do not look for how your brothers can help you, but for ways that you can be of help to your brothers. You always look to give, rather than to receive. All of this may seem very idealistic, and in some cases it's just that. But it is an ideal that all clubs profess and are always striving for in principle and practice. You should be aware of the "Golden Rule" of conduct while traveling in club circles: if you give respect, you will get respect. If you act like an asshole, you will be treated like one.

Participation

It is important for you to understand that it is the patch holders who run the club, not the officers. This may seem a moot point to some, but it can't be overstressed. This is not to say that the officers don't deserve respect from the other patch holders. These members have shown leadership qualities and have probably been in the club for quite some time. They are in office to carry out the wishes of the membership in a timely and efficient manner, as it is not always possible to get the members together to make decisions or take action.

Officers are elected to act as spokesmen for the club and perform various responsible tasks, but they don't run the club. When they speak or act on club matters, it is in a manner that they believe that the members of the club would agree upon, if a quick vote were taken. If an officer doesn't understand the membership's feelings about various matters, then he is out of touch with his brothers and should step down. This is a critical point because the strongest and most representative form of rule is one in which the power comes from the bottom up. If things were the other way around and the leaders or officers continually dictated down the chain of command, a sense of apathy and noninvolvement would eventually set in.

If this were to happen, the individual patch holder would have no intuitive sense of his club's direction and would hesitate when he feels that he should act in the best interest of the club. Having little or no say in what is going on destroys a man's motivation to get involved or voice his own opinion. It would also drain his feelings of unity with his club brothers. Without such unity, a brotherhood cannot exist. Remember that the strength of a brotherhood rests with the membership at the bottom of the chain of command and is passed up. This is why aggressive participation is such a prized quality that is expected from the patch holder and is looked for in the prospect.

Levels of Commitment

When a man earns his patch, it does not mean that he has reached the ultimate goal and from that point he can kick back and coast. Moving from hangaround to prospect to patch holder is not climbing from the bottom to the top, but rather more like climbing a constantly ascending slope, and in time becoming a stronger and more committed brother. A man's prospecting rocker, and later his patch, are merely presented in recognition of what he has demonstrated along the way. In this fashion, the more senior the patch holder is in the club and the more he experiences, the more of a brother he should be to all.

Purpose of prospecting

Prospecting is not an initiation as you would find in a fraternity. It is instead a period of training that is sustained until the prospect, in every sense, conducts himself as a patch holder. It's a time in which the man's attitude is conditioned so that he displays a sense of responsibility and respect toward the patch holders of the club, without which he will not develop a sense of brotherhood. He is educated in basic motorcycle club protocol and etiquette.

He is given time to develop the habits that are basic to good security and good communications: to get the man into the habit of participating; to give his family time to adjust to the demands of the club; to experience and learn an essential degree of humility; and to become accustomed to trusting the judgment, at times blindly, of those patch holders who will someday be his brothers. To break the man of habits, those that are self-centered and self-serving. The list could go on, but the point here is to demonstrate that prospecting has definite objectives and that a prospect will go nowhere in the club if he is not aware of this and does not apply himself to those ends. It's not possible to make a checklist of what is expected from a prospect in all cases. There isn't any formula for success, but the key is ATTITUDE. Everything else can be learned in time, but a man's attitude comes from the heart.

The testing of a prospect may come in many ways. It may be planned or spontaneous. In any event, when a prospect is given a task, the patch holder is going to be looking for the man's attitude and the spirit in which he carries out the task. The prospect should be alert and always attentive in looking for more to do. If he is ever in doubt of his priorities or he can't find something to do, he should ask.

The patch holders know which of the prospects hustle, and those are the prospects that are spoken of with the greatest pride and respect. It is also the way by which confidence and trust are developed. These are the seeds of brotherhood. Remember that you will be prospecting for the whole club and not just one individual or individual chapter. The patch holders of one chapter are always held accountable for the actions of a patch holder of another chapter. It is, therefore, only right that the patch holders of all chapters have a hand in developing the prospects on their way to becoming a full patch holder.

Some Do's and Don'ts

As a prospect, strive to conduct yourself as a responsible patch holder at all times. Always display a positive attitude. Participate as much as you think is acceptable; then participate more. If you see a patch holder of your club that you have not met, take the initiative to introduce yourself. Always introduce yourself as Prospect (your name). At all gatherings, make it a point to circulate when you have the time to do so and greet every patch holder who is there. Anticipate the brothers' needs and offer to supply them. Don't wait to be told what to do, and don't get overly friendly with someone who is not a regular acquaintance of the club.

If someone outside the club has questions, refer him to a patch holder. Never give out a patch holder's name, phone number, address, or any personal information to anyone outside the club. Never give out any information about the club itself to outsiders. This includes, but is not limited to, where the club is based, how many members are in the club, etc. Always be security minded, look around and see what's going on around you in public places and report anything that seems suspicious. While in public places, always conduct yourself with your association with the club in mind. Remember that what you do, people will remember — good or bad.

Never let a patch holder walk off alone in an unsecured area. If he is going out to his car, his bike, or even just out to get some fresh air, go with him. Watch his back at all times. If you are at an open function and pick up on some negative attitudes, especially from another club, quietly alert a patch holder immediately. Keep your ears and eyes open and feed any information that you may pick up on to a patch holder, especially information regarding another club. Remember that you are a prospect twenty-four hours a day. Your association doesn't go "on" and "off" with your colors.

Remember that you are every patch holder's prospect, not just your sponsor's or just your chapter's. Never wear your colors out of your area without your sponsor's approval, and never out of state unless you are with a patch holder. If two or more patch holders are having a private conversation, don't approach them within earshot, especially if they are talking with a patch holder of another club. If you need to interrupt, put yourself in a place of visibility and wait to be acknowledged. If it is important that you interrupt, ask another patch holder to break in for you.

Never use the term "outlaw club" when speaking to a member of another club. Never lie to a member of another club. If you are in a situation where you are asked about the club or its membership, it is acceptable to say "that seems like club business, and I really can't talk about it." If this doesn't put the subject to rest, offer to put him in touch with a patch holder for him to speak with. Always show respect to a patch holder of another club. Even though he is with another club, he has earned his patch; you have not.

Always carry a pen and paper, a watch, and a calendar. Frequently ask the patch holders how you are doing and if there's anything you should be doing differently. Never ask when you may be getting your patch. Never call a patch holder "brother." He's not your brother. Never call a patch holder of another club "brother." He is not your brother, either. Remember, your patch is earned; it is not given to you.

Never bring a personal friend or a stranger into the presence of patch holders without asking permission to do so first. At an open function, never turn your back to a patch holder of another club. This is not so much for safety reasons, but as a show of respect. Always show respect and courtesy to patch holders of other clubs. Don't come across like you want to be best friends. Be professional in such encounters; keep it short, then move on. Keep away from women associating with other clubs.

Never be quick to walk up to a patch holder of another club in a public setting, even if you know him well and the clubs are on friendly terms. If you want to greet him, walk up slowly and wait for him to indicate that he wants such a public display to take place. He may be on some club business and may not want to give the general public the impression that the clubs are on such friendly terms. If he looks like he's going to ignore you, accept it and keep your distance. The best approach is always to wait for them to come to you, and to let everyone else see that.

Learn what different parts of our patch represent and what the different color combination of yours and other clubs represent. As you can see, there is a lot to think about. This decision is probably one of the biggest you'll ever make. Be absolutely sure this is for you and GO FOR IT!

Bylaws of the USA Bandidos Motorcycle Club

As of June 2002

(This document was handed out to all members.)

1. Requirements for a Chapter:

- Five (5) member minimum – One (1) "Charter Member"
- Charter Member = 10 years.
- Keep pictures and information on all members.
- Hold weekly meetings.
- $25.00 per month, per member, to National Treasury (by the 1st of each month).
- Probationary Chapters (new) will pay a one-time donation of $1,000.00 to National Treasury.
- Probationary Chapter members' bikes and titles will be pledged to National Chapter for the first year.

2. Patches:

- Only a top and bottom rocker, Fat Mexican, 1% diamond, and MC patch should be on the back of your cut-off. It should be visible from 150 feet.
- A 1%er diamond will be worn over the heart.
- Anything else is up to the individual.
- "Year patches" & "buckles" are not to be given early.
- National can grant a "Lifer" patch or membership on a person-to-person basis.

- One "Property Patch" per member. If she rides her own bike, it is NOT to be worn while riding with or around patcholders or prospects. It should not be worn in public without her "old man" in view.
- There is no limit on "property belts."

3. Do's:

- Labor Day and Memorial Day are MANDATORY RUNS.
- A Chapter may leave one (1) member behind from a mandatory run. A member on medical leave or a Life Member is that member. This is for security reasons; that person should have access to a phone as much as possible.
- When you are traveling, you should attend your host chapter's meetings.
- You must abide by those chapters' by-laws and policies.

4. Don'ts:

Things that will cost you your patch:
- You don't lie.
- You don't steal.
- This includes "ol' ladies" as well.
- Needle use will not be tolerated.
- Neither will smoking of any chemicals – coke, speed, mandrax – if it didn't grow, don't smoke it!

5. Motorcycles:

- Each member will OWN at least one (1) Harley Davidson or facsimile of at least 750cc.
- No more than 30 days a year down time.
- After 30 days, that members' chapter will pay National $500.00. Have a good reason? Ask for more time.
- Road Captains should inspect all bikes regularly.
- If you are visiting another area, chapter, state, or country, and

you borrow another brother's property (bike, tools, money, etc.), you are responsible for the return of that property. It will be returned in as good or better condition than when you borrowed it.

6. Membership:

- Hangaround period to be determined by chapter president.
- Harley Davidson motorcycle or facsimile capable of meeting the demands of "pledge" period.
- Members must be at least 21 years of age.
- Sponsor — May be individual (preferably charter member) or may be sponsored by chapter as a whole.
- Sponsor: Do not turn your pledge loose without help. If you think enough of him to sponsor him into this club, it's up to you to teach him the right way, the BANDIDO WAY. If you're not ready to sacrifice your time and share your knowledge, don't do it. The simple things — "Who's the neatest M.F. in the world?" Or don't wear your patch in a vehicle. Trivial things that will get a prospective BROTHER run off.
- Pay $275.00 to National Treasury.
- Pledge bike and title.
- Be voted in as pledge by chapter (100% vote).
- Receive your patch or rocker.
- DO YOUR TIME.
- Prospect: 6 months MINIMUM.
- Probationary: 1 year MINIMUM.
- This man is pledged to the whole BANDIDO NATION, not just one chapter or area, city, or state. He will attend every meeting, party, bike event, or gathering of any kind in his area where Bandido patcholders will be present.
- He will not miss any National or Regional runs, especially funerals.
- This club is about sacrifice. Get used to it! His motorcycle should

be in up-and-running condition his whole pledge period, ready to go anywhere. In other words, NO DOWN TIME!

- Pledge is not eligible for vote if there are any outstanding debts, chapter, national, or private (inside club). He should start into this club on a level playing field.
- After the mandatory time period has passed and the sponsor feels the pledge is ready, a meeting should be called. All surrounding chapter secretaries should also be notified (in advance).
- The Pledge should be voted in by a 100% chapter vote. Club members outside the chapter should have a chance to voice their opinions. The pledge's sponsor should base his decision on these things, for he is the one who will have to face it if things go foul. It is a lifelong commitment: DON'T RUSH IT.
- Charter Member is 10 years of unbroken service.
- National may grant leave of absence – this is not automatic. Two (2)-year members are eligible for transfer only if both presidents involved have agreed and a $50.00 fee is paid to National Treasury.

7. Suicides:

- Any brother who commits suicide WILL NOT be allowed to have a BANDIDO funeral . . .

8. Other National Fees:

- New Patch Fee $275.00
- Transfers $50.00
- New Charter $1,000.00
- 30-Day Downtime Rule $500.00

Projects & Job Assignments for El Secretarios

March 2001

(This is a document I prepared as a guideline.)

- Money
- Commissary program & inmate affairs
- USA website
- USA website – graveyard
- USA website – history of the club
- T-shirts
- All other merchandise (except T-shirts)
- Life Insurance
- Support clubs – members list & e-mail list & phone list & club list/cities
- Patches & stickers
- Newsletter
- Travel arrangements for the national chapter
- World e-mail list
- USA secretary list
- USA phone list
- Time in club – members & chapters – actual date of entry into club
- Legal issues & oversight of all criminal cases
- Public Relations issues

- Club tattoos – uniform rules & regulations worldwide
- Dress shirts - uniform rules & regulations worldwide
- PBOL guidelines – merchandise & patch
- List of deceased brothers – each chapter – gravesites for same
- Business – incorporation & trademark administration
- Funeral guidelines – one guy from every chapter (however you can get him there) for any funeral; two guys from each chapter within 500 miles (on bikes); every chapter sends flowers or money for each funeral.

Edward's Projects & Job Assignments for National Chapter

March 2003

(This is a sample list of tasks I performed regularly.)

- Keeper of the USA phone list, USA e-mail list, USA fifteen-year member list, and USA support club chapter/member list.
- Keep tabs on the Fat Mexican trademark.
- Monitor most internal federal criminal cases (Bandidos members) and some state criminal cases.
- Provide occasional internal travel arrangements worldwide.
- Provide occasional national public relations services.
- Provide suggestions for forms of communication between the national chapter and the national chapter members.
- Provide suggestions for forms of communication between national chapter and all United States chapters.
- Provide suggestions for design changes to the USA website.
- Provide suggestions for legally structuring the club's financial affairs.
- Provide emergency backup for publishing the USA newsletter.

Bandidos Motorcycle Club Active Chapters

As of August 2007

AUSTRALIA

Adelaide

Ballarat

Brisbane City

Cairns

Downtown

Geelong

Gold Coast

Hunter Valley

Ipswich City

Melbourne

Mid North Coast

Mid-State

Noosa

North-Vic

Northside

Sunshine Coast

Sydney

Toowoomba

BELGIUM

Antwerp

Tongeren

CANADA

Calgary, Alberta

Toronto East, Ontario

Toronto North, Ontario

Toronto South, Ontario

Toronto West, Ontario

Winnipeg, Manitoba

DENMARK

Aalborg

Copenhagen

FrederiksvÆrk

Gladsaxe

HelsingØr

HillerØd

Holbeck

Horsens

KØge

NÆstved

Roskilde

StenlØse

ENGLAND

Guernsey

Jersey

FINLAND

Harjavalta

Helsinki

Hyvinkaa

Lohja

Nokia

Tampere

FRANCE

Annecy

Annemasse

Avignon

Cannes

Grasse

Marseilles

Nice

Strasbourg

GERMANY

Aachen

Allersberg

Berlin

Berlin Centro

Berlin Eastgate

Bochum

Bremen

Cologne

Cottbus

Dinslaken

Dortmund

Duisburg

Essen

Gelsenkirchen

Hamm

Ingolstadt

Kaiserslautern

Kassel

Lauchhammer

Madeburg

Mannheim

Munich

Munich Northside

Münster

Neubrandenburg

Oldenburg

Osnabrück

Passau

Perleberg

Recklinghausen

Rheinbollen

Siegen

Starnberg

Stralsund

Ulm

Unna

Wanne Eickel

ITALY

Catania

Florence

Meran

Messina

Pisa

MALAYSIA

Kuala Lumpur

NORWAY

Drammen

Frederikstad

Kristiansand

Oslo

Stavanger

SINGAPORE

Singapore

SOUTH AMERICA

Costa Rica

SWEDEN

Boras

Falun

Gothenborg

Halmstad

Helsingborg

Seffle

Stockholm

THAILAND

Bankok

Bankok Eastend

Pattaya

Samui

UNITED STATES

Albuquerque, NM

Albuquerque North, NM

Albuquerque South, NM

Albuquerque West, NM

Alamogordo, NM

Amarillo, TX

Austin, TX

Baytown, TX

Beaumont, TX

Bellingham, WA

Birmingham, AL

Billings, MT

Biloxi, MI

Black Hills, SD

Boot Hill, NE

Bremerton, WA

Carlsbad, NM

Centro, NM

Chelan County, WA

Cloverleaf, TX

Corpus Christi, TX

Dallas, TX

Delco, ID

Denver, CO

Denver Central, CO

Denver South, CO

Dothan, AL

East River, SD

Eastside El Paso, TX

Elko, NV

El Paso, TX

Everett, WA

Fort Worth, TX

Gallup, NM

Galveston, TX

Grand Junction, CO

Hill Country, TX

APPENDICES

Houston, TX
Houston North, TX
Houston Northwest, TX
Houston Southwest, TX
Houston West, TX
Huntsville, AL
Jackson, MS
Jefferson County, TX
Kerrville, TX
Lafayette, LA
Lake Charles, LA
Laredo, TX
Las Cruces, NM
Las Vegas, NV
Lawton, OK
Little Rock, AR
Longview, TX
Lubbock, TX
McAllen, TX
Missoula, MO
Mobile, AL
Montgomery, AL
Mount Hull, WA
New Orleans, LA
Oahu, HI
Oklahoma City, OK
Panhandle, TX
Panhandle North, TX
Plainview, TX
Pueblo, CO
Rapid City, SD
Roswell, NM
Ruidoso, NM

Rupert, UT
San Antonio, TX
San Antonio Centro, TX
San Antonio West, TX
San Antonio Northwest, TX
San Antonio Southwest, TX
San Leon, TX
Santa Fe, NM
Seattle, WA
Seattle South, WA
Seattle North, WA
Shreveport, LA
Skagit County, WA
Tacoma, WA
Toele, UT
Tres Rios, WA
Tri-Cities, WA
Truth or Consequence, NM
Tulsa, OK
Tulsa North, OK
Waco, TX
Whatcom County, WA
Yakima, WA

Bandidos Support Club Chapters
August 2003
(No Updates Available)

Name of Club/State	City	Members
ALABAMA		
Pistoleros	Auburn	5
Pistoleros	Birmingham	6
CMA	Birmingham	2
Soldiers of the Cross	Birmingham	3
Wayward Wind	Birmingham	5
Pistoleros	Dothan	2
Pistoleros	Huntsville	
Pistoleros	Jasper	5
Iron Hawgs	Jasper	5
Pistoleros	Mobile	4
Soldiers of the Cross	Mobile	12
CMA	Mobile	2
Alabama Riders	Montgomery	5
Pistoleros	Montgomery	5
ARKANSAS		
Ozark Riders	Eureka Springs	7
Ozark Riders	Rogers	6
COLORADO		
Peligrosos	Denver	16
No Names	Grand Junction	5

Los Bravos	Denver	11
John's Guys	Pueblo	12

LOUISIANA

West Bank	Baton Rouge West	5
Louisiana Riders	Baton Rouge	6
Louisiana Riders	Bogalusa	4
West Bank	Point Coupee	7
Hole in the Wall	Lafayette	5
Road Shakers	Acadiana	7
Rat Pack	Lake Charles	12
Grey Ghosts	Minden	3
Grey Ghosts	Nacadoches	4
Louisiana Riders	New Orleans	6
Grey Ghosts	Shreveport	14

MISSISSIPPI

Asgards	Biloxi	6
Asgards	Gulfport	6
Pistoleros	Hattiesburg	5
CMA	Jackson	10
Pistoleros	Jackson	2
Asgards	Kiln	6
Asgards	Pascagoula	6
Mississippi Riders	Tupelo	5

MISSOURI

Hermanos	Jamesland	11

MONTANA

Hermanos	Kallispell	5
Hermanos	Missoula	4
Amigos	Ronan	1

NEW MEXICO

Native Thunder	Acoma	3
German MC	Alamogordo	9
Black Berets	Albuquerque	9
Native Thunder	Albuquerque	4
Bandoleros	Albuquerque	4
Pacoteros	Artesia	4
Native Thunder	Dine Nation	2
U.S. Vets	Hobbs	10
Regulaters	Roswell	7
Bandoleros	Sante Fe	6
Bandoleros	Truth/Consequences	3
US Vets	Tucamcari	7
Native Thunder	Zuni	3

OKLAHOMA

OK Riders	Tulsa	9
OK Riders	Shawnee	8
OK Riders	Comanche	9
CMA	OKC	2

SOUTH DAKOTA

Hermanos	Sioux River	5
Ghost Dance	Pine Ridge	6

TEXAS

Iron Riders	Amarillo	28
Companeros	Austin	10
Iron Riders	Borger	29
Southern Pride	Beaumont	3
Border Brothers	Brownsville	20
Rebeldes	Corpus Christi	10
Macheteros	El Paso	4

Del Fuego	El Paso	5
Coyoteros	El Paso	6
Amigos	Estralla Sola	3
Rebel Riders	Fort Worth	14
Aces & Eights	Fredericksburg	12
Amigos	Galveston County	8
Macheteros	Hill Country	5
Los Dorados	Hill Country	5
Soldiers of Jesus	Houston	10
Amigos	Houston State	5
Amigos	Houston East	5
Amigos	Houston North	8
Amigos	Houston West	4
Southern Raiders	Houston West	5
Los Malos	Jefferson County	
Renegades	Laredo	4
Aces & Eights	Levelland	37
Desperados	Longview	8
Los Cabboleros	Killeen	5
Amigos	Montgomery County	13
Los Riders	Plainview	39
Macheteros	San Antonio NW	14
Southsiders	San Antonio SW	12
Westsiders	San Antonio	9
Campesinos	San Antonio	9
Malditos (Bad Lance)	San Antonio SW	9
Texas Wheels	Waco	80
Equestrians	Waco	12

WASHINGTON

Warriors	Everett	7
Destralos	King County	5
Amigos	King County	8
Hermanos	King County	4

Hombres	La Costa	4
Hombres	Olympia	4
Amigos	Pierce County	10
Hombres	Seattle	6
Amigos	Snohomish County	9
Hombres	Snow Valley	4
Hombres	Tacoma	6
Hermanos	Tacoma	5
Destralos	Thurston County	5
Hombres	Wenatchee	4
Canyon Riders	Whatcom County	11
Unforgiven	Yakima	6

WYOMING

Hermanos	Gillette	5

47 Support Clubs   **Total Members**   **929**

Bandidos Motorcycle Club Inactive Chapters
June 2005
(No Updates Available)

CITY	STATE	COUNTRY
Atchison	Kansas	USA
Champaign	Illinois	USA
Cheyenne	Wyoming	USA
Devil's Mountain	Washington	USA
Elkhart	Indiana	USA
Edmonton	Alberta	Canada
Findley	Ohio	USA
Ft Smith	Arkansas	USA
Ft Wayne	Indiana	USA
Gillette	Wyoming	USA
Goshen	Indiana	USA
Haywarden	Iowa	USA
Juneau	Alaska	USA
Kingston	Ontario	Canada
Los Alamos	New Mexico	USA
Monroe	Michigan	USA
Montreal	Quebec	Canada
Opelika	Alabama	USA
Pascagoula	Mississippi	USA
Phoenix	Arizona	USA
Quebec City	Quebec	Canada
Silver City	New Mexico	USA
Springfield	Missouri	USA
Texas City	Texas	USA

APPENDIX H

Newspaper Articles